# Saipan

Also by Bruce M. Petty
and from McFarland

*New Zealand in the Pacific War: Personal Accounts of World War II* (2008)

*At War in the Pacific: Personal Accounts of World War II Navy and Marine Corps Officers* (2006)

# Saipan

## *Oral Histories of the Pacific War*

BRUCE M. PETTY

McFarland & Company, Inc., Publishers
*Jefferson, North Carolina, and London*

*The present work is a reprint of the illustrated case bound edition of* Saipan: Oral Histories of the Pacific War, *first published in 2002 by McFarland.*

Library of Congress Cataloguing-in-Publication Data

Saipan : oral histories of the Pacific War / by Bruce M. Petty.
p. cm.
Includes index.

**ISBN 978-0-7864-4244-7**
softcover : 50# alkaline paper ♾

1. Saipan, Battle of, 1944. 2. World War, 1939–1945 — Personal narratives. 3. World War, 1939–1945 — Campaigns — Mariana Islands. I. Petty, Bruce M., 1945–
D767.99.S3S243 2009
940.54'26 — dc21 2001044840

British Library cataloguing data are available



Manufactured in the United States of America

*McFarland & Company, Inc., Publishers*
*Box 611, Jefferson, North Carolina 28640*
*www.mcfarlandpub.com*

To my mother, Betty Faris Petty,
who thought I should be a writer long before I did.

# *Acknowledgments*

I would like to acknowledge the hundreds of people who shared their time and memories with me. Although not all of their oral histories appear in this volume, much of what I learned from them does.

I would also like to thank my wife, Dr. Daniele Lonchamp-Petty, for being the main financial support for the family while I obsessed over this book. She has been more than a wife and the mother of our three children; she has been my best friend.

My friend and editor *par excellence*, Dr. Beret E. Strong, deserves special mention. Not only has she edited every page of this book, but she did so with a soft touch that always left me on a high. Not once did any of her slash and burn marks leave me with feelings of despair. She, more than anybody else, helped me maintain my enthusiasm for this project from beginning to end. Beret is not only an accomplished writer in her own right, but an award winning documentary film maker. Even if she were not my editor I would value her for her friendship.

I would also like to thank Tee Abraham of the Northern Marianas College for the help she gave me early on in this project. She made it possible for me to contact and interview many members of the Chamorro and Carolinian communities.

Dr. Dirk A. Ballendorf of the University of Guam almost adopted me from the moment I met him and shared my plans for writing this book. He has been extremely helpful in clarifying some of the details of Micronesian history, and he probably saved me some embarrassment in the process. I can't thank him enough.

Wakako Higuchi, also of the University of Guam, likewise has been an enthusiast as well as a wonderful friend. Her more than twenty years of research on the Japanese in Micronesia have added to my knowledge. More than once she has cautioned me about Americans who write about the Japanese in Micronesia and get it wrong. I hope this volume doesn't let her down.

I would also like to thank Col. Hiroshi Shiraishi, Chief of Military History at the Staff College, Japan Ground Self Defense Forces. He and his staff contributed names and biographical information on Japanese military officers who served in the Pacific during the war. He also helped dispel numerous myths held by islanders at a time when knowledge of world events was limited.

The Office of Historic Preservation on Saipan has been helpful from the very beginning of this project. Deserving of special mention are Joseph P. Deleon Guerrero, historic preservation officer; Scott Russell, deputy historic preservation officer; and Lon Bulgrin, archeologist. Also from HPO, I would like to thank Juan Diego Castro Camacho (Familian Wambo)—always a good man to have along during my many hours of exploring the jungles of Saipan for remnants of the past, and Susana Rabauliman

I would also like to thank the following people for their contributions, large and small: Samuel McPhetres, Rose Manibusan of the War in the Pacific Museum on Guam, Paul Chancy Oberg of the Northern Marianas Museum of History and Culture, Elizabeth Diaz Rechebei, Yong Taek Lee, Jennings Bunn of the Naval Museum on Guam, Warren Nishimoto from the Center of Oral History at the University of Hawaii, Dr. Theodore Cook, and his wife, Haruko Taya Cook. Also, Dr. Kathy Broome Williams, Francis Hezel, Sr., John Tweedy, Juan A. Camacho on Navy Hill (Saipan), and Capt. James B. Johnson, USNR (Rt.), former Naval Administrator of the Northern Marianas and lifelong friend of the Chamorro and Carolinian people.

I beg the forgiveness of anybody I may have left out.

# *Table of Contents*

## *9. The Army Air Force*



## *10. The Home Front*

# Introduction

Saipan was the site of one of the bloodiest battles in the Pacific during World War II. The island is less than fifteen miles long, but for more than three weeks during the summer of 1944 a tsunami of fire and steel swept this small island, leaving tens of thousands dead, scattered across a landscape that was broken, and burned and smelled of rotting flesh. Even today, more than fifty years after the battle, one can find skeletal remains scattered along the jungle floor and in limestone caves. Hundreds, perhaps thousands, more rest entombed in caves and tunnels scattered throughout the island—caverns incinerated by flame throwers and sealed with explosive charges. Some more accessible caves and tunnels were simply made into time capsules by bulldozers that piled tons of rock and dirt over the entrances, leaving their terrified human inhabitants to suffocate or die of thirst and hunger.

The generation of islanders who remember the days before the storm, and the storm itself, is rapidly passing. Many from the generations born after the war know little or nothing about the lives of their parents and grandparents as subjects of the Japanese Empire or how their lives today are the direct result of what happened more than fifty years ago.

Few Americans born after World War II have heard of Saipan, or any of the other bloodied islands of the Pacific War. Yet two Marine Corps divisions and one Army division fought to take and hold Saipan. U.S. forces suffered more than 14,000 casualties. More than 3,000 Americans left the island in coffins. After the island was declared secure, it became a major staging area for the invasions of Iwo Jima, Okinawa and the big planned invasion of the Japanese home islands. During and right after the fighting for Saipan, hundreds of thousands of Americans were stationed on the island or passed through it as the fighting moved north.

Today the jungle has reclaimed much of the island, covering the ugly scars of war. Once again it is peaceful and quiet. The sunsets are beautiful, and without the interruption of clouds of acrid smoke. There is no longer the rattle of machine guns, nor the thunder of exploding shells. Yet if you probe into the hills and pull back the foliage you can still find the detritus of the battle that tore this island apart more than a half century ago. Less visible are the human scars and frail human emotions that rest below the surface.

In gathering the material for this book through personal interviews, I have asked people to recall events that took place more than fifty years ago. But the terror and trauma of war is not easily erased, not even from the mind of a child.

My first interview resulted from a chance meeting with a woman in her mid-sixties of mixed Japanese and Chamorro parentage. During the course of our conversation I learned that she was born and raised on Saipan, and that most of her family was killed during the fighting for Saipan. Of the ten children in her immediate family, she was one of only three to survive. In addition to her siblings, Vicky Vaughan, formerly Setchan Akiyama, lost members of her extended family—aunts, uncles, cousins, and a grandfather.

Vicky and I met several times after our first encounter and discussed the possibility of recording and publishing her story. She was hesitant at first, but finally agreed. She later told me that she didn't like holding her memories inside. On numerous occasions she had tried to talk to her surviving brother and sister about it, but they didn't want to remember. She attempted to tell her own grown children, but they made her stop because they didn't like to see their mother cry. This was an opportunity to tell a wider audience. It was to be a catharsis.

# D-Day 15 June, 1944

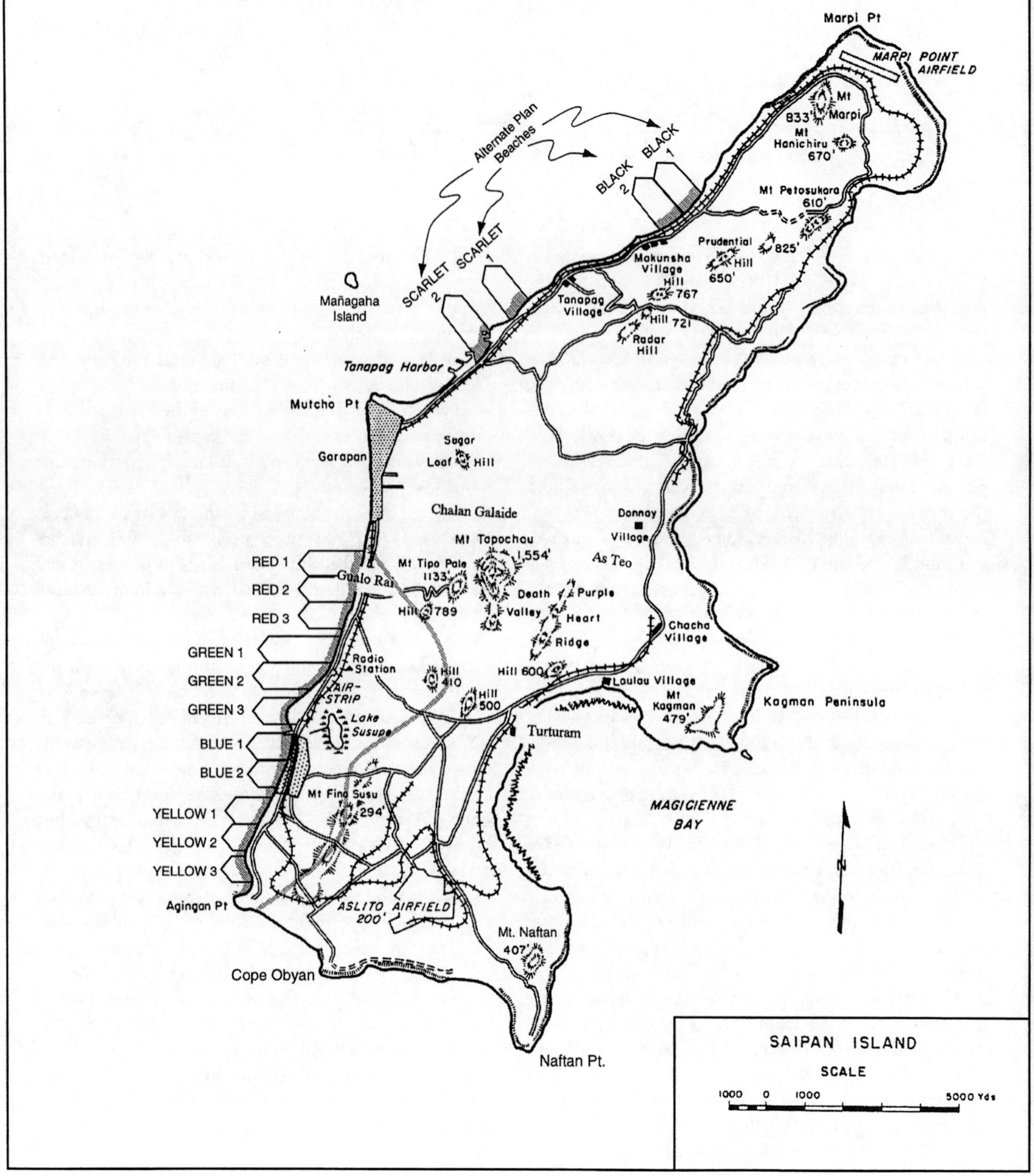

My interview with Vicky proved to be the pattern for almost all of the others. It actually consisted of three interviews. The first one lasted about two hours and was punctuated by tearful breaks. She told me later that after we finished she had one long cry. She confessed that she still missed her father, who became separated from the rest of the family during the early days of fighting on Saipan and was never seen again.

After each session I sat down and listened to the taped interview, transcribing it to my computer. After our third session I had a draft of her story, and we sat down to go over it together. Her oral history went through five drafts before she was satisfied her story was accurately told. Most of the subsequent interviews I did with other people required two to four sessions of interviewing, with a total of four to seven writings before interviewer and interviewee were satisfied.

In every instance I have attempted to corroborate the stories of the interviewees. I have tried to find other people who knew the interviewee at the time of the events in the interview. I have also made reference to documented evidence whenever possible.

## *Where the Story Begins: A Wheel with Many Spokes*

Saipan is part of the Mariana Islands, an arc of islands in the Central Pacific. Saipan is the second largest island in the Marianas chain, Guam being the largest. All of the islands of the Marianas are volcanic in origin. There are twenty-eight islands altogether if you count all of the islets. The northernmost island in this chain is Uracas. Uracas is just south of the Tropic of Cancer and is the closest of the Mariana Islands to Iwo Jima, where another famous and bloody battle was fought on the road to Japan. In geological time, the southernmost of these islands are the oldest and are today void of active volcanoes. From Anatahan Island north, all of the islands are young enough to have active volcanoes. Maug is actually three islets, a product of one high volcanic island that exploded before recorded history. In 1981 the volcano on Pagan Island erupted, forcing the few inhabitants of that small island to flee. Though the more southerly islands of the chain — Saipan, Tinian, Rota, and Guam — have no active volcanoes, earthquakes are common.

It is believed that the ancestors of the present native population came from Southeast Asia by way of the Philippines. The first European to make landfall in the Marianas was Ferdinand Magellan in 1521. However, it wasn't until the year 1565 that Miguel Lopez de Legaspi claimed the islands in the name of Spain. By 1749 the Spanish had relocated all the Chamorros from the Northern Islands to Guam in a successful effort to pacify and Christianize them. Rota was the only one of the islands north of Guam where a number of Chamorro families successfully avoided relocation to Guam. (Their unique history will be discussed later.) As a result of this effort, the Chamorro population was reduced from a pre-contact population estimated to be around 40,000 based on archaeological and historical evidence, to near extinction less than 200 years after they were first discovered by Magellan.

The Refalawasch, or Carolinians, were the last of a long line of Pacific Islanders to emigrate to the Marianas. The first recorded emigration from the Carolines was in the early nineteenth century after the Carolinians' atoll homes were decimated by a series of natural calamities. With permission from the Spanish authorities on Guam, these people were allowed to settle on Saipan, founding the village of Arabwal, now Garapan.

Throughout the rest of the nineteenth century and into the twentieth, the Chamorro people and new waves of Carolinians continued to return to the northern islands. However, as late as 1876 there were still no more than an estimated 1000 people living on Saipan. This new Chamorro culture resembled only slightly the pre-contact one. Now, they were more Spanish and Filipino in culture. Catholicism was the cement that bound them to their new identity.

The majority of the islands are uninhabited today, although in recent years some local families have sought to repopulate a few of them. During Japanese times all of the islands with arable land, including tiny Aguijan (Goat Island), were populated and exploited. Sugar cane was the number one cash crop on the more southerly islands, while copra and other crops dominated the islands to the north.

## *1914: The Japanese Period Officially Begins*

In 1854 when Commodore Matthew Perry opened Japan to the world it was still a feudal nation locked in centuries of isolation. Fifty years later it was a modern industrialized nation. It defeated a major western power in

Opposite: *Saipan Island on D-Day. From* Saipan: The Beginning of the End *by Major Carl W. Huffman, USMC (Historical Section, Headquarters, United States Marine Corps).*

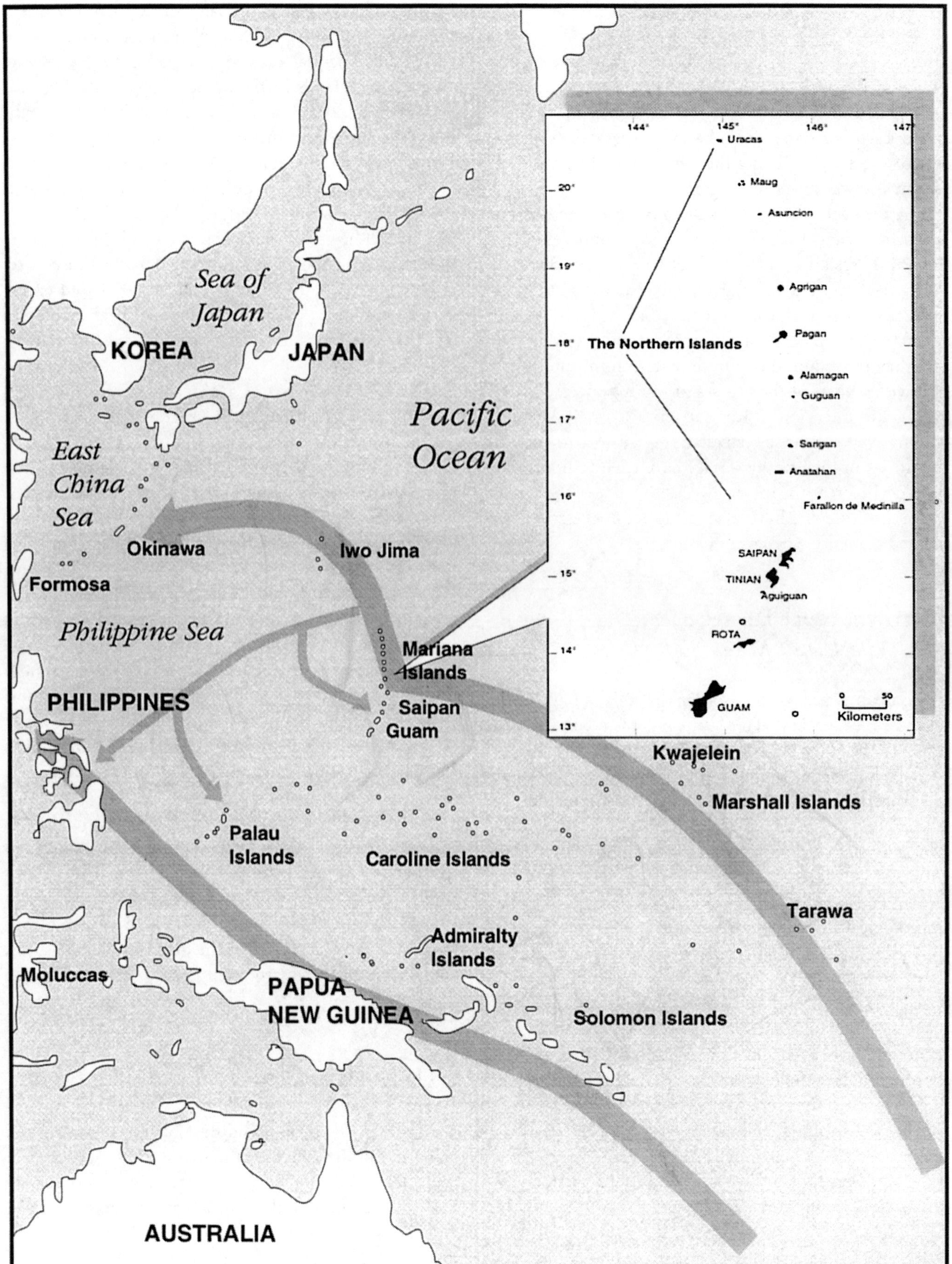

Sea of Japan
KOREA
JAPAN
Pacific Ocean
East China Sea
Okinawa
Iwo Jima
Formosa
Philippine Sea
Mariana Islands
PHILIPPINES
Saipan
Guam
Kwajelein
Marshall Islands
Palau Islands
Caroline Islands
Tarawa
Admiralty Islands
Moluccas
PAPUA NEW GUINEA
Solomon Islands
AUSTRALIA
144°
145°
146°
147°
20°
19°
18°
17°
16°
15°
14°
13°
Uracas
Maug
Asuncion
Agrigan
Pagan
The Northern Islands
Alamagan
Guguan
Sarigan
Anatahan
Farallon de Medinilla
SAIPAN
TINIAN
Aguiguan
ROTA
GUAM
0
50
Kilometers

*Part of Garapan, one of Saipan's larger villages, as it looks today. Restaurants, karaoke bars, and souvenir shops, patronized for the most part by Japanese tourists, are commonplace.*

the Russo-Japanese War of 1904–1905, gained access to Manchuria, and annexed Korea in 1910.

On August 4, 1914, Great Britain declared war on Germany. Japan had been an ally of Britain since the two nations signed a secret agreement in 1902. Although Japan did not actively participate in the fighting in Europe except for convoy and anti-submarine duties in the Mediterranean, it did take advantage of Germany's weakened position in Asia and the Pacific. Soon after hostilities in Europe began, Japan sent a naval squadron to attack German naval forces in the Western Pacific and occupy German-held islands. The German squadron in the area rendezvoused at Pagan Island in the Northern Marianas, then dispersed to the Indian Ocean and South America without making any contact with Japanese forces. In October 1914, Japanese naval forces took control of all German-held islands north of the equator without loss of life to either side. Thus, in 1914, we see the beginning of the first Japanese period in Micronesia, and the first period in the history of the islands of a modern, booming economy.

Japanese individuals and companies had had a presence in Micronesia since the late nineteenth century. However, with these island territories now under Japanese suzerainty, other companies with strong support from the Japanese government began moving into the area. Japanese, Okinawan, and Korean laborers were also brought in. The jungle was beaten down and pushed back. Wherever possible, these jungle islands were turned into sugar cane fields, orchards, and gardens. Phosphate discovered on Rota was also exploited by the Japanese. For the first time in their history the Chamorros and Carolinians became minorities on their own islands.

There was no major attempt on the part of the Japanese to exploit the islands' commercial potential until World War I was over and the Treaty of Versailles had

Opposite: *The Western Pacific, with an inset showing the Mariana Islands.*

*What the jungle looks like today on Saipan where it has not been replaced by development for the tourist trade.*

been signed. Japan was not sure it would be allowed to retain the former German colonies until world leaders met on the subject following the cessation of hostilities. With the Treaty of Versailles a mandate system was created whereby the islands would be administered, but not owned, by Japan. Without the knowledge of the United States, this had earlier been agreed to by Great Britain, France, Japan, and Russia in exchange for Japan's participation in the war. The United States was the only major power to oppose the agreement. President Wilson finally accepted the terms of the agreement but only after Japan agreed to join the League of Nations and administer the islands under the mandate system. This Japan readily agreed to since it was a *de facto* recognition of Japan's new position as a major power on the world stage. Regardless of this mutually-agreed-to system, the United States remained suspicious of Japan's growing power and influence in the region. From this time on U.S. military planners focused their attention increasingly on Japan in possible scenarios of future hostilities in the Pacific.

One of the terms of the League of Nation's mandate was that Japan could not fortify the islands. This they did not do until war broke out between the United States and Japan in 1941, when Japan was no longer a member of the League.

Although part of the mandate required Japan to submit yearly reports to the League of Nations on the progress of Japan's administration of Micronesia, the requirement did not include on-site inspections. The mandate also required that these territories be open to the trade and commerce of all nations, but Japan effectively closed off the waters of Micronesia to other nations, further feeding the suspicions of President Wilson and future American administrations.

Even individuals seeking passage to the South Seas on Japanese vessels met with frustration. Those who persisted and succeeded were seldom allowed to leave ship at their multiple island stops. Among the few who did succeed was American journalist and writer Willard Price. He spent several months in Micronesian waters in the mid–1930s, and even managed a month long stay on Yap where he and his wife were the guests of Jesus and Mecaila Untalan. The Untalan family was originally from Guam but had emigrated to Yap like many other Chamorros during the German administration (1899–1914). One of their daughters, Filomena, was later executed by the

Japanese along with her Filipino husband and two small children (1944).

At the time of the Japanese takeover of the Northern Marianas, the Chamorro and Carolinian population was less than 3,000. The Japanese introduced free education and health care. However, under the Japanese, the primary purpose of education was to teach Japanese language and culture to the Micronesians, who were also trained to serve as carpenters, nurses, teachers, blacksmiths, and so on. Except in rare cases, higher education was not available to the local population. Upward mobility was not part of the grand scheme the Japanese had for the islanders. In spite of this, members of the local population did participate in the economic boom that came with the massive Japanese presence. Most Chamorros and Carolinians profited simply by renting out their lands to the Japanese. Then, as today, the economic boom depended on the importation of "non-resident workers."

## *Things Begin to Change*

By 1943 the Japanese started to became indifferent, even hostile to the local population. Those Chamorros and Carolinians still living in the villages of Garapan and Chalan Kanoa were forced out of their homes and onto their ranchos to make room for the growing population of Japanese soldiers and sailors. Shops once open to the entire population became restricted to Japanese only. Locals were forced to survive on farming and fishing and were also required to provide food for the Japanese.

As the war in the Pacific came closer to the Mariana Islands, the Japanese began sending their civilians back to Japan and bringing in troops from Manchuria, Korea, and the home islands. At this stage in the war American submarines dominated Pacific waters. The toll on Japanese shipping was tremendous. Many of the ships carrying Japanese civilians home and soldiers and supplies to Saipan were sunk with great loss of life. While close to 30,000 Japanese military personnel died during the battle of Saipan, as well as an estimated 10,000 Japanese civilians, countless others also perished at sea in attempts to escape the coming conflagration or arrive to participate in it.

The year 1942 provided a series of victories for the Japanese throughout Asia and the Pacific. However, by 1943 the Allies had stopped the Japanese on all fronts. The Japanese found themselves digging in and trying to hold on to what they had gained. As the Pacific War turned more and more bleak for the Japanese, they found themselves either cut off or retreating on most fronts. They became increasingly desperate and paranoid. In many cases they turned hostile to the local peoples, and there was a constant search for spies. Any number of characteristics could lead to a person being suspected or even arrested and executed for spying. If a person had a lighter complexion than most, or a long, thin nose; if he or she spoke a foreign language or was found to possess foreign language books; if a person had tattoos, was of European ancestry, or had a European name; any of these factors could and did put individuals and their families at risk. Having a radio in one's possession, especially during the last years of the war, was an almost certain death sentence.

Even Japanese nationals were occasionally suspect, especially if they had lived overseas, were found to have radios, or spoke a foreign language. On Saipan a Japanese man by the name of Ikuta (first name unknown) was held in the local jail right up to the time of the American invasion. Some sources say his English was so good that he was used to interpret for a number of American pilots also held in the jail at that time. With the exception of two American pilots, all of these prisoners were released at the time of the American invasion in June 1944.

## *"Proper Place"*

In the early 1940s the Japanese Ministry of Health and Welfare employed approximately forty scholars and researchers to put together a document called "An Investigation of Global Policy with the Yamato Race as Nucleus."* It was completed in 1943, and rationalized Japanese policies that had long been in effect. The overall conclusion of this study was that all ethnic groups and nationalities had their "Proper place," with the Japanese at the top of this conceptual pyramid. This concept of "proper place" included a perceived need for racial purity and for avoiding interracial marriage. However, the Japanese had been in Micronesia since the late 1800s, and individuals tended to adopt the ways of their new environment. Like other expatriates, Japanese who made their homes in the faraway islands of Micronesia married into local families.

By the 1920s larger numbers of Japanese, especially from Okinawa, began to emigrate to these islands, now under a League of Nations mandate. They came as individuals, but also as couples and families. Even those who arrived single could find partners of the same nationality. Nevertheless, there continued to be interracial liaisons and marriages. Most were between Japanese men and

*Dower, John W. *War Without Mercy*. New York: Pantheon Books, 1986.

Micronesian women, but Japanese women also married Micronesian men, though not without protest from family members in most cases. In one case, the offended parents sent their young daughter back to Japan in a desperate move to prevent her from becoming the bride of an amorous Chamorro suitor by the name of Enrique Castro Dela Cruz. The young man in question proved even more desperate. He joined the local boxing team and became proficient enough that he was able to compete with his team in Japan. Once in Japan, he abandoned his boxing ambitions and searched until he found his partner. The two of them then booked passage for another island group in Micronesia. After the birth of their first child they returned to Saipan to confront her parents with their fait accompli. The bride in question died in 1996. Her offspring are my neighbors.

## *Part I — Micronesian Voices*

All Micronesian cultures have a long oral tradition. Almost all of the extant written history of the area has been produced by people from the outside. As has been pointed out by Professor Dirk Ballendorf of the University of Guam and others, Pacific Islanders have only recently begun to produce, to any significant extent, a written literature of their own.* In the first part of this oral history, I have attempted to give voice to the people of Micronesia.

Most of the people I have interviewed live in the Mariana Islands. However, before and during World War II many people now living on Saipan, Rota, and especially Tinian lived in other parts of Micronesia such as Yap and Palau. Some natives of the Marianas found themselves as far away as the Malay Archipelago (present day Indonesia) and Papua New Guinea.

Many of those who survived the conflagration that swept much of Asia and the Pacific during World War II eventually made their way back to the islands of their ancestors. Others, thinking their island homes destroyed and their families dead, made new lives for themselves in other parts of the Pacific and Asia.

A good example of the latter is a Chamorro by the name of Daniel Aldan. He was sent to Indonesia by the Japanese to work during World War II. At war's end he heard that Saipan had been invaded and destroyed. Assuming that his family had been killed during the fighting, he elected to stay in Indonesia, where he married and started a second family. It was not until the mid–1980s that Mr. Aldan returned to Saipan for a visit, only to discover that his first wife was still alive. She, likewise, had remarried and started another family.

This book is an attempt to take an oral tradition and give it new life and longevity. Here, the oral becomes literary. Perhaps these oral histories will be preserved and shared with an audience beyond the Pacific waters where these dramas took place. Their stories, for the most part, are not based on documented evidence. They are based on what people remember, and what they think they remember. For many who witnessed the violent deaths of friends and family members, this last half-century has been a long climb out of a dark hole. Going back has been a catharsis for some, a return to that dark hole for others.

What are the islands like today? In the course of writing this book I had the privilege of spending time on several. Saipan I have already described to some extent. A word or two about the others follows.

### Rota (Luta)

Like most of the islands in Micronesia during World War II, Rota, which lies between Guam and Tinian, never experienced a ground invasion by the United States. The Japanese civilian population before the war had reached 5,000. When Rota surrendered to U.S. forces in September 1945, there were almost 3,000 Japanese military personnel, roughly 6,000 Japanese civilians, and 790 Chamorros.

By mid–1944 few ships came to Rota, and those that did carried Japanese military personnel and their supplies. American bombers from Guam and Saipan released their fiery and explosive cargos on Rota when their missions had to be aborted. American fighter planes were over the skies of Rota almost every day, shooting at anything that moved. It was so dangerous that most activities, including farming and fishing, had to be done at night. Food became so scarce that the entire population was put to work growing sweet potatoes, corn, and other fast growing crops, almost all of which were confiscated by the Japanese military. The Chamorros were forced to go into the jungle and sustain themselves on what they could gather or capture. This included fruit bats, coconut crabs, and small birds.

Nearly everybody on Rota, both indigenous and Japanese, lost all possessions during the early days of the bombings. The clothes they had were the clothes they wore the day they fled into the jungle. There were no medicines for the sick, eventually not even for the Japanese. Filth and disease reduced the population. Few babies born

*Ballendorf, Dirk Anthony. "Interpreting the Cultures of Micronesia: Three Paradigms of Pacific Historiography." *Journal of the Pacific Society of Japan*, v. 13, n. 2, July, 1990, pp. 1–8.

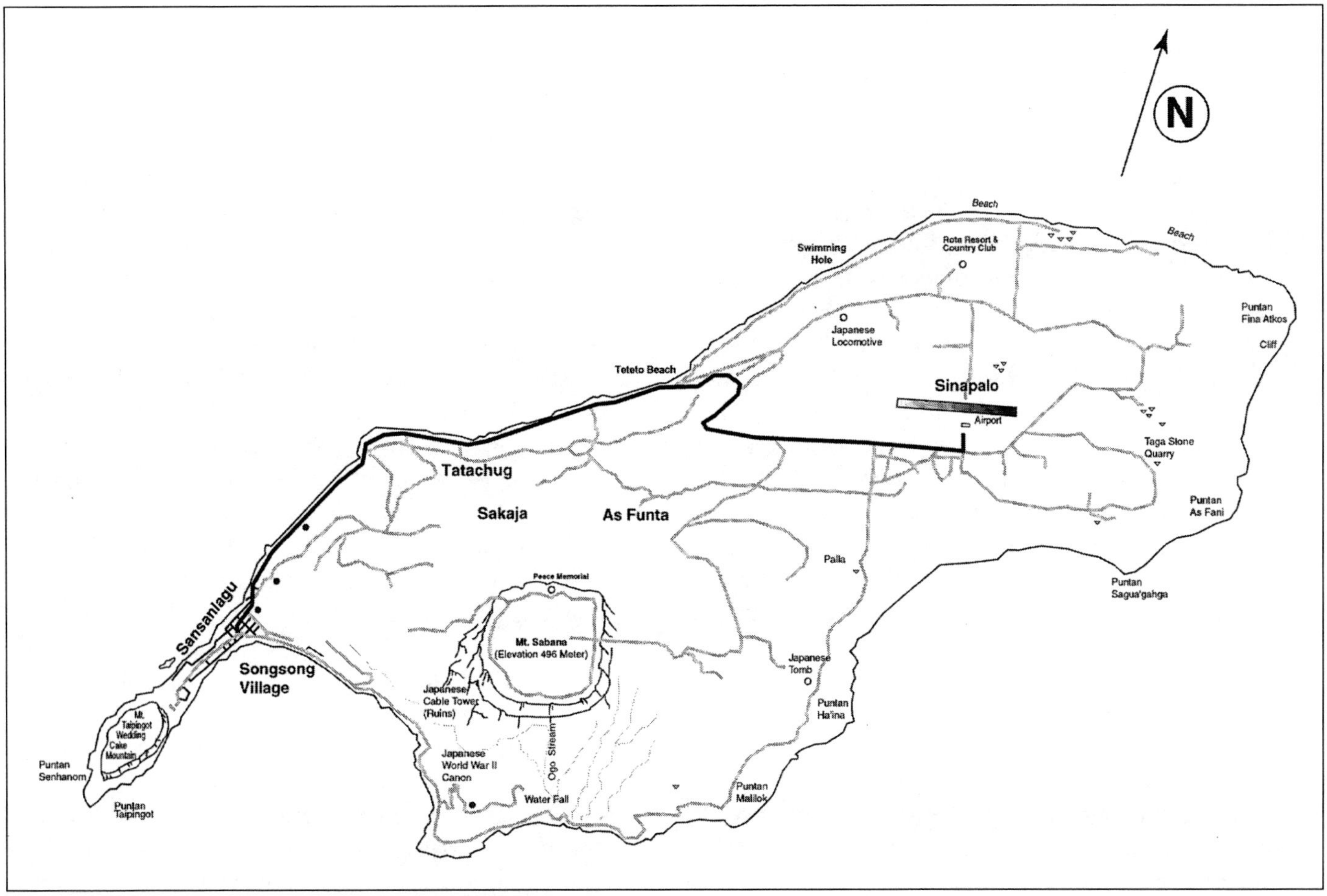


*Rota, which lies between Guam and Tinian.*

during the last fifteen months of the war survived. In most cases mothers could not produce enough breast milk to sustain life.

To make life even more miserable, the populace had to live in constant fear of the Japanese military. The Japanese were on the lookout for signs of disloyalty among the native population, and the Chamorros circulated rumors of Japanese plans to kill all of them in order to have more food for themselves. (This was a common fear among islanders in other island groups throughout Micronesia during the last years of the war.)

I think Rota is the most beautiful of the inhabited Mariana Islands. The people are friendly and the pace of life is much slower than on neighboring Guam and Saipan. The entire population is still only a few thousand — less than during Japanese times. A Japanese millionaire has more or less adopted Rota. He has built a golf course and contributes to community projects. There are a few hotels, but none of them punch holes in the skyline as hotels do on Saipan.

From the airport to the main village of Songsong is a modern road. When I first went there with my wife and children in February of 1996, we thought we were the victims of mass mistaken identity. From every car we passed, people waved at us. We wondered who they thought we were until some friends told us that greeting everybody you pass is a Rotanese custom.

## Tinian

Tinian for the most part remained unpopulated until the 1920s, when the Japanese began to exploit the island for the production of sugar cane. Because of its relative flatness compared to Saipan, and its abundance of water, Tinian soon produced more sugar cane than Saipan. From the 1920s until the invasion of Tinian by U.S. Marines in July 1944, the population was dominated by Japanese, Okinawans, and a few Koreans. With a few exceptions, the small number of Chamorros living there at the time disappeared during the fighting. It is presumed that they were killed.

One of the exceptions was the family of Kancho Shimabukuro. He was an Okinawan married to a Chamorro by the name of Maria Borja. They along with their young son, Joaquin, were on nearby Aguijan Island during the fighting and so survived. An older son, Antonio, was serving in the Japanese Army on Rota. Antonio and his parents would not see each other again until 1952 when Antonio, then living on Saipan, discovered his family had been repatriated to Okinawa, the place of his father's birth.

Even before the island was declared secure in the summer of 1944, Naval Construction Battalions (Seabees) began work on what would become North Field and West Field. By the war's end Tinian would boast the biggest and busiest airport in the world. It was from the six air strips on Tinian and the two on Saipan that the new B-29 bombers began a nonstop air war against the Japanese home islands. In August 1945, the *Enola Gay* took off from North Field to drop the first atomic bomb on Japan. *Bock's Car* dropped the second one a few days later on Nagasaki.

After World War II, Chamorros from other parts of the Northern Marianas and Yap Island were promised land on Tinian as part of a homestead program then administered by the U.S. Naval Administration. Most of the people living on Tinian today are post-war transplants, or their descendants. The northern 80 percent of Tinian is a U.S. military reserve. North Field is still visible from the air, and part of West Field is being used as an airfield for small planes that bring in passengers from Saipan, Rota, and Guam. Most of the buildings used by the U.S. military during World War II were sold to the Micronesian Metals Corporation as scrap, and tangantangan now grows where they once stood. The People's Republic of China has built a multimillion-dollar casino complex on the southern part of the island. Its long term effect on the island and its people still remains to be seen.

## Guam

The Philippines and all of Micronesia, including the Mariana Islands, fell under Spanish rule in the late sixteenth century. In 1898 Spain found itself at war with the United States. In addition to losing the war, Spain lost the Philippines and the island of Guam. Of all the islands of Spanish Micronesia, the U.S. wanted only Guam, which would serve U.S. ships, then fueled by coal, as coaling station between Hawaii and the Philippines. In 1899, the remaining islands of Micronesia, including the Northern Marianas, were sold by Spain to Germany. The German presence in Micronesia was short-lived, lasting only until 1914, a mere fifteen years.

Guam was never heavily fortified or manned by large numbers of American military personnel. This was partly due to the restrictions placed on the U.S. Navy by the Washington Naval Treaty of 1921–1922. On December 8, 1941 (Dec. 7th in Hawaii), Japanese planes from Saipan bombed Guam. On December 10, Japanese Army troops landed and took control of Guam. They encountered minimal resistance from the outnumbered U.S. forces and the small group of armed Guamanians that made up the Insular Force Guard. Thus began one of the most tortured periods in the modern history of Guam and its people. The fact that Guam had been an American colony, and many Guamanians were openly pro–American, made the next two and a half years especially difficult for the people of this small island.

With the new Japanese civil administration and a small force of Japanese military garrison personnel, Chamorros from Saipan and Rota were brought to Guam to serve as "interpreters." Some worked with the Japanese and Guamanian civil police and the Kempeitai (Japanese military police). Some also taught in the schools. The Chamorros from the Northern Marianas, having been under Japanese rule for almost thirty years, spoke Japanese as well as their native Chamorro language, and were thus considered indispensable in the Japanese administration of Guam. When Guamanians were arrested and interrogated by the Japanese authorities, there was always a Chamorro interpreter from the northern islands present. Interrogations almost always involved beating and torture, often administered by fellow Chamorros from Saipan and Rota. Few Chamorros from the northern islands who found themselves in these situations were volunteers. They were there by order of the Japanese military. To refuse would have resulted in their own imprisonment and death, and possibly that of members of their families.

Guamanians suffered more than beating and torture at the hands of the Japanese and their Chamorro interpreters. Many were killed while in custody. Some were taken out and shot, while others were decapitated. During the war crimes trials that were held on Guam after the war, almost all of the Chamorros from Saipan and Rota who survived the fighting were tried, convicted, and sentenced to prison terms.

In the 1950s and 1960s the people of the Northern Marianas displayed a strong desire to reunite with Guam and become American citizens. However, the people on Guam voted down the idea in an unofficial poll taken in 1969. The role played by Chamorros from the Northern Marianas during the Japanese occupation of Guam is thought by many to be one of the primary reasons for this failure to reunite the people of the Mariana Islands.

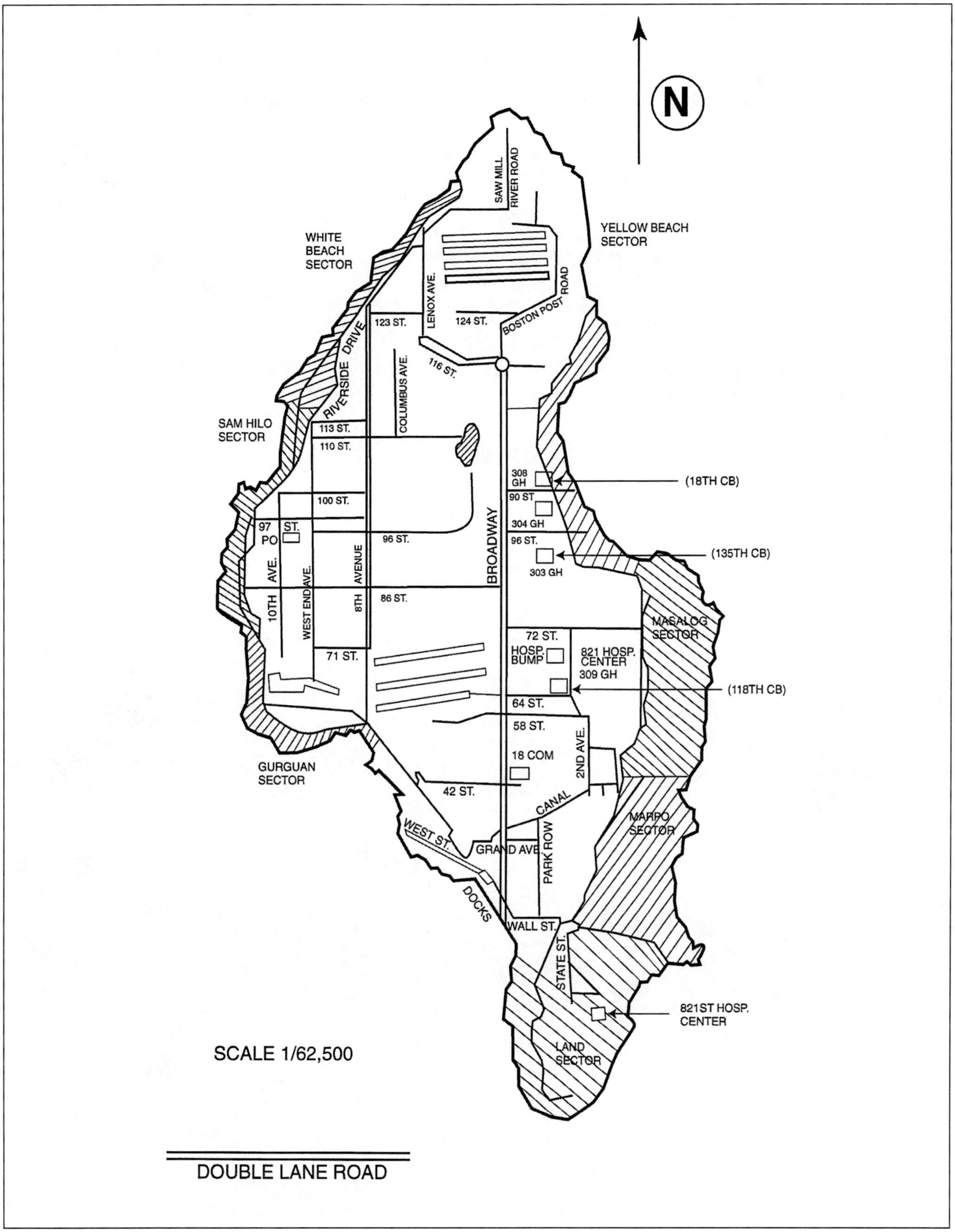


*After Tinian was secured by U.S. Marines, the Seabees took over and named the streets and roads they constructed after those in Manhattan.*

Top: *North Field on the island of Tinian had four runways, with another two to the south of the island, and two more on Saipan. From these bases the United States launched its devastating B-29 air raids against the Japanese home islands, which culminated with the dropping of two atomic bombs on the cities of Hiroshima and Nagaski.* Bottom: *One of two atomic bomb pits found at North Field, Tinian.*

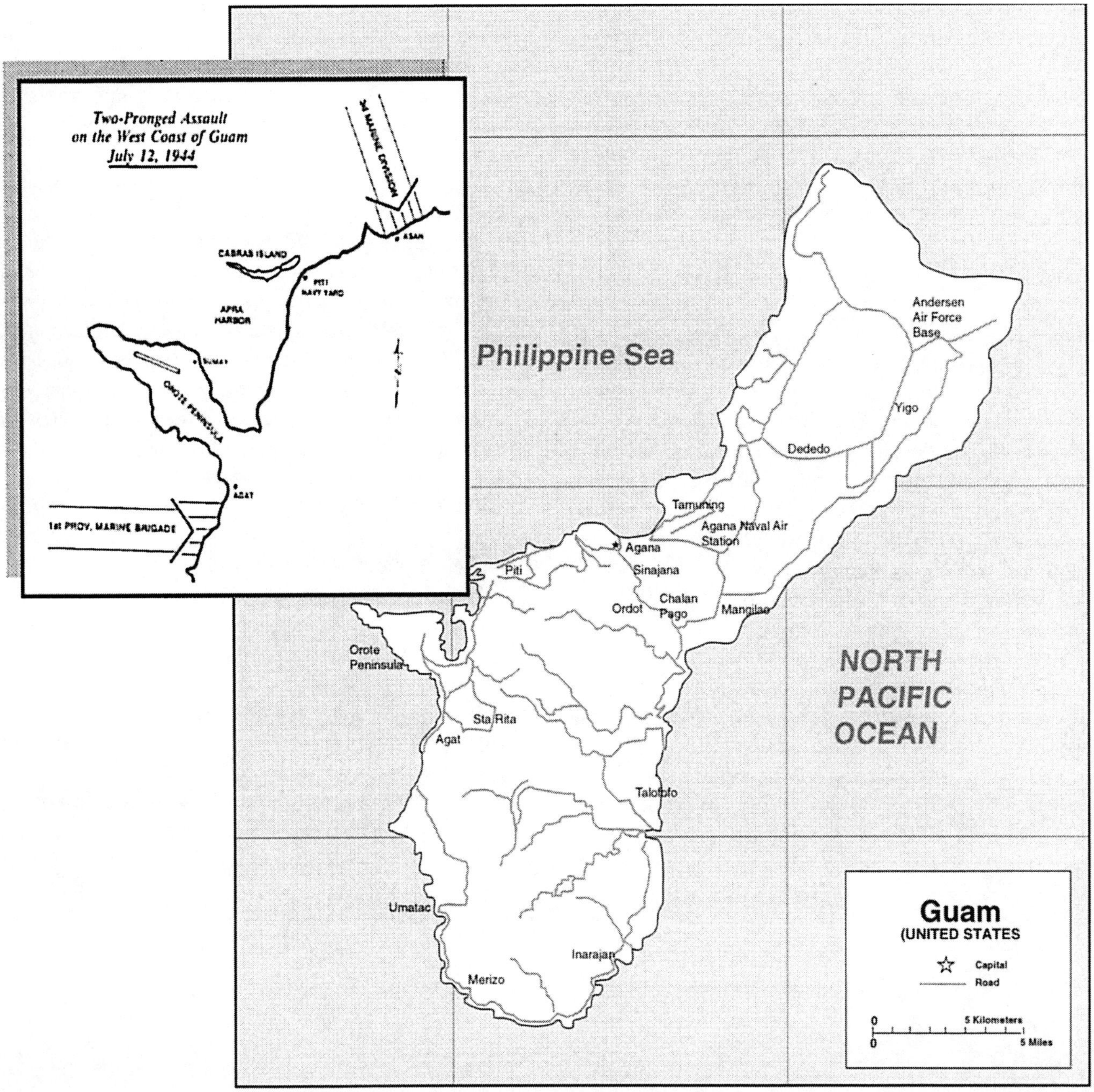


*Map of Guam. (Used by permission of Dale Barker, veteran of the First Armored Amphibian Battalion.)*

## *Part II — American Voices*

In June and July of 1944, U.S. forces invaded and conquered Saipan, then Tinian. Guam was liberated that same July. Today, many American veterans can look back and see that they participated in an event that was much bigger than they were. Some want to be remembered for the part they played. Others, like their island cousins, have spent a lifetime trying to forget.

Unlike the islanders, many of the U.S. servicemen I have interviewed have been able to refer to diaries, regimental histories, cruise books, and other documented sources in recounting experiences during World War II. This has allowed them to compare their memories with documents noting dates, names, and places of actual events when taping their oral histories.

### American Soldiers and Marines

When I arrived on Saipan in June of 1994, the island was preparing for the fiftieth anniversary of the battle for Saipan. Most of the major pre-war Japanese sites and

World War II sites had been cleaned up. Signs had been erected to guide first-time visitors as well as returning veterans. I met several veterans at the airport, in restaurants, and in hotel lobbies. I found that many weren't sure they wanted to be back. One ex–Marine I met at the airport baggage claim told me that the only reason he had come back was because of his son, who was living and working in Japan. His son wanted to come to Saipan, but he did not.

## Liberation

When the bombs began to fall and the shells began to explode, I doubt that inhabitants of the Northern Marianas, or other parts of Micronesia, saw liberation in all of the death and destruction. During the previous thirty years there had been peace and a prosperity. Now, suddenly people were being killed, homes destroyed, livelihoods torn away. A way of life was about to give way to another that nobody could even guess at.

I doubt that the soldiers and Marines who found themselves struggling ashore and being shot at in June of 1944 thought of themselves as liberators. As one Marine Corps veteran of the fighting on Saipan told me, "We didn't come here to liberate anybody. We came here to kill Japs!"

The term "liberation" might have more meaning on the island of Guam, where the people suffered grievously under the brief but terrible Japanese occupation. The majority of Guamanians today see themselves as American citizens and have no desire to change the status quo, although many would like to have Guam's status changed to something other than U.S. territory. A small minority on Guam, as in Puerto Rico, would like complete independence.

Some of what I have shared above came to me through document research. However, most of it came to me from the many interviews I did, not all of which are included in this book. It holds true, especially with veterans of front line fighting, that events of more than fifty years ago are still difficult, and sometimes impossible, to talk about. Many American Marine and Army veterans have told me that though they were willing to share memories with me, there were some memories they would hold with them to the grave. As one former Marine told me, "Many of us have spent the last fifty years trying to forget." I thank those who have taken the time and painful effort to go back to their youth to share a part of history that took place before many of us were born.

These oral histories are not the narratives of generals and admirals. You will not find grand strategies arrayed before you, nor will you find the thoughts of political giants who molded and shaped the rest of the twentieth century. These are stories known only among small circles of family and friends, circles whose radii grow smaller with each passing year. However, the bit parts they played were on a grand stage, and much of the script was written by people in faraway places.

# PART I

## Micronesian Voices: Oral Histories of Pacific Islanders

# 1 Saipan

## Japanese Father, Chamorro Mother

VICKY VAUGHAN

*Vicky Vaughan was born on Saipan in 1933. Her father was a Japanese immigrant, and her mother was a native Chamorro. After the war Vicky attended the American Dependents School on Saipan along with a select group of other locals. She was one of the first two natives of Saipan to win a scholarship to the University of Hawaii. Upon graduation from UOH she returned to Saipan where she briefly taught school. She soon met and married an American serviceman. She then moved to Chicago where she worked as a social worker, and raised five children. She returned to Saipan in 1992, where she now lives.*

My name is Victoria Delos Reyes Akiyama. I was born January 7, 1933, in Garapan, Saipan. Some older people still remember me by my Japanese name, Setchan. My father was Japanese and my mother was Chamorro. My father's name was Tomomitsu Akiyama (Pedro) and he came to Saipan from Yamanashi Ken, near Tokyo. He first came to Saipan in the 1920s when he was still a student. I am told that when he arrived all he had was his bed roll, a pair of chopsticks, and a rice bowl. He met my mother on this trip. He returned to Saipan after he finished his studies, and they married. My father became a Catholic, and to the best of my knowledge never saw Japan again. As a young girl, Saipan was my entire world. It never occurred to me to ask my father why he came to Saipan. Why should I? I was happy. My world was defined, safe, and secure. How was I to know that it would be torn apart, and never put back together again?

My mother's name was Abelina Sablan Reyes and she was the third of nine children. She married my father when she was only seventeen or eighteen. Before she died she gave the world seven children. I don't remember much about my mother. She died when I was only five years old. I remember when relatives came over to perform the rosary; I would hide under the table and watch. I also remember sitting on my mother's death bed, surrounded by other family members and having our pictures taken. The last thing I remember about my mother is her casket being taken from the house.

After my mother died my father married my aunt and had three more children, two girls and one boy. Of the ten children in our family only three of us survived the war. I have a sister who still lives in Saipan, and a brother who lives in California with his wife. Neither one of them will talk to me about what happened to us during the war. I have five children of my own now, but they don't want to talk about it either, because they don't like to see their mother cry. But, I need to talk to somebody.

I had an older brother, but I never knew him because my mother took him to Japan so that he could continue his education. He was supposed to return to Saipan but never did. From our two story house in Garapan we could look out across the lagoon, and past the harbor entrance. Sometimes ships would be sunk by American submarines within sight of our house. One day a ship was sunk just outside of the entrance to the

*Vicky Vaughan (Setchan Akiyama) as she looks today, with the author's children.*

lagoon. My father was frantic because he thought my older brother was on board. As it turned out, he was not on that ship, or any of the ships that tried to make it to Saipan. However, after that day my father turned over part of the house to shelter the survivors of sunken ships. I found out after the war that my oldest brother was in the military and died in the Philippines.

I was a happy child. I never wanted for anything. Our house was not far from the old Garapan Church. We lived close to an air raid shelter that still exists on Beach Road. When American planes started bombing Saipan in February of 1944 we would always go there. One of my older brothers, Shiuichi, was killed during one of these air raids. I don't know the whole story of what happened. He was hiding in a cave with a friend. During a lull in the bombing he left the cave and, according to the friend, a boulder fell on him and crushed his chest. However, this was never confirmed. We never found his body. Like so many, he just disappeared.

Just before the invasion of the island, my father left for some important business in the Marpi area. He was always such a busy man. But I remember, as busy as he was, he always had time for me. One of my last memories of my father was the two of us having a bicycle race on Beach Road in Iliyang. He was such a wonderful man. He must have known that something was going to happen because he made me responsible for his important papers, and he asked one of his friends to look after us if anything happened to him. However, one of the sons in that family was a soldier, and just before the Americans landed he shot and killed everyone in his family. Only their Carolinian maid survived, and it was through her that we knew what happened to them.

On the night before the invasion we fled Garapan. We had a farm in Iliyang where National Office Supply is now, but my stepmother insisted that we go on to Aslito where we had another farm, and she knew my grandparents and other family members to be. After the war somebody told me that my father came back to Garapan looking for us, but we had already left, and when he could not find us at Iliyang he must have assumed that we were all dead. I carried my youngest sister, Elpedio, on my back, and in my arms were the documents that my father had entrusted me to carry to a safe place. All together we were seven, me, my stepmother, and five siblings. I was also responsible for two younger siblings, both of whom wanted to be carried. We walked along the beach where we saw soldiers planting mines. Then we moved inland towards Aslito. We had to stop and take cover from time to time because of the shelling.

When we got to Aslito we went to the house of my uncle, William S. Reyes. Before the fighting reached us we had dug a hole and covered it with palm logs and dirt, but the soldiers took that, and the only place left to hide was under my uncle's house. I remember hearing one of my cousins say, "Oh, look! They are fighting." But, I was busy concentrating on what I had been taught, "Stick your thumbs in your ears, and cover your eyes with your fingers." The next thing I remember is the house disintegrating and catching fire. My sister Teruko just disappeared. I never found any trace of her after that. I looked over to where my stepmother and baby brother were. His head was cracked open and his brains where hanging out. I am sure he was dead, but his lips were still moving as if sucking on his mother's breast. My grandmother and stepmother were both wounded. I was untouched at the time, so I started dragging the wounded away from the burning house and into one of the covered foxholes. I saw my aunt Carmen. She was dead, and someone had laid her body on a box and folded her arms across her chest. Not far from her was my brother, Jose. He had a small hole in his chest, but when I rolled him over his back was shattered. He was trying to hold up his pants when he died, because I had taken his belt. In the same foxhole where I dragged the wounded were two soldiers; one of them had part of his face missing and maggots were crawling around inside. He said to me, "I am a soldier; I am supposed to die. You can come in." He then left with the other soldier. In the foxhole one of my cousins was praying. She was full of holes and blood kept spurting from her wounds. She complained of being hot, and took her clothes off, and tried to wring the blood out. She died shortly after. I watched so many members of my family die that day. I saw another cousin with her stomach ripped open. She

*The wedding photograph of Tomomitsu (Pedro) Akiyama, father of Vicky Vaughan a.k.a. Setchan Akiyama, and Abeline Reyes Akiyama, mother of Vicky Vaughan (on Saipan sometime in the 1920s.)*

*Akiyama Family Photo: Taken sometime in the early 1930s. From left to right are Shiuichi (Jesus) Akiyama, Osamu (Antonio) Akiyama, Setchan (Victoria) Akiyama — the baby in the arms of her mother, Abelina (Maria) Sablan Reyes Akiyama, Galo Reyes (Vicky's maternal uncle), Mariko (Maria) Akiyama (sister of Vicky), Arizumi Akiyama (Vicky's paternal uncle), Mitsunori (Max)— Vicky's older brother who lives today in northern California.*

kept trying to push her intestines back in with her dirty hands. I sat at the entrance to the foxhole trying to protect them from further harm. It was some time later; I don't remember how long it was, I felt something hot on my back. They were using flame throwers, and my back had been burned. I screamed hysterically.

When the Americans captured us they treated our wounds on the spot, then transferred us by ambulance to a makeshift hospital at Camp Susupe. I was laying face down on a stretcher in an ambulance so I saw very little of the carnage around me. Before we left the foxhole for Camp Susupe I remember that everything around us was burned. My stepmother had a broken shoulder, and it was in a cast. We were in the same tent at Camp Susupe one night when the air raid warning siren went off. I was so scared that I jumped out of my cot and onto my stepmother. I must have landed on her broken shoulder, because she screamed. When I was able to get up and move around they allowed me to visit my grandmother in another tent. People were always dying in that tent, but she survived.

In Camp Susupe we were always hungry. I think that is where most of us tasted Spam for the first time. Sometimes American soldiers would call us over to the barbed wire fence and give us chocolate. We were provided with no shelter. We had to make our own with whatever materials we could salvage. Pieces of rice sacking might be all we had for a door. We were all covered with lice. We must have looked like monkeys at times, all sitting in a line picking bugs out of the hair of the person in front of us. We had to be on guard at night because sometimes American soldiers would come into camp looking for young women.

While we were still in Camp Susupe people, even friends and relatives, told me I could no longer speak Japanese. I had spoken Japanese all of my life; now people were telling me I couldn't. The Japanese were all dead, or in camps like us. The Americans were in charge now. Because I was half Japanese people who used to be my friends started calling me names like "Tojo."

I think I must have been in a state of shock during those days. I was able to function, but I could not and did not shed a tear. I asked around about my father. Some people said that he had stopped by their cave, but did not linger for long. One of my cousins told me that she last saw him at a cave in Talofofo, but that was the last time anybody saw him. Even though I watched most of my family get killed, I still had hope that my father was still alive, and that he would take care of me, and all would be well again. In Camp Susupe there was a Mr. Guerrero. He told me one day that my father would come the next day. As a young girl I was always taught to look up to and respect adults. You could always depend on them; they would never lie to you. All that next day, and for some days afterward I sat outside my shelter and waited and watched, but my father never came. Ever since then I have been suspicious of people. After more than fifty years I still miss my father.

## My Two Families

### Sister Antonieta Ada

*Sister Antonieta Ada lost her Japanese family, with the exception of her older brother, during the fighting on Saipan in 1944. She joined the Mercedarian Order of the Catholic Church in 1963 and is a graduate of St. Mary's College in Leavenworth, Kansas.*

My Japanese name was Nishikawa, Kimiko. My Chamorro name is Antonieta Ada. I don't remember my Japanese mother's maiden name, but her first name was Nami. My mother and father had six children and I was the second youngest. Of my immediate family only my oldest brother and myself survived the war.

My father's first name was Tsunetaro and he shredded and dried tapioca for export to Japan. I am told it was used to make some kind of liquor. I think he was also a lawyer. He would ride his bicycle from our home in Laolao to his office in Garapan, and come home on weekends and holidays and for the harvest. My mother pretty much ran the farm. She worked very hard, getting up early in the morning. When I got up to go to school she would be back in the house preparing breakfast, her clothing wet from being in the fields. I don't remember my Japanese mother ever saying much. She was a quiet woman. The only thing I recall her saying to me was, "Never tell lies. Liars grow up to become criminals." She said that to me and my brothers and sisters many times.

My father had a good friend. His name was Juan Martinez Ada, and his wife's name was Ana Cepeda. Mr. Ada was like the mayor of all the Chamorros and Refalawasch (Carolinians) during the Japanese period. He had farms in Chalan Kiya, Chalan Laolao, and Laolao Bay. He was very wealthy in those days. The Adas only had three children, and two of them died while still young. Their one surviving son died during the war in Camp Susupe. He had spent many days in a shelter during the fighting and probably died from the effects of hunger and disease. Mr. Ada, because he and my Japanese father were such good friends, asked my Japanese father if he could have me. I was two years old at the time. My Japanese father agreed. At first I was very confused. I didn't know who my real parents were.

*Sister Antonieta Ada, M.M.B.*

On special Japanese holidays my Japanese father would come to my Chamorro home in Garapan and bring me Japanese food. I remember thinking to myself, "Who is this man, and why does he bring me Japanese food?"

In those days the Japanese had better schools than the Chamorros and Refalawasch, so my Japanese father decided that when I came of school age I would live with my Japanese family during the school year, and my Chamorro family on weekends and vacation. So you see, during those early years I was not sure who my real family was. It was when I started to go to school that I realized that I had two families.

In those days we traveled mostly by bull cart and sometimes by truck. The only time we traveled on the sugar cane train was between Garapan and Tanapag for the Fiesta of the Virgin Mary of Remedios. Sometimes on the weekends I would go with my Chamorro family to our farm in Chalan Laolao. We would spread mats on the ground. This was a time for singing and playing games. I guess what I remember most about my Chamorro family is going to church and learning how to pray. My Ada family was always reminding me that I was their daughter and that I should help them when they became old. But after the war, when I was about fourteen or fifteen, I knew that God had a purpose for me. I felt that he was calling me. I told my mother that I wanted to join the Mercedarian Order, but she told me, "No, you just like to go to the convent because you have friends there. You have to be very smart and work very hard to become a sister." "Besides," she used to say to me, "you are my only daughter. You have to take care of me until I die. After I die, then you can become a sister." But I didn't know when she was going to die, so when I was about twenty-seven, which at that time was a late age for joining a religious order, I went against my mother's wishes. In December of 1962 I arrived in Kansas City, Missouri, to attend St. Mary's College. However, a friend advised me to join the Mercedarian Order first, then complete my education. I took her advice and as a result did not start college until September of 1966. I graduated in 1970 and returned to Saipan in August of that year. While I was away my mother, Ana Cepeda Ada, died and was buried before I even knew about it. In those days the mail was not very good. In the end I guess you could say that I failed to carry out the one wish my mother had of me. Only God knows how much I suffered on account of this, but at the same time I had to trust that everything was in God's hands. He will reward whatever we do for his love.

Before the invasion of Saipan it was very peaceful here. There was not much crime like we see today; fighting, killing, and stealing. Everybody helped one another in those days. If you wanted to build a house, friends and families came to help you, but that was more of a Chamorro and Refalawasch custom. The Japanese worked harder. The Chamorros were more relaxed; the Japanese more businesslike.

Life started to change several years before Saipan was invaded by the Americans. The Japanese closed our church. The Sisters who ran a school for girls set up a makeshift church in the basement and church services were held there.

Our home was at Laolao Beach and I went to school in Chacha (now called Kagman). Just before the actual invasion took place I remember seeing several trucks with Japanese soldiers drive up to our school. They went into the administration building, and the next day we had to take our classes under a mango tree. Later, when the bombs began to fall, classes ended for good. All that remains of the school today are the steps going up to the classrooms.

One day when we were on a hill near Laolao, behind our farm, we could see American planes bombing Aslito Field. The fires they caused burned for several days. On another occasion I watched two planes beyond Laolao Bay. One of them caught fire and crashed into the ocean. The soldiers said that the Americans would invade Saipan at Laolao Bay, so they planted mines under water, but they later floated to the surface.

When the fighting started my Japanese family and I hid in a cave above our property in Laolao, but we were between two anti-aircraft batteries, and my father decided that if we were to survive we would have to move to a safer location. He knew there was a big cave near Chacha and that it was full of food. So, one night we left in two groups. Three of the older children left first because my father felt that they could move faster. We never saw any of them again. The rest of us left later. It was not until the year 1995 that I found out that the brother just above me in age was killed by a bomb or shell in the Marpi area. I discovered this from an Okinawan woman who used to work on the farm of my Japanese father in Laolao. There are Okinawans who lived here before the war. Some of them come back almost every year to pray for those they lost during the war. They have their own memorial in Marpi. The reason they had never contacted me before was because they didn't know my Chamorro name. I still don't know how they found me, but when they did they invited me to the hotel where they were staying. Some of them were my classmates when we were very young and they still remembered me, but I didn't remember them.

There were lots of people at Chacha, so after only one night we moved again, this time to the Talofofo area. By then the enemy was closing in on Talofofo and we had to move again. We traveled at night and hid during the day, but even at night the ships fired off flares that lit up the night. I remember very little conversation among us in those days. We were just running and hiding. From Talofofo we went to Banzai Cliff. I think now that my father was taking us there to jump off with all of the other people. However, when we arrived somebody yelled that the enemy was coming, and we all ran. My father new the area pretty well and took us to a cave close to the ocean. There were several soldiers and other people there. I don't know how long we stayed in that cave, but my little brother fell ill while we were there, and died.

One night my father and oldest brother went out from the cave to find water and food. They were passing by a sugar cane field when a machine gun opened fire on them. My father was hit in the legs. Both he and my brother laid face down on the ground until the firing stopped. Then my brother carried my father back to the cave where he died later that night. A Japanese soldier helped my brother bury my father under a tree somewhere near the cave. Many years later my brother came back to Saipan to find my father's bones. He was sure that he could find my father's grave because he was buried under this tree, but the tree was no longer there and my brother finally had to give up. Instead of bones, he returned to Japan with small stones, one for each family member lost in Saipan.

With only three of us left my mother decided that we should return to our farm. We left at night but had gone only a short distance when once again a machine gun started to fire in our direction. My mother was hit. The rest of us fled, thinking my mother had been killed. We later found out that she had only been wounded, but laid in the open for three or four days before American soldiers found her and took her to Camp Susupe. The rest of us ran — I don't know where. At some point my brother and I became separated.

Later that night I heard voices speaking Japanese. When I came closer I found Japanese gathering sweet potatoes from a field. They invited me to join them.

I was in the jungle looking for food one day when I heard somebody coming, so I hid. As the person drew closer to where I was hiding I peeked around a tree to see who it was. I couldn't believe it; it was my older brother. Both of us remained with the other Japanese until our supply of food became very low. By then the Americans had loud speakers that we could hear from where we were hiding. They told us to come out and they would give us food and water. The woman who invited me to join the others was a natural leader. Even the Japanese soldiers among us listened to her. She was the one who pointed out that we had little food left and that we should surrender. I really don't remember anything about the soldiers we surrendered to. They all looked alike to me in those days. However, I do remember the American soldiers who would come to Camp Susupe and give the children candy and gum, but I was older and didn't want to get involved with them. I felt some hatred towards them; they killed my mother and father. Later, when I was older, I learned not to hate. I was luckier than most because I had my Chamorro family. The Adas loved me and were very good to me.

Camp Susupe was awful; just tents with sand for floors. I think the Japanese at Camp Susupe were not treated as well as the Chamorros. The Chamorro camp seemed to have better accommodations and better food. I was not in the Japanese camp for long because my Chamorro father, Juan Ada, came to get me. I saw my Japanese mother only once after my arrival in Camp Susupe. She was very weak and could hardly talk. She died not long after that. Because I was a girl I was allowed to stay with my Chamorro family, but because Japanese law prohibits a male child to be adopted by non–Japanese my brother was repatriated to Japan.

At first only farmers were allowed to leave the camp to tend to their crops, but they had to return at night. Eventually we Chamorros left Camp Susupe and moved into buildings in Chalan Kanoa that were not destroyed during the fighting. One day my cousin, who was maybe twenty years old, and my brother came to my home in Chalan Kanoa. My cousin said, "They are sending us back to Japan. Do you want to come with us or stay here?" It was a very difficult decision for me to make, but because I loved my Ada family so much I decided to stay in Saipan. My brother did not protest. My cousin said, "Okay, you stay if you like and when things settle down in Japan I will come back and get you if you change your mind."

Saipan for many years was made off limits by the U.S. military, so it was very difficult for Japanese to visit. I don't think Japanese were allowed to return to look for the remains of loved ones until sometime in the 1960s. Over the years I tried many times to make contact with my brother in Japan. I wrote letters to the Japanese consulate in Hawaii asking them to help me find my brother, but nothing ever came of my efforts. Then one day a Japanese Navy training ship came to Saipan. My cousin, who was then living in Yokosuka, sent me a letter through one of the student sailors on board this ship. Of course I wrote back immediately and sent my letter back to her through this same person on the ship. I asked her to find my brother for me. We eventually made contact. He was living about two hours from Tokyo in Saitama Prefecture. I later took a ship to Japan to see my brother, but I had forgotten my Japanese and he did not speak English, so you can imagine what a difficult reunion we had. We communicated with our tears. Some years after I had joined the Mercedarian Order I returned to Japan and lived there for eleven years as a missionary. That was 1977 to 1988. I relearned my Japanese language and Japanese culture at this time. In 1988 I returned to Saipan, where I still live.

## Escolastica

### Escolastica Tudela Cabrera

*Escolastica Tudela Cabrera was born in Saipan in 1930. Her ancestry is Spanish, English, and Chamorro. She is one of thirteen children born to Vicente Ramirez Tudela and Rita Diaz Borja. She started her own business in Saipan at the age of nineteen, was a member of the municipal legislature in 1963, and can still be found today at Esco's Bake House on Capitol Hill. She is married to Gregorio Camacho Cabrera, and they have thirteen children.*

My father worked for the Germans in the phosphate mines on the island of Angaur. When the Japanese took over in 1914 he continued to work in the mines for the Japanese. The whole time my father worked on Angaur he would send food and money to his parents on Saipan. Sometimes it would take as long as six months for a letter or package to go from Angaur to Saipan. He returned to Saipan in 1929 after sixteen years of working in the phosphate mines. I was born the following year, 1930.

Even though my father was away from Saipan for so long he was still close to his parents. The reason he came back was because they were getting old and they needed him to help take care of them. While he was still on Angaur he asked his father to save a piece of land for him so that he would have a place to live and support his family.

On Saipan our house was in Garapan near where China Town is today. My mother's family had some land in As Teo and my father and mother farmed that. From our house in Garapan it took them four hours by bull cart to get to the farm, so they would leave on Monday and come back to Garapan on Saturday. They grew coffee, tapioca, and tobacco—everything by hand. My father and mother worked very hard. Because my parents were away at the farm all week, the older children had the responsibility of raising us younger ones. When they came home on weekends my father would stretch out on the floor and we children would massage his muscles, then he would tell us stories. He

*Escolastica Tudela Cabrera in 1945. Having survived the war, along with most members of her family, she went on to become an independent-minded and successful business woman. (Courtesy of Escolastica T. Cabrera.)*

told us about the Germans and how strict they were. If somebody committed a crime like stealing a cow during German times they had to walk through the town with a sign around their neck that told what they had done wrong, then they were sent to one of the northern islands to do work, like plant coconut trees.

I went to Catholic school for a while, then I went to a Japanese school for Chamorros and Carolinians. The Japanese wanted us to learn Japanese language and customs. Every morning we had to go to the Genja (Shinto Temple) to bow and pray towards Japan. I was one of the top ten in my class, and when the teacher had to leave the class I was given a red and white arm band and put in charge of the class. If the students acted up while the teacher was gone I was held responsible. If we did something wrong our Japanese teachers hit us, sometimes with a ruler, sometimes with a leather whip. I was once struck across the ear, and two students actually died from beatings they received from teachers. One was in 1942 and one was in 1943. In 1942, when I was in the second grade, the teacher beat a Carolinian girl and she died. Her name was Soledad Repeki. A year later this same teacher beat another student, who also died. His name was Alejandro Cabrera. People went to the police to complain about the killings, but they don't listen to Chamorros and Carolinians. They just tell us to go away. Nothing was done about that teacher. He was a big man, very mean. My husband who started school a couple of years before me had a different teacher and he said his teacher was very nice.

In 1943 the Japanese started to expand Aslito Field. They used forced labor to do the work, all by hand. One of my brothers was among those forced to work there. They were not paid, and were given very little to eat, only some rice and water. Sometimes at night my brother would come to our farm asking for food. In 1942 they closed our school and put us to work carrying sand for the airstrip they were building in Susupe, down where the Civic Center is today. I had to carry bags of sand on my back. I was twelve years old then. The Japanese would tell us Chamorro people nothing about the war and I couldn't read kanji. People were

*Escolastica Tudela Cabrera today. Here she is standing outside her home on Capitol Hill. "Esco" still owns a small market and bakery, the last of many business enterprises she has established and owned over the years since war's end. Today, her children run the store. (Photograph courtesy of Pedro C. Sablan.)*

very quiet, but when they started building the airfield I knew something was coming. The Japanese started to ration food. They gave us coupons.

My husband's brother, Antonio Camacho Cabrera, and my brother, Manuel Borja Tudela, were sent to Guam to be interpreters once the Japanese had taken over from the Americans. One time a Japanese officer had a Guamanian hung by the neck and then told my brother to beat him. The man died. After the Americans came back in 1944 they rounded up all of the Chamorros from Saipan who had worked for the Japanese. There was an investigation and [people were] put on trial. All of the Chamorros—there were twelve or fifteen—were sentenced to life in prison. But Chamorros are all Catholic, so the families of these men came to Guam and apologized. My mother went to the wife of the man that my brother killed and apologized. When she came home she was crying. She got down on her knees and prayed. After eight years in prison they were all paroled.

While on Guam my brother married a Guamanian and they had one son. She came to visit us once in 1948, but when she returned to Guam she divorced my brother. My brother would never talk about what he did on Guam during the war. My brother-in-law, Antonio, disappeared during the fighting on Guam. Nobody knows what happened to him.

One day before the actual fighting started on Saipan I was down by the lagoon buying fish; this was about five o'clock in the afternoon. I think that was in 1943. There were dark clouds and it looked like a big rain was coming. I remember looking out towards Managaha, the small island in the lagoon. A Japanese ship was coming into the harbor when it suddenly blew up. Many people were killed on that ship. There were also two Chamorros on the ship returning to Saipan after going to school in Japan. One was Joaquin Sablan and the other was Francisco Cruz. They both survived.

In June of 1944 when the fighting started on Saipan I was on our farm in As Teo. Japanese soldiers would come there to bathe and wash their clothes in the spring. There was one Japanese soldier who liked me and told my father that he wanted to marry me after the war, but my father didn't like him; he didn't trust him. I think he was on Guam before coming to Saipan because he would bring us things like American soap. He borrowed our sewing machine sometimes and when he returned it he would bring us a big spool of thread. He told us that the Americans would kill everybody except the young girls. The girls they would take to the ships to be geishas, but I never heard of American soldiers taking advantage of girls, at least not 'til after the war.

We were lucky because we had many caves on our farm. We hid in one that was very big, but the Japanese came and kicked us out. They wanted to use it as a hospital cave. We had to go to a smaller one. We couldn't even stand up inside it. There were about forty-five of us in there. It was very tight, but nobody complained. We stayed there for nineteen days.

There was a spring near our cave so we had plenty to drink. One day when all of the men went to the spring to get water there were American soldiers nearby. They fired their guns and all of the men threw down their containers and ran back to the cave, but nobody was killed. When one of my older brothers got back to the cave he asked my father, "What does God-damn-son-of-bitch mean?" My father laughed.

We were more afraid of the Japanese than the Americans. There was a Japanese soldier next to our cave and he kept cleaning his gun, taking the bullets out and putting them back in. When a big piece of shell hit next to his head he ran away, and so did the Japanese in the big cave.

Some of the women wanted me to go and tell the Americans that we were in the cave but I was afraid. The Japanese were above our cave firing down at the Americans with machine guns and rifles, and the Americans were firing back. I didn't want to go out. Then some Japanese came by our cave with their big swords and said if anybody went to the Americans they would cut our throats.

My father, who was also a cobbler, made a door over the front of the cave with a dried cow skin. Then this American captain came and kicked down our door. My mother's voice was the first to come out. She was saying, "Paz Chamorro men, Catholic men, Christian men!" She kept repeating that. One of my brothers had been to Guam and he knew a few English words. He said, "Never mind. Hello friend." He kept repeating that. Then that captain asked if anybody spoke Spanish or Japanese. My father spoke Spanish and all of us spoke some Japanese. The captain then talked into his radio and some soldiers came; I think they were Mexicano. They were very interesting. All they wanted to know was, "Where is the priest; where are the nuns?" They were afraid that the Japanese were going to kill the priests and nuns. I don't know why but they were afraid that the Japanese would think they were spies and kill them. Then my father gave the Americans one of my brothers to go with them. His name is Jose. The soldiers gave him a uniform and a helmet. They used him to speak Japanese and get soldiers to surrender. He was gone for more than one month. My mother was crying every day, "Where is my son? Where is my son? Maybe he is dead." She complained to my father, "Why did you give my son away?"

Before the war during Japanese times things were peaceful. Most Japanese people were nice, but there was not much opportunity for Chamorro women. We could marry, or if not marry, be a housekeeper. But when the fighting started the Japanese became mean. We became like slaves— forced labor. Then the Japanese really treated us like third class citizens. They would come to our farm and take whatever they wanted. If we protested they would threaten us. They didn't take advantage of Chamorro women because they had Korean and Japanese women in Garapan.

Before the war we never saw an American. We didn't know about American culture. When we were still in Camp Susupe we could go out and work. One Chamorro girl met an American soldier and they wanted to get married, but there was this Spanish priest who had been on Saipan since before the war. He was a Jesuit, and he wouldn't marry them. He told us that if a Chamorro marries an American the family of the Americans will think them ugly like puppies. He always told us that Americans should marry Americans, Chamorros marry Chamorros, and Carolinians marry Carolinians. His name was Father Jose Tardio. He was only here for a couple of years after the war, then another priest, a Capuchin, took over. His name was Father Arnold Bendowski, and he stayed here for thirty years. He did not prevent Chamorros and Carolinians from getting married to Americans.

During Japanese times we had nothing. When the Americans took over we had a better life. They gave us Social Security and Welfare. But I don't like these laws about child abuse. I have many friends who were arrested because they disciplined their children. In Chamorro custom we spank children if they do something wrong so they will grow up to be good. Sometimes we use a whip made from the cow's tail. I told my children if they do one thing wrong they get one hit. If they do two things wrong they get two hits. My father always told me don't hit on the head because that is an important place, and don't break bones. If the skin is bloody, that is okay because it will heal. Also, American culture says that when a child turns eighteen years old he can marry, or not listen to his parents. That is not a part of our culture. In Chamorro culture you stay at home until you get married. I have one daughter, she is forty-five and she is still with me because she is not married. Now, Chamorro and Carolinian children when they are eighteen they go and do what they want. American culture has weakened the traditional Chamorro family.

When I was sixteen, this is after the fighting, I went with my brother, Torcuato, and worked in the handicraft shop. It was run by Juan Blanco. This was on consignment. We did pandanas weaving and wood carving, and the Americans would come there to buy. We made very good money that way. In those days people working for the military only made thirty-five cents a day. That was maybe ninety percent of the people, and they complained about people making handicrafts making so much money. Because of that we had to stop and go out and find another kind of work. I learned how to sew, then one of the officer's wives started a beauty parlor. She offered me fifty cents a day plus tips if I would work for her. I eventually learned the business and when she left the island she offered to sell the business to me for $500. That was a lot of money in those days. I had to get a loan, but I paid that loan back in six months.

## The Fisherman's Son

### Juan Blanco

*Juan Blanco is a seventy-three-year-old native of Saipan. His father, Juan Taitano Blanco, came to Saipan from Guam at the turn of the twentieth century along with his wife, Antonia Aquon Blas. He was one of the first natives of Saipan to attend school in Japan during the Japanese occupation of the Mariana Islands. Upon his return to Saipan in 1939 he was allowed to continue his studies at a Japanese high school and graduated near the top of his class. After Saipan had been taken from the Japanese by U.S. forces, Juan worked for the U.S. Military. He was Speaker of the House from 1960 to 1962 during the Trust Territory days and was manager of the Bank of America on Saipan, from 1947 to 1970.*

In 1934 a number of professors and students from different universities in Japan came to Saipan to look around. They went to Japanese schools and the one native school, and saw that the school system was segregated. I'm not sure but I think they decided then to select a native student to take to Japan to study; this was on a trial basis. I was a student president and one of the top students in my class. They talked to my teacher and he selected me to be the one to go. I think my father had something to do with it as well. You know, even though he was born on Guam he had a talent for languages. He learned to speak Japanese well and many Japanese liked him because of that. They asked my parents if they could take me to Japan to study. My father, after consulting with my mother, agreed to let me go. I was the only native student to go at that time. Later, other native students followed.

I remember the day I boarded the ship to go to Japan. I was happy and sad at the same time. I was the only Saipanese on board, but I was treated very well. It took us seven days to reach Japan and I was seasick most of the way. That is what I remember most, being sick. They had to send the doctor to see me. I traveled to Japan with the son of the family I would stay with for my first two years in Japan. The family name was Mori. The son's first name was Atsusi. He was older than me by nine years. My first two months in Japan were the most difficult for me. Every night I pulled the blanket over my head and cried. I missed my mother and Tony, my younger brother. My first day in school the teacher introduced me to the students. They were surprised to see that I wasn't black and that I was not a cannibal. They took my picture because they had never seen anybody from Saipan. But after that they treated me very well.

I arrived in Japan in August; it was still summer, but by November it started to get cold. Japan in those days was a poor country. The house I stayed in didn't have a heater and I had never experienced cold weather before. All they had to keep warm by was a hibachi in which they burned coal. The Mori family had a small store attached to the house. They sold cigarettes, sembei

*Juan Blanco (center, holding ball) at age ten in 1934 at the Hayashi-cho Elementary School in Koishikawa, Tokyo.*

*Juan Blanco, left, with other former staff of Nanyo Kohatsu, the sugar company in Japan. Beside him, left to right: T. Watanabe, T. Hoshino, and K. Takashima.*

(small rice crackers), and vegetables. One of my duties around the house was to clean the floor with a rag and cold water. In the winter my hands would swell and hurt.

I lived with the Mori family in Tokyo for two years. Then my sister Elizabeth came to Japan along with two other Chamorro girls, Rufina Muna and Maria Arriola, to go to nursing school. After two years of living and going to school in Tokyo I moved to the city of Shimizu about halfway between Tokyo and Osaka. I stayed with a Dr. Narushima and his wife. They had a big house and no children, so it was just me, my sister, and the two other Chamorro nursing students. I was very happy there. The Narushimas treated me like their son. Mrs. Narushima would stay up with me late at night while I did my homework, feeding me pieces of fruit and giving me encouragement. Every year when I go back to Japan I go to their graves and pray. I still have close contact with my Japanese classmates from Shimizu. I go to class reunions and many of them come to visit me in Saipan.

By 1939 Japan was at war with China. My father heard about this on Saipan and became concerned for my safety. I didn't feel I was in any kind of danger but my father did, so he told me to return to Saipan.

When I arrived back on Saipan I was allowed to continue my studies in the Japanese school system, but I had to have a Japanese name, so they called me Seiichi Kamiyama. I don't know why; probably because Chamorros where not supposed to go to Japanese schools.

In Japan there was no discrimination against me, but on Saipan things were different. In those days on Saipan, Japanese and Okinawans were first class citizens, Koreans were second class citizens, and Chamorros and Carolinians were third class citizens. I was treated pretty well except sometimes when I beat Japanese and Okinawan students at wrestling. Chamorros were not supposed to be better than them at anything.

All of my teachers were very good to me except for one, but that is not important; he was very Japanese. You see I worked very hard in school and made good grades. I was near the top of my class and when I graduated in 1942 I thought I would be on the honor roll, but the Japanese had a rule that only Japanese could be on the honor roll.

One of my Japanese teachers was like a father to me. His name was Mr. Yoshida. He came to my house after I graduated and explained to my father why I was not on the honor roll. I cried when I found out, and my father was very sad. That was in December 1942.

After graduation I applied for a job with the Japanese Civil Service. Mr. Yoshida checked on my application and found that because I was not Japanese I would not make the same salary as a Japanese even if they accepted my application. So then he went to the management of Nanyo Kohatsu Kaisha (NKK), the South Seas Development Company. In Japanese times that was the sugar company. Mr. Yoshida told them about me, that I spoke Japanese fluently, and that I had graduated from Japanese schools. They told my teacher that they would be happy to have me in their company and I was hired into their staff management training program. I received a salary equal to that of the Japanese and I was treated no differently than anybody else. I stayed with the sugar company until the Americans invaded in June 1944. Mr. Yoshida survived the war. He wrote to me in

*Juan Blanco, left, with a former classmate, standing beside their school monument in Sugarking Park, Saipan, 1999.*

1947 to see how I was doing. I wrote back but never heard from him after that.

Maria, one of my sisters, married a Japanese. She was a twin, and she and her Japanese husband are still alive and live on Guam. His name is Kamiyama, just like the name they gave me in school, though there was no connection. This guy Kamiyama was the first son of a Shinto priest in Tochigi, north of Tokyo. In Japan the firstborn son gets everything when the father dies, but when Kamiyama was a young man he came to Saipan. While on Saipan he met my sister and fell in love with her. So he gave up his inheritance to stay on Saipan and marry Maria. He asked many times for permission from his family in Japan to marry her. They finally gave it to him and his younger brother inherited his role as first son. This happened while I was going to school in Japan. I only heard about it after my return to Saipan.

I used to read Japanese newspapers so I knew there was tension between the United States and Japan. I remember Japan wanted to have access to oil and other natural resources in Indochina and the United States prevented that. I think that is what started the war. Japanese propaganda kept saying that Japan was winning, but I knew that Guadalcanal had been lost and after that I became suspicious about Japanese claims of victory.

We had our home in Garapan, but in 1941 or 1942 the military chased us out and took our house. We had property in Susupe where Camp Susupe used to be. My family stayed there until the American invasion in 1944. During the actual invasion I was separated from my family. The sugar company I worked for took over construction of the airfield in Marpi. I was up there in February 1944, when the Americans first bombed Saipan. I think they were B-24s. They dropped a few bombs in our area but not many. After that I saw dog fights in the air many times. Several planes crashed at sea and on Saipan. I heard about two American airmen who were shot down and captured. They were later killed, or that is what I heard.

Later, we left Marpi to escape the bombings. There is a large cave not far from Calabara cave. There were maybe 1,000 Japanese in the cave. I stayed there for about two weeks. There was a large boulder in front of the mouth to that cave, and one day while I was in there with my NKK co-workers a bomb landed between that boulder and the mouth of the cave, killing many people. My sister Concepcion, who was in another part of the cave, survived. I found her afterwards and we went to another cave in the Marpi area. Concepcion and I hid in that cave until the Americans arrived. Some soldiers walked right past our cave without seeing us.

We had plenty to eat. The Japanese soldiers had lots of canned food; luxury food, corned beef, tuna, salmon, and things like that. But water, that was the problem; we ran out of water and that is when we decided to surrender. The Americans separated me from my sister and took her to the Chamorro camp at Susupe. They thought I was Japanese, and put me in the Japanese camp for two weeks before I was able to convince them that I was Chamorro.

There was an American I met while I was in Camp Susupe; I think he was from Kansas. His name was Lt. Russell Stevens. He spoke very good Japanese and was a very nice fellow. We maintained contact for a long time after the war. I think he is dead now. He helped me get back with my family. Fortunately, all of them survived.

After about a month in Camp Susupe I was given a job by the Americans. It was a hard job. I had to carry Japanese ammunitions out of caves where they had been left after the fighting. Then I was made a kitchen helper at thirty-five cents a day. My friend Lt. Stevens knew I spoke some English that I had learned in high school, so he got me a job managing the handy craft shop that was very popular among U.S. military people.

When I think about it I did pretty well under both the Japanese and the Americans. I didn't suffer too much. The worst part for me right after the war was the sanitation. The flies and the mosquitoes were terrible.

# The Policeman

## Gregorio C. Cabrera

*Gregorio C. Cabrera was born in October of 1925 to Ramon Taisague Cabrera and Concepcion Campos Camacho. Gregorio was born on the island of Angaur in Palau. At the time his father was working in the phosphate mines under the Japanese. His mother returned to Saipan with the family while his father remained in Angaur, not returning until after World War II.*

On Angaur I remember my father operated a machine that loaded the phosphate onto ships. I didn't go to school while we lived on Angaur, but I do remember I used to go to the mountains with my friends to catch chickens and wild monkeys. We sold the monkeys to the Japanese. I think they took them back to Japan. The soil on Angaur was very good but I don't remember much farming being done there. In the mountains the papayas were very big, not small like on Saipan. When we came back to Saipan we took a ship to Palau, then to Saipan. When we arrived on Saipan my mother took me to register for school, but it was too late in the year so I had to wait until 1933 to start school. On Saipan we lived in Garapan with one of my father's brothers. In those days we ate locally grown fruits and vegetables, things like bananas and breadfruit. We also raised pigs and chickens. We didn't eat rice; that was only for the Japanese. We didn't have the habit of eating rice. We were still under the Spanish influence. We ate mostly corn meal tortillas. In those days we didn't have the health problems that we have today. Diabetes was a word we never heard. We worked hard and walked everywhere. People weren't fat then. We didn't party like we do now.

My family owned land in Gualo Rai. We rented most of it to the Japanese. Before the war we had no problems with the Japanese. When the Japanese forced us out of our home in Garapan we moved to our land in Gualo Rai. A Mr. Koyamada was the principal of our school; he was also my teacher. When he was not teaching our class, Nicolas Diaz acted as a substitute teacher. After I graduated from school in 1938 I worked for a construction company called Sagami-gumi. We built the Japanese Navy headquarters in Gualo Rai. There is a garment factory there now. After that I worked in a tapioca starch factory (Nanyo Tapioka Kaisha). I worked there a very short time, maybe eight months. Then I worked in a soap factory (Oshima Soap Factory) for two years and eight months. That was just before the invasion of Saipan.

One day all of my friends were called to the Japanese headquarters. They wanted people to work on Aslito Airfield. I wanted to be with my friends so I went too, but without telling my boss at the soap factory, Mr. Saito. I was already on the truck to go to Aslito Field when Mr. Saito came looking for me. I saw him ride up on his bicycle. He told the Japanese organizing the work detail that I did the work of two men, so they pulled me off the truck and put two men in my place. I went back to the soap factory.

The reason I went to work in the soap factory was because my brother, Jose, who worked there before me was sent to Guam by the Japanese to be an "Interpreter." Just before Pearl Harbor the Japanese picked my brother and nine other Chamorros to go. This was on December 7, 1941 [December 6th Hawaiian time]. They were sent on a fishing boat. When they arrived near the coast of Guam they were put ashore in two smaller boats. The boat that my brother was on arrived safely on the beach and the five people on board hid in the mountains. The other boat capsized in the surf. A Guamanian Chamorro saw these people and reported them to the local police. The five people on this boat were arrested and interrogated. They told the authorities that the Japanese were going to invade Guam at 0800 the next day, and they were supposed to be there before the invasion to act as interpreters when the Japanese arrived. These five Chamorros were locked up in a jail and told that when the Japanese arrived they would be taken out and shot. But when the Japanese arrived everybody ran away and nobody in that group was killed. My older brother, Antonio, was on Guam at this time serving as a policeman. We never saw Antonio again. When the Americans returned to Guam in 1944 my brother, Jose, was arrested and sent to the stockade because he worked for the Japanese. He came back to Saipan in 1949.

I was in Tanapag when the Americans first bombed in February 1944. The planes saw some Japanese soldiers and horse carts moving down the road so they dropped a bomb there. I saw one Japanese child killed by that bomb. A rock hit her in the head. That was only one bomb. Before that I saw eight planes very high. I think they were taking pictures before the invasion.

When the pre-invasion bombardment started in the afternoon on June 11, 1944, I was at our home in Gualo Rai. The Japanese had several guns below our ranch, but when the bombs started to fall the gunners ran away. The Japanese said they were going to the mountains, so my whole family went with them. We went to Mt. Tapochau. From there we could see all over. On the second day I could see a ship on the north side. A big gun from Managaha [an islet in the lagoon on the west side of Saipan] fired at the ship but did not hit it.* That same day the American ships shot at Garapan.

My family stayed on Tapochau for three days, then we went to Chalan Galaide. At Chalan Galaide there were lots of Chamorros and a priest and some sisters. From there we went to As Teo and stayed there for more than a week. In that valley the Japanese had a field hospital. After maybe two days a small plane circled over As Teo. Then ships shelled the valley. No Chamorros died from that, but two did die when planes strafed the area. Antonio Manalisai and Victoria Tudela Borja died in their house when the planes strafed it.

I was with a friend when a plane strafed us. My friend, Manuel Villigomez, was grazed by a bullet just above the eye. I told him, "Why is that blood coming up?" He said, "I don't know." He didn't feel anything. So I took my towel and wrapped it around his head.

*Gregorio "Gorro" Cabrera, husband of Escolastica T. Cabrera, seen as he looks today outside his home on Capitol Hill. He, along with other island men, was recently honored by the U.S. Marine Corps for services rendered to their new country after Saipan was secured from the Japanese but while the war was still raging. The last organized Japanese resistance did not end until December 1945, four months after Japan surrendered. (Photograph courtesy of Pedro C. Sablan.)*

After that we went further north, in the direction of Talofofo. One group went towards the beach and my group went to Tanapag. There were maybe thirty people in my group and we stayed in the Tanapag area until the Americans arrived. The Japanese launched their banzai charge [Gyokusai] while we were hiding there. The Japanese tried to get behind the American lines by going into the water in the lagoon. We could hear them yelling. This is by what is called Lower Base today, or Puntan Flores. The Japanese had a sea plane ramp there.

One woman in our group died. Her name was Celia Cabrera Reyes. She had given birth not long before and I guess she was weak. There was the remains of a house near us, and hiding under the house were five Japanese, four adults and one baby. The Americans killed everybody under there except the baby. A Chamorro who was hiding under a dried cow hide was run over by a tank. His head was crushed. Serafin Borja was his name. I was there with him, but when I heard the tank coming I left and went into a covered hole. Joaquin "Oma" Sablan was killed by a machine gun about the same time.

We didn't surrender until the next day. The night before we surrendered I could hear a baby crying. He was saying, "Obu." In Japanese that means "I'm

**Probably the* USS Maryland, *or* California.

hungry," or thirsty. It was that baby who was under the house with the four dead Japanese adults. When we surrendered the next day I told the American soldier, "We have a baby over there." So the soldier told me to go get it. Only I went because maybe the soldier was afraid there was a Japanese soldier hiding there. I didn't know that baby's mother but her sister was married to a Pangelinan. That baby is Mitch Pangelinan, and he is still alive.

Shortly after I surrendered I worked for the U.S. Army laying a communication cable from Chalan Kanoa past Gualo Rai to a place called Falipe. We had a digging machine and a jackhammer to do the work. We usually quit work every day at about 4:30 in the afternoon. One night some Japanese soldiers who were still hiding in the jungle went to the bathroom in the hole we were digging and they smashed the machine we used to dig the trench. We had to take it to the shop to be repaired and another machine was brought in so that we could continue with our work. Before this incident they didn't put any guards on the machines, but that night they strung a line along the length of the trench and hung tin cans from it. At one end of the trench the Americans put a guard with a machine gun. That night the Japanese came back. They touched the line with cans hanging from it and alerted the guard. He fired at the noise and the next morning when we came to work there were two dead Japanese by the trench. One of the American soldiers turned the head of one of the dead Japanese. Then he opened the mouth and saw that he had some gold teeth, so he took his gun and hit that dead Japanese in the mouth and broke his teeth. He took the gold teeth, wrapped them in tissue, and put them in his pocket.

At Camp Susupe I served as a policeman. I helped guard the Japanese civilians at Camp Susupe. Each guard detail was made up of one U.S. Marine and one Chamorro. We were to make sure no Japanese came in and none left. One day an old lady who had a farm in Chalan Kiya found a note written in Japanese in her shack. It was held down by a rock so that the wind wouldn't blow it away. The lady couldn't read Japanese, so she took it back to camp. The Americans translated it. It said, "Wait for me in the camp tonight. I am going to bring you something." So that afternoon all of us policemen were called to the office. We were told to get our uniforms and guns because some Japanese would be trying to sneak into the camp that night. They did come. We could hear them coming through the grass. However, they must have become suspicious because they turned around and began running. One of the Chamorro guards said, "Hold it!" The Japanese wouldn't stop, so both the Chamorro and the American guard started shooting. One of the Japanese was shot in the back and the bullet came out his chest. He died in the road. The other one was hit in the leg and forearm, but he kept running. We found him hiding in an eggplant field. Even before this incident, Japanese soldiers were coming and going from Camp Susupe. They tried to take things to the Japanese civilians and they stole supplies from the military.

After the war I worked as a policeman for nine years, then I quit to help my wife with her business. Before I resigned as a policeman we caught two Japanese who were still hiding. That was in 1953. Nobody ever suspected that there were still Japanese hiding out on the island. People who had farms in the area knew that somebody was taking things but they never suspected Japanese soldiers. The night before they were discovered some Chamorros were hunting coconut crabs near where the Japanese were hiding. The Japanese threw rocks at them and the Chamorros ran away. They were scared because they thought Taotaomo'na [ancestral spirits] were doing it.

The next day, Felix Borja, who worked in the power plant, went to his ranch to feed the pigs and chickens before going to work. While he was going back to work in his Jeep he saw a fruit bat fly across the road and land in a tree. At that time we were allowed to have guns, so he stopped and took his shotgun from the Jeep and went into the jungle looking for the bat. On the ground he saw where somebody had gone to the bathroom. Going further, he saw two Japanese. They saw him too, but Felix ran away. He was scared. From there he went to the police station to report what he had seen. That morning a call went out for everybody to report to the office whether they were on duty or not. We all went home, put on our uniforms and got our guns.

At that time the Marianas were under the U.S. Naval Administration. Twelve men, myself included, went looking for these Japanese that Felix reported seeing. The Japanese were on top of a rock that was maybe eighteen or twenty feet up and twenty-four feet around. They had camouflage netting over the top. We shot in the air and told them to put their hands in the air. I told them if they lowered their arms we would shoot them. Me and Antonio Benevente went up to take them. They were wearing nothing but sadi [loin cloths]. They were later returned to Japan. I have not seen them since.

We have one Japanese friend who comes back every year. We met him many years after the war when he came back to Saipan. He was looking around our property and we asked him what he was looking for. His name is Mr. Kanga. He was an administrator in the Japanese secret police, the Kempeitai. During the war he was with Captain Oba and his men. More than a year after we first met Mr. Kanga he returned to Saipan with Captain Oba and some of the surviving members of his band of holdouts.* Captain Oba came to our house several times while he was here and we had long talks about the old days. Captain Oba is dead now, but Mr. Kanga comes to see us whenever he is on Saipan.

I liked the Japanese before the war because they treated us like people, but as the war got close their attitude changed. They would hit the Chamorros.

**Captain Oba and his men did not surrender until December of 1945, four months after Japan officially surrendered. Captain Oba and some of his surviving group returned to Saipan in 1986 for a visit.*

After the war, when the Americans took over, if you were a Chamorro from Guam you got a good salary, but if you were a Chamorro from Saipan you got a lower salary. During the Trust Territory days the Americans were very slow to improve the economy and the education on Saipan. Some children wanted to continue their education on the outside because on Saipan there was nothing. Some children wanted to go to college but the Trust Territory people said they could not. We couldn't even travel without permission from the Naval headquarters on Guam. Things started to get better when we became a Commonwealth. A lot of that had to do with the Japanese coming back with money. A lot of people are millionaires now from selling their land, but not us.

# Messenger Boy for the Japanese Police

## Manuel T. Sablan

*Manuel Tenorio Sablan was born on Saipan in 1928. After the fighting was over on Saipan he worked at a number of different jobs for the U.S. military. During the U.S. Naval Administration of the Northern Marianas he served as the sheriff of Saipan from 1956 to 1965. When the islands were administered as a Trust Territory he served as the director of Public Safety until his retirement in 1978.*

My father's name was Jose Palacios Sablan. He was born in 1905 and during the Japanese times he worked for the Japanese post office. He died when I was five years old, so I don't remember much about him.

My mother was a housewife and a seamstress. She would take orders from both Chamorros and Japanese and work at home. She had five children before my father died. I was the oldest.

I started going to the Japanese school in 1936 and finished the fifth grade. I did fine in school. In spite of all the talk about Japanese discipline, as long as you followed the rules you were fine. The only time you were punished was when you violated the rules and regulations.

The school had a curfew for students and it was very strict. Nobody was to be out on the street after seven o'clock at night. The funny part of it was that every morning the teacher would ask us, "Was anyone on the street after seven o'clock last night?" Knowing that we would be punished if we said yes, most of us would raise our hands if we had been out after curfew, because we were afraid to lie even if there were no witnesses.

The Japanese teachers were also very strict in the use of the vernacular — our native language. You didn't use it even at home. My mother spoke very little Japanese, but I had to talk to her in Japanese because that was what we were taught. On the following day, just like with the curfew, the teacher would ask us, "Did anyone use the vernacular last night?" Again, knowing that you would be punished if you raised your hand, you just told the truth. Even if you used only one word that was not Japanese you were expected to raise your hand. When I say punishment, I'm not talking about being kicked or something like that. You might get a knuckle on the head, or a ruler on the hand. But, I never forgot my Chamorro language because my mother was always speaking to me in Chamorro and I always answered back in Japanese.

When I graduated from school in 1942 I was very fortunate. I was asked by my teacher if I would like to work for the Japanese police as a messenger. There were two other boys who were also asked. Their names were Jose Tenorio and Jesus Salas. Jose and Jesus were both very nice. We got along well with each other. The native policemen were making thirty yen a month. As messengers we were making more than those policemen. It is funny, but it is true. We made forty-five yen a month. In fact one of the native policemen really got mad at us once. He said, "Why do you guys have to make so much money? You're just running around on a bicycle." But you could survive on thirty yen in those days.

All three of us worked as messengers for the Japanese police from August 1942 until June 15, 1944. Sometimes I worked for the chief of police, cleaning his house. His name was Sato. That was his last name; that's all I remember. The one Japanese policeman I remember best was Mr. Hirasawa. He survived the battle, and has visited Saipan twice since then. I have never met anyone nicer than this individual. When he was on duty he would call us in to talk and joke around. He survived the battle and the Americans made him chief of security for the Japanese being held at Camp Susupe. You see, we had over 90,000 people on Saipan before the war. But you know something, we had only two police officers on night duty at any one time. One stayed in the office, and one walked his beat in the whole Garapan area. That is how disciplined the people were before the war. People were afraid to commit any crimes.

Another thing, as messengers for the police department we were given bicycles. You know, if you didn't have a bicycle you couldn't go any place. Even given the small size of Saipan, before the war if you didn't have transportation you hardly knew your neighbors. Besides, people were very busy. They had to work hard to survive. I didn't even know Garapan until I started working for the Japanese police, because before that I left home at five o'clock in the morning and went to school. I came back at two o'clock and stayed at home the rest of the day. If you were lucky, and you had some money, you could go to night school. That was the one exception to the curfew. If you were caught on the street after seven o'clock at night, and you could justify where you had been, then they wouldn't take you in.

We had a lot of Koreans on Saipan. They were mostly laborers. Working at the police station, I was there when people were arrested and brought in. Many of them were Koreans who were rounded up at night. I don't know why they were arrested, but the police would beat them up or sometimes just slap them. It depended on the individual policeman who was on duty.

One time I witnessed a Korean guy getting the water treatment from a Japanese policeman. He was taken into a back room. They had the person lie down. Somebody had to hold his feet and another person held his head, then another person poured water down his nose so he couldn't breathe. I don't know what the guy did but I wouldn't want to be in his position. You see, there is one thing about Japanese times—you don't know and you don't ask. I didn't even know about the bombing of Pearl Harbor. I didn't know the United States was at war with Japan. I knew some Chamorros were sent to Guam on 8 December 1941, but that is all I knew. At the time, I didn't know why they were sent.

During Japanese times Chamorros, Carolinians, and even Koreans were not allowed to drink liquor—only Japanese and Okinawans. So if you got caught drunk on the street, or caught drinking for that matter, they would send you to jail for twenty-nine days without going to court. Again, that all depended on who the officer on duty was. That guy Hirasawa I was talking about, I don't remember him ever sending anybody to jail.

We had a house in Garapan but the Japanese occupied it when they started bringing in troops. My mother had to take the rest of the family to our farm in Fina Sisu in the Aslito area of Saipan. I stayed in Garapan with the Japanese police. Even before this, when I started working for the Japanese police we had a room where we slept at the police station. We didn't go home to our families when we were off duty. After my family was moved out of Garapan I didn't see them until after the battle. I was worried, but what could I do? My father was dead, but like I said, my mother was a seamstress, and we had a Japanese couple leasing a room in our house in Garapan.

About two weeks before the Americans invaded Saipan the Japanese started evacuating their wives and children to Japan. Even the wife of the civilian chief of police was preparing to leave. I know, because I was involved in the packing of her things. There were two ships, you see. One was the *MV Santos*, and one was the *MV America*. Now, the *MV America* was for the hotshots' wives. The *MV America* was at Charlie Dock, and the *MV Santos* was in Garapan. All of the ordinary civilians were put on board the *MV Santos*. A week later we found out that the *MV America* was torpedoed and went down. The *MV Santos* was also hit, but managed to reach Japan. Everybody on the *MV America* was assumed killed, including the wife of the police chief.

I was at the police station in February 1944 when the Americans first bombed Saipan. I learned a couple of days later that the sugar refinery was hit hard. I knew then that there was a war going on between the Japanese and the Americans. I heard these things. I didn't ask, I just heard them. That was one thing about the Japanese times—you never asked questions. I also heard the

*The old Japanese Jail in Garapan, Saipan, where numerous American pilots were held before the invasion. The last two American Navy pilots held here died before they could be liberated, one as the result of friendly fire. The other one was severely beaten, then decapitated by one of his jailers. Their remains were discovered by U.S. Marines as they moved into the area on their advance north along the west coast of the island. Autopsies were performed on their remains to determine cause of death, and pieces of clothing with their names stenciled on them were also found.*

police talking about some Americans in a rubber boat who were picked up in the Talofofo area and brought to the jail. I got on my bicycle and rode down to the jail house. Because of our relationship with the Japanese police we were allowed to go in and out of the jail. Not many people could do that. So sure enough, I went to the jail and this truck pulled up. There were four Americans. They were blindfolded, and their hands were tied behind their backs. They were white and extraordinarily big. Their hair was gold. At first I didn't even know they were Americans.

At that time there was a Japanese prisoner in the jail who spoke English, and was used as an interpreter. His name was Ikuta, and I found out later that he was arrested for spying for the Americans. There were all sorts of rumors, like he was picked up in Garapan for using a small radio, but I don't know really what the true story was. My wife lived next door to him in Garapan when she was a young girl, and she said that he was arrested when they found some communication equipment in his house. He was an old man, probably in his sixties. I think he died during the fighting — during the bombardment. I never found out much about those Americans. We went back to the jail about a week later and they were gone. The same old Japanese man told us that the Americans were sent to Japan.

Later the Japanese brought in two more American pilots. I think it was about a week before the Americans invaded Saipan on June 15. We heard rumors that they had been brought here from Truk Lagoon. When we heard about this we decided to go to the jail and take a look. It was in the evening. One of the Chamorro police officers, I believe it was Antonio Cabrera, told us not to go, but we went anyway. We sneaked in and we saw the two Americans in two different cells. One was sitting in the corner holding his stomach as if he were in pain. The other one was just walking around the cell, smiling and talking. Of course, we didn't know what he was saying. He got shot in the arm; he showed us the wound.

Joe Tenorio was always carrying money. So Joe says, "Let's get some bread and give it as a gift to the American." But, we didn't know what to say to this American. We just looked at him and used hand signals. We tried to tell him to wait until dark and we would bring him food. However, when we came back that night with the bread one of the guards saw what we were going to do and told us not to.

There was another prisoner at the jail who was from Palau. We met with him in the hills several days later. When the Americans started shelling Garapan, all of the prisoners were let out. He told us that the Americans had died. The roof came down on one of them during the shelling, and the other one was beheaded by one of the Japanese. I found out later the name of the Japanese who killed the American with his sword. His name was Nitta-bucho. Bucho for the Japanese police is a high rank, probably a captain.

The police station was in Garapan just above where the Kristo Rai Church is now. During the bombing we hid in a manmade cave behind the police station. On June 15 we stayed in there from about one o'clock in the afternoon until around five o'clock at night. The police station was on a hill, so we could see most of Garapan from there. When we came out of the cave that evening not a building was standing. That was when Joe Tenorio suggested that we head for the mountains. So we just took off. We didn't tell anybody. We just waited until dark, then the three of us took off for the mountains.

First we went to a place called Fanaganan (near what is called Navy Hill today). However, once we got there we decided to split up because my mother and her family were in the Aslito area, and Jesus Salas' family was in Chalan Kanoa (southwest end of the island, where the Marines landed). Joe's parents were in Tanapag (northwest end of the island). I told Joe to go find his parents, and Jesus and I left together to find our families. Jesus and I got as far as Iliyang (south of Garapan) and couldn't go any further because fuel storage tanks were burning all over. So that same evening we went back to Fanaganan, then to Chalan Galaide (near Mt. Tapochau). Along the way there was a lot of shelling, and sometimes we had to hit the ground. In Chalan Galaide we had a very close call. In fact we saw one guy get killed by an exploding shell.

From Chalan Galaide we decided to move to the St. Lourdes area (east side of the island) and that is where we ran into Joe again. I couldn't get to Aslito from that side of the island either. That whole area was burning. So we decided to walk to Tanapag and look for Joe's parents. There were a lot of Japanese soldiers going in the same direction. We managed to get to Tanapag and find Joe's mother and grandfather. Then we all walked back to St. Lourdes that same night. We didn't want to stay in Tanapag because there were fuel tanks burning up there. We stayed in some caves at St. Lourdes for about two weeks. Then the Americans started bombing the area, so that night we walked to Talofofo (northeast coast). A woman named Victoria Tudela Borja was killed when an American plane strafed the house she was in. I know now it was a P-51. We went into the house after the plane left and found her lying there dead.

On the way to Talofofo we saw dead people all over the place. When we got there we couldn't find any caves to hide in, so we decided to start digging in the ground. We had no shovels, no picks, just a machete. So we cut some wood and used that as picks. We dug into a slope — all of us, and finally we dug enough for ten or fifteen people. We were fortunate because my father's cousin, Gregorio Sablan, was with us and he could speak English. We had only sugar cane to eat while we were there, and we surrendered on that spot on July 4, 1944. I'll never forget that date. There was a lot of shooting in the area the night before we surrendered. But the following day it was so quiet; not a noise. A Japanese soldier passed by and said, "The Americans are coming!" He took off, and we just waited. There were a lot of trees between the road and where we were hiding. We could see the Americans, but they couldn't see us. Someone yelled to Mr. Sablan, "There are some Americans outside!" I guess the old man panicked, or something, because instead of coming out, he ran back into the cave. He finally came out and said something in English. We put up a white flag — not a white flag, just a piece of cloth on a stick — and we all went out. The Marines surrounded us, I guess to make sure we didn't have any weapons. We were pretty lucky to have somebody with us who could speak English. Everybody was searched — I mean everybody except the women. We had to wait there probably an hour, then they brought trucks up for us. We had to walk about a few hundred feet until we came to a level area where the trucks were. They took us all directly to Camp Susupe.

In Camp Susupe I couldn't find my mother even though she had been picked up earlier. She was picked up three days after the invasion. That was the most difficult thing for me, not being able to find my mother. Even when I was in the caves, I was thinking about my mother and my brothers all the time, more than anything else.

Camp Susupe was big and we weren't authorized to walk around. I found my mother maybe a week later. She was over close to Lake Susupe. I was so happy. Everybody was so happy. We hugged and cried. I don't remember what we said.

It was hard in Camp Susupe. There really wasn't much of a place to sleep. Some of us men had to sleep on the ground with just a blanket, but under a tent. We hadn't eaten anything in two weeks except for some sugar cane, and you would think that you could eat a whole pot of whatever, but after just a few bites you became full; you couldn't eat any more. I was in Camp Susupe from July to October 1944 hauling water to the camp using a bull cart and five gallon cans. I did that until October 24. That is something I can't forget.

October 24 is when I started working at the 369th Station Hospital in San Vicente. They needed locals to help with the patients, mop the floors, and go up to the galley and haul food for the patients. We washed the patients and helped the nurses with the bandages. Some of the patients were very badly wounded. You know, we worked from five o'clock in the morning until seven o'clock in the evening, sometimes later. We were paid ten dollars a month, but we appreciated it. We were fed there, and given a place to sleep. One Sunday a month we were driven to Chalan Kanoa to see our families. But I enjoyed it. That is where I started to learn English.

We were taking care of wounded soldiers from Iwo Jima and Okinawa. They were all brought here. I was there doing that until sometime in 1945.

About a mile away from the 369th was another hospital for the Japanese. I saw one of the Japanese policemen there I used to work for. He was very badly injured. We tried to talk to him, but he just looked at us.

The bad thing about Japanese times was that if you didn't have employment, if you didn't have property to farm, you were in big trouble. But the good thing was that we Chamorros helped one another. In other words, if you had a neighbor who needed help you had to help him even if you weren't related. So people survived because of that. One of the good things about the Japanese times was that you knew what not to do. The system was so rigid, so strict, you could not afford to make a mistake, knowing the consequences.

## Provisional Marine

### Cristino S. Dela Cruz

*Cristino S. Dela Cruz is a seventy-one-year-old man of German, Spanish, and Chamorro ancestry. In 1944, at the age of seventeen, he was recruited by the Fourth Marine Division as a Provisional Marine to help locate Japanese stocks of ammunition that he had helped hide before the invasion of Saipan. He was finally recognized for his services in 1983 by the Commandant of the Marine Corps.*

We had friendly relations with the Japanese until the war started between the Japanese and the Americans. Then the Japanese became mean. I had an uncle, Gregorio Sablan, who drank too much beer and sake one time. He told some Japanese who were renting a house from our family that Imperial Japan was no good, and he was sent to prison for seven years for that. Then the Americans invaded and all the prisoners were released and told to find shelter.

After I graduated from school I was recruited by the Japanese Imperial Army. They taught me how to load ammunition and move guns around. I did that for three years. When the Japanese took over our house in Garapan we moved to my uncle's farm in Fina Sisu. (Fina Sisu is a ridge of high ground just east of the beaches where the Marines landed on 15 June 1944.) I was hiding there with my family when the fighting started. There were twenty of us altogether. We hid in a hole for one week before the Americans captured us. That was from 11 June until 18 June. We survived on coconuts, salted fish, and rice. Before we were captured two of my sisters were killed by a bomb. There were many Japanese all around us on Fina Sisu. When the Marines came near our hole I looked out and I could see their faces were painted with camouflage so they looked like tigers. They waved to us to come out. My older brother, Gabriel, was excited about getting out even though there was still a lot of fighting going on around us.

The Marines pointed us to get on a truck, but when I looked at my brother he was covered in blood. He told me that he was in pain. A sniper must have shot him when we were surrendering. I helped my brother get on the truck. He fell on the floor of the truck and blood was coming out. He was dead. The truck driver took us to the Fourth Marine Division cemetery where Hopwood Junior High School is now. The chaplain asked me to get my father. Then the Marines assigned two Japanese POWs to help us bury my brother. While we were lowering my brother's body into the grave the two POWs dropped their end and my brother's head hid hard on the bottom. When this happened I became so mad, I yelled at the Japanese, "You are not supposed to do that! My brother is not an animal! You Japanese are prisoners of war! You cannot treat us like that anymore!"

I looked around and found a branch from a burned tree, then I went looking for the two Japanese. I wanted revenge for what the Japanese did to my brother. I found one of them and pushed him. "You son-of-a-bitch, you!" I hit him twice; then I hit him twice more. "You Japanese no good. I will kill you Imperial Japanese." I hit him again, then the American MP came and pulled me off of him. If they had not come I think I would have killed him, all because of my sudden temper.

The chaplain told me to go with my family, so I followed them into the camp. I did not go far. It was still daylight, and I sat down. The sun went down and still I did not move. All I could see were truck lights coming from the direction of the ocean. I was still there at nine o'clock thinking about what I did. I was feeling bad because I beat that Japanese and because of what happened to my brother. I could still see that bullet hole in my brother from front to back. Then I saw silhouettes coming towards me. They were searching for somebody by the light of a cigarette lighter. There were seventeen Marines and they were looking for me. When they found me they waved for me to follow them. They took me to their command post. I could see inside the tent. An American officer was interrogating a Japanese officer. After the interrogation the American officer called me in. I didn't know what he is saying because I didn't know English. Then he called in an American soldier who spoke Spanish. Through this other soldier the American officer asked me if I was the one who beat the Japanese. I said, "Yes." He said, "Did you beat him because you don't like Japanese?" I said, "Yes. I don't like Japanese!"

After that I talked about many things. Then I showed him the map I had in my pocket. It was the map I used to mark where I put Japanese ammunition. I told him I would show him where these hiding places were. He was very happy and this calmed me down because I thought I was going to be punished for beating the Japanese prisoner. The American officer told me that if I could show them where the Japanese ammunitions were stored it might save lives and shorten the fighting. He then told the Spanish-speaking soldier to go with me to get my mother's blessings. I told my mother what I was going to do. She was so worried. She told me not to go because I might get killed. I said, "Please mother, let me go. If the Japanese surrender it will be a good fortune for Saipan. I want to help." She was upset because she had already lost four children, but I kept on insisting.

After I received my mother's blessing they gave me a uniform but no gun. They put me in a Sherman tank. There were seven of us inside. I took them up to Tuturam.* We had to zig-zag because of Japanese artillery. One shell hit the tank, knocking off the tread. The tank was laying on its side but we got out through the turret. After we all escaped the tank another shell hit it and it blew up. We then got on an amphibious tractor. Not long after this an MP stopped us because there was some heavy fighting just ahead. This was in Papago near "Death Valley."

I was with the Fourth Marine Division, and for five days we didn't move because there were many Japanese. Some of us got under a truck to hide. Remember, they wouldn't let me have a weapon at that time. Maybe over 300 Marines died during those five days. It was hand-to-hand combat. Over 1,000 Japanese died there. They charged us with bayonets. One Japanese was killed right in front of me, and when he fell his bayonet hit me in the arm and cut it. Then a piece of metal from a fragmentation grenade hit me in the other arm. I was treated in the field. When the colonel saw that I was wounded he gave me permission to carry any kind of weapon I wanted. I was very happy. I wanted a bazooka so I could kill many Japanese. My partner, who was my interpreter, asked me why I wanted a bazooka. I said to kill many Japanese. He said a bazooka required many men to carry ammunition and load it. After that I chose a Thompson submachine gun. It held thirty rounds. I only had my gun for a few minutes when some more

**Now the village of San Vicente.*

Japanese came at us. Everybody was shooting without aiming. We shot like that for maybe ten minutes. They kept coming even if they were hit. Some got inside of our lines. At that time we were between the Fourth Marine Division and the Twenty-seventh Army Division.

I knew where many of the caves were and I would yell at the people inside to come out and surrender. Sometimes they would and sometimes they would not. Sometimes they would come out as if to surrender then they would throw hand grenades. But I always had backup, and I would signal them when to shoot or not to shoot. After somebody surrendered from a cave and nobody else came out, just to be safe a flame thrower team would blast the cave. This was all after the big fighting in Papago, but in the same area.

We then moved east to the Kagman* area and fought our way up to As Teo, then to Marpi where "Suicide Cliff" is. That is where I first met Guy Gabaldon.† I knew him for only a few minutes, but when I next saw him in 1989 I recognized him as that Marine I met in 1944. I saw him in the police station when I went to get my driver's license. I saw him from forty feet away. He saw me too, and came closer. When we were about five feet away he recognized me. I said, "Mr. Gabaldon?" He said, "Dela Cruz?" Then we shook hands and hugged. He had captured several hundred Japanese and was getting ready to take them to the south of the island. I think that is probably why I remembered him forty-five years later.

I saw many Japanese civilians jump off the cliffs. They hit the side of the cliff on the way down. If they surrendered Japanese soldiers would try to kill them. I spent seven days in the Marpi area looking for Japanese who might still be hiding there. We didn't find anymore. After that I returned to Fourth Marine headquarters and stayed there for one month. I went to Camp Susupe to see my family. My mother was so happy to see me alive. I told her that my Marine buddies always protected me because they knew I was not a trained fighting man. Then my mother took me to a small shack that served as a chapel and called one of the priests. He blessed me and I thanked Christ. I held my mother's hand and we walked out.

I left the military after that and was enlisted into the newly formed local constabulary. In 1953, while on rotation to Tinian, it was discovered that there was still a Japanese soldier in hiding on Tinian. Somebody had found his shack near a swamp and he was growing some tobacco there. I went there with a small group of armed men and took him alive. I told him to come out with his hands up or I would kill him. I told him that three times before he came out. I asked him if there was anybody else. He said, "No." I asked him several more times, but each time he answered that he was the only one. So then, I took my M-1 carbine and emptied a clip into his shack. I started to load another clip, but when I looked up at the Japanese he was crying. When I asked him why, he told me that I had destroyed his only supply of soy sauce. I told him to never mind because he would find plenty of soy sauce on Saipan. His name was Murata Susumu, and he was repatriated to Japan. I never received any medals for my service with the Marines, but I don't regret what I did because it gave me my country.

*Known as Chacha before the war.*

*†Guy Gabaldon was in the Second Marine Division. He was seriously wounded by a Japanese straggler, and earned the Navy Cross for heroism. Gabaldon returned to Saipan in 1980 with his wife and family, and lives in a house close to one of the beaches where he first landed as a young Marine in 1944.*

# Arrested by the Kempeitai

## David Sablan

*Mr. David Sablan is the son of Elias Parong Sablan and Carmen Mangarero. He graduated from high school on Guam after World War II, and stayed on Guam for eighteen years, eventually becoming sales manager of an automobile dealership. He later became assistant manager of the Guam branch of the Bank of Hawaii. Mr. Sablan returned to Saipan in 1965, where he is still active in the business community. He is president of the Saipan Chamber of Commerce at the time of this writing.*

My father, Elias Parong Sablan, who was part Carolinian, went to Yap during the German times to go to school. He studied English and communications.* I remember in 1938-1939 taking a ship down there with the whole family to visit his sister, who was married to a Yapese. Her name was Jacoba. She was married to Isidro Flawau. Isidro was a son of a high chief on Yap, but they moved to Saipan sometime before the war and he, like my father, worked for the Japanese in the sugar

*Yap was the center for all trans–Pacific underseas cable connections.*

industry. Later, after the war, they moved to Guam in order to educate their children.

When the Japanese bombed Pearl Harbor they also invaded Guam. My father was recruited by the Japanese to go with them along with several other Chamorros. He knew Japanese and Chamorro, and the Japanese needed interpreters. I will never forget; we were all crying because Dad was leaving to go to war. He left on the 7th of December, 1941. He was given a choice of staying after the invasion or returning to Saipan. He was among the few Chamorros who returned soon after the invasion. He was there a month at the most. It was not something he wanted to discuss afterward.

During the war there were American submarines a few miles off Saipan and they were sinking Japanese ships as they came into the harbor. There were a lot of Japanese military who ended up here without clothes, without guns, without food. There were also natives who were going to school in Japan and were returning on those ships. As a result there was an unexpected population of military personnel on Saipan, so the Japanese moved to close down the Catholic Church and use that as a barracks. Some of the bigger homes owned by the natives in Garapan were also taken over by the Japanese and we were among those victimized by this move. We ended up moving to our ranch in Chalan Kiya. We stayed there until the American invasion. We had a bull cart and we packed up everything we owned and hauled it to our ranch in several loads.

My father had bought my older sister an organ

*The surviving children of Elias Parong Sablan and his wife, Carmen Mangarero Sablan. They survived, for the most part, on nothing but sugar cane, while hiding in a cave near Mt. Tapochau on the island of Saipan.* Top row, left to right: *Rudy, Mariano, Henry, Ignacio, and David.* Sitting, left to right: *Merced, Maria, and Magdalena. A younger sister, Eugenia, died in Camp Susupe, shortly after their rescue by three Marines. She was four years old.*

because she was a music teacher. We moved that to the ranch along with our books— my grandfather's books and my father's books. We put everything in a thatched hut we built. Then right after the Americans first bombed Saipan in February 1944 — this was the worst part for us— the Kempeitai (Japanese military police) came to our ranch early one morning and woke us all up. They took all the books out, tore them all up — slashed them with their bayonets and burned them. My sister's organ — they ripped it apart.

We weren't sure what they were looking for, but later we found out that they were looking for some kind of communication equipment. They suspected my father of being a spy for the Americans. You see my sister used to play the organ at night to console everybody because of the rather strange life we were living, and some Okinawans that were living near us thought that we were sending messages to the Americans. We found out later that the Kempeitai had surrounded our place and waited all night hoping to catch us sending signals. When they didn't succeed they arrested my father, arrested my sister Maria, my uncle, Mariano Guerrero, and another man, Juan Concepcion, who was living with my uncle. They took them all to the jail in Garapan and for two solid days they interrogated them. Then they let my sister, my uncle, and the other guy go, but my father was kept in jail for the next two months. We were allowed limited visitation during those two months. It was very traumatic for all of us. My father told us after he was released that they held a bayonet against his neck and said, "Admit that you are an American spy!" But he never admitted it. The Japanese asked him, "Do you like America or Japan?" My father said, "I like the Germans, because they educated me." I think the fact that my father participated in the invasion of Guam gave him some credibility and they gave him credit for that.

While he was in jail the Japanese brought in a downed American pilot and my father was used to help interpret for him, but my father never saw the pilot after that. The Japanese finally released my father, and within weeks the Americans landed on Saipan.

While my father was still in jail we built a shelter on the ranch, a hole covered with coconut logs and dirt. This was under a mango tree. After we completed it the Japanese started using this area to store barrels of gasoline; I don't know why. When my father was released from jail he said, "We better leave here because if we continue to stay here the Kempeitai might return and they will behead me." So we all packed up our clothes and moved up to another ranch. That was a place called Kannat Tabla, a place owned by my cousin's family, the Semans. But after only one day my father was still not satisfied that we would be safe, so we packed up our stuff again and went to a cave that my father remembered. There were about fifty of us, the Seman family, ourselves, the Cabrera family, and a couple of others. We all ended up in this cave for fear that if the Japanese came they would definitely kill my dad. We found out later that the Kempeitai did return to our ranch looking for my father.

We were in that cave for three weeks. We did a lot of praying. In the cave there was a small hole that gave us a panoramic view of all of southwest Saipan and we could see ships as far as the horizon. We could see the landing craft coming toward the landing beaches.

Two days after we moved into the cave the grass above the cave caught on fire and it got to be so hot inside that we couldn't bear it any more. So my father said, "Okay, let's go down to the farm of the Iglesias family." So we went down the cliff to that farm to get some water and get away from the heat only to find shells falling all around us. When we got inside the house we started praying while bombs were exploding all over the place. The shrapnel was flying all over, even cutting the trees down. My father decided we should go back to the cave. My grandmother and a few others were too weak to climb back up so they stayed. My grandmother said, "If I'm going to die, I'll die here." But as we found out later, she lived and was taken to Camp Susupe with the others. On the way back up we hid under a rock overhang, and during that time we could hear Japanese and American voices, and the crash of metal. It was about four in the morning and the Japanese were having a fight with the Americans below us. It was a miracle that none of us were killed. The rest of the time we were in the cave we had no communication with anybody.

While we were in the cave all we had to eat for those three weeks was sugar cane. Early every morning the able bodied men, maybe half-a-dozen of them, would go out to a field and cut sugar cane for the rest of us. After we had been in the cave for about another two or three weeks the men who went out to cut sugar cane ran into a Japanese patrol, so they hid for a while. Then they came back after the sun was already up, about eight o'clock in the morning. Some Americans on ships saw the movement of these men up there and started shooting shells into our area. Some of those shells exploded right outside of our cave. The noise just about busted our ear drums. This was followed by a patrol of Marines. There were three of them sent up there. They found the crucifix that we had placed outside the cave, but they couldn't see the cave because you had to crawl over this big rock to get to it, and the opening to the cave was very small. But then a baby in the cave with us started to cry and that gave them assurance that there was a cave nearby. So they stood there with their guns and one of the Marines said, "Without fear, with your hands up, come out." He said that in broken Japanese. Because of what the Japanese told us—that the Americans would do terrible things to us if we were captured—we thought of killing ourselves.

This cave was huge. It was kind of unique because you had sort of a living room, then a lot of little cavities. In the cavity where my family hid there was a large drop off, and that is where we were going to jump and just forget about living.

One of the Marines was getting ready to throw a hand grenade into the cave. Once again he said in broken Japanese, "Without fear, with your hands up, come out." That is when my dad popped out and said in English, "I surrender!" And the Marine said, "Oh, you speak English." My father said, "Yes, a little bit." Then the Marine said, "By any chance is your name Elias Sablan?" My father said, "Yes." And the Marine said, "We've been looking for you because some of the people already captured and down in the camp said that you speak English and can help us translate, or interpret for the Japanese that are there." At that point my father yelled back in the cave for everybody to come out.

One of the people in the cave, Joaquin Crisostimo, had a boil on the back of his neck. When one of the Marines took out his first aid kit Crisostimo thought he was going to be killed, but what he was really going to do was fix the boil on his neck. They gave us water and we saw that one of them had a rosary around his neck, so we figured they were good guys. They were not out to kill us. We were questioned on the spot about whether or not there were more natives in the area, but we didn't know of any, so they marched us down toward the west side of the island were the camps were. On the way they told us to be careful because there were still Japanese in the area. While we were coming down off the mountain my dad started talking to one of the Marines and he asked him what his name was, and he said, "John Sullivan." The other one was Engle, and the third one was George Prevost.

While we were still in Camp Susupe my father got me a job with the Navy working in the Supply Department without salary, just to learn English. The storekeepers—the petty officers—taught me how to speak English, word by word, you know, "This is a broom. This is a mop. This is a coffee pot," because I used to make coffee for them. They gave me some size four Navy shoes, and they bought me a bicycle so I could go to the post office and pick up the mail. I had a pass that took me to the Korean camp and the Japanese camp. One of the Navy storekeepers I remember was Joe Sowerby. We corresponded after the war. He used to send me goodies at Christmas time. He later showed me copies of some of the letters I sent to him. You wouldn't want to see them. They are full of typical Navy-influenced vocabulary, if you know what I mean. Every other word was a profanity.

I had a younger sister, Eugenia, who died in Camp Susupe. She was about four years younger than I was. She seemed fine while we were in the cave, but in Camp Susupe she ate some bad food or something. Her belly became big and she died. That was very emotional for us because we had all survived the ruin of war, then to have her die.

After the war ended in 1945 I became a telephone operator on the midnight to 6:00 A.M. shift, and during the day I strung telephone lines. I did that until 1947 when my dad finally decided that I should get an education. He sent me to Guam where I stayed with a Sanchez family while I went to school. It was rough in those days because the Guamanians didn't care for the Saipanese. They thought we had been pro–Japanese during the war. After the ordeal that my father had gone through—after what my whole family had gone through—and to be branded "pro–Japanese" was something I just didn't understand. I was always being threatened and had to run away to keep from being beaten up. I had a hard time. They called me things like, "Japanese lover."

Guam had an outdoor movie theater in those days, and sometimes I would go to see a movie. But even before it was over I would leave and run like hell to keep from being beat up. I never stopped to fight; I always ran. That is why you will find me very fit today, because of all the double time I used to do.

I was fourteen years old then and I had to do a lot of work for the Sanchez family. I helped them renovate their home. I had to empty the bed pans every morning. They didn't have an indoor toilet in those days. I had to feed the pigs, and I was given a gallon of water to shower with every day. To make friends I joined the Boy Scouts. That helped keep me from getting beat up. I went from Tender Foot all the way to Eagle Scout.

Also, while I was going to school I would visit the prisoners from Saipan who were being held for crimes

*David Sablan with the three Marines who saved him and his family in 1944 on Saipan.* From left to right: *George Prevost, Gene Engle, David Sablan, and John Sullivan. Dave is pointing to a map of Saipan where they first met during the final days of fighting on Saipan. The photograph was taken in the early 1980s at a Second Marine Division Association Reunion in Seattle, Washington. Mr. Sablan is a lifetime associate member of the SMDA.*

they had committed on Guam during the Japanese occupation. I had nothing else to do on Sunday after mass, so I would go and visit them.

I left Saipan in 1947 and didn't move back until 1965. Because of the political status of my father — he was the mayor of Saipan at that time — I was privileged to fly into Saipan periodically on a Navy plane and visit my family.

After I graduated from high school I married a local girl and settled down on Guam to work and make a living. As the years passed people would still come up to me and ask if I knew this guy from Saipan or that guy. I would hear stories about how they were mistreated by somebody from Saipan during the Japanese occupation, or about a family member who was killed. I would say I was sorry for what happened. I was apologizing for everybody.

After the war my father was appointed chief of police. He held that post until the assigned mayor of Saipan passed away. The mayor's name was Gregorio Sablan, and that was sometime in early 1945. My father was appointed by the Commander [of the] Naval Forces Mariana Islands, a rear admiral. It later became an elected post and my father served as mayor of Saipan until he lost the election in 1954. The U.S. Navy then elevated him to the post of United Nations observer. Then every year he went to New York with the United States Mission to the U.N. to report on the political, economic, and education progress of the Northern Mariana Islands.

That first year, 1955, my father had a U.S. Navy captain as an aide or guide. The media then got into the act and he was written up in the *New Yorker* magazine. Among other things he was asked what he wanted to do while in New York. He said three things. He said he wanted to go to Yankee Stadium to see a baseball game, so they took him there. The second thing was he wanted to have some rice, because he missed having rice. The third thing was he wanted to find John Sullivan. He was then taken to Washington, D.C. — to the Pentagon, to search out John Sullivan of the Marine Corps. They narrowed it down to three names. When my father got back to Saipan he gave me the three John Sullivans and their addresses, and I wrote to all three. One John F. Sullivan responded in such detail that I knew this was the John Sullivan that had brought us down from the cave in 1944.

In 1957 I had an opportunity to travel with three Capuchin Fathers going home to the United States on triennial leave. I bought a car on the West Coast and drove cross country with the priests. We called on John Sullivan in Burlington, Illinois. At this time John and I updated each other on questions that were never answered during the war. The priests that were with me were so intrigued with all of this that they called the local paper. The media came out and interviewed me and I made the headlines in Burlington. We were only going to stay there for a day, but ended up staying for several. John invited some of his ex–Marine Corps friends and neighbors to come over and meet me. John told me that during the rest of the fighting on Saipan he had become separated from Engle and Prevost and he thought they had been killed. However, through my efforts with the Marine Corps I was able to locate both Engle and Prevost. They were still alive, and in 1982 we all met in Seattle, Washington, where the Second Marine Division Association was having one of their annual gatherings. I was made an associate member, and at that reunion I was the guest speaker. It was there that I met Engle and Prevost for the first time since the war, and John Sullivan was there too. Up until that time John Sullivan had given up on ever seeing them. He thought they had been killed somewhere during the mopping up of the island. Unfortunately, my father never got to meet back up with John or the other Marines in that group.

## Carolinian Elder

### Felipe Iguel Ruak

*Felipe Ruak was born in Tanapag Village on Saipan in 1932. After World War II he went to schools on Guam and in Papua New Guinea. He was selected to attend a special class on radio broadcasting at the East-West Center in Hawaii, where he graduated at the top of his class. He worked for several years at the U.S. Navy radio station on Saipan. During the years when the Northern Mariana Islands were a "Trust Territory," he went to work for James B. Johnson in the Land Commission Office, later becoming senior land commissioner. He is now retired but remains active in the community as a teacher of traditional Carolinian men's dances.*

My father, Jesus Ubet Ruak, was born on Chuuk Island* but I don't know when. My mother, Rosa Iguel, was born on Tinian. Her parents had migrated to Tinian from one of the outer islands of Chuuk called Nomonuito Atoll. When my father married my mother he had to become a Catholic and adopted the first name "Jesus." This was after my mother's family moved from Tinian to Saipan.

My mother passed away after the war. I was not here to see my mother when she died because I was on Guam attending school. I was her youngest child.

When I was growing up during Japanese times I went to Japanese school. I would walk from our village of Tanapag† to Garapan where the school was. We had to get up early in the morning to be sure that we would be at the school before the actual hour that school began. My first teacher's name was Muramoto-sensei. His teaching assistant was Mr. Juan Reyes, who was a Chamorro. When I went to second grade, my teacher was Kawasima-sensei. I was never late for school because I was afraid of being punished. The Japanese would hit you on the back, and if you kept on doing bad things they made you get on your knees and put your arms straight above your head. You might have to stay like that for a hour without moving. But before they punished you they would always ask you why you did it. It was scary to lie to the Japanese, because if they thought you were lying they would punish you even harder.

I did not finish second grade because the war started. They let all the students stay at home because they didn't know when U.S. forces might come and they didn't want the students to be at school when that happened. So the school was closed, and not knowing the meaning of war, I enjoyed myself. One unfortunate part of this was that the Japanese military needed all of the buildings that we had here on the island, so they asked all the people to move away from the village. And since my mother and father were not actually Saipanese we had no other place to go. However, some Chamorro friends invited us to stay at their farm. That was in the Saddok Dogas area, not far from Tanapag Village. We were there with my stepbrother, Francisco, my sister, Luciana, her husband, Joaquin Taisague, my mother, and my father's godson, Jose Kani Teigita. Also, our church was closed so that the church building could be used for storing supplies. The Japanese soldiers dug trenches all over the village. As a young man growing up I didn't know anything about war, so I just enjoyed myself with my mother and my sisters. My father and some other men from the village were taken away by the Japanese military to work. Believe it or not, they were never paid.

We relied on local foods, like bananas, breadfruit, tapioca, and sweet potatoes. For water we had to catch rain. We couldn't go fishing because we were restricted by the Japanese military. Sometimes we went hungry, but there was nothing we could do about it. I complained to my mother, but all she could do was ask me to be a little more patient. Sometimes people would

*Formerly known as Truk in what is now the Federated States of Micronesia.*

†*Talaabwogh was the original Carolinian name, later mispronounced by the Japanese, then further mispronounced by the Americans.*

come by with sugar cane and they would offer me some. That would help take away some of my hunger and thirst. Sometimes the American planes would fly over Saipan. When they did, the men working at Aslito Airfield would run away. My father was one of them. One time when he ran away he came to see us, and maybe he stayed a little bit too long, because by the time he reported back he was very late. He was punished. The Japanese made him put his hands on top of his head, then they hit him with long sticks. My father fell down; his ribs were broken. He stood up and they slapped him around some more. He could walk afterward, but very slowly. When he breathed they could see that something in his side was moving in and out, so they let him go. Some relatives brought him home. There was nothing to carry him on, so they put his arms around their shoulders and walked with him. He died early one morning just before the Americans landed. Planes were flying around, and there were ships all around the island. He died because of the beating. That was June 1944, just before the Americans started dropping down bombs.

I liked my father very much; he was a good friend. After the beating he couldn't lie down because of the pain. He could only sit, and he was like that for two or three weeks before he died. When he wanted to sleep I piled pillows on my lap and he would lay his head on the pillows. I was with him almost constantly during those last weeks. When he had been sitting up too long he would bang his fist on the table to get my attention. When I came near him, he would smile and laugh. Then he would ask me to sing a song to him. He liked traditional Chuukese songs.

My sister, Luciana, would sit at the door with her baby. Her husband was somewhere working for the Japanese. Luciana was afraid to go near my father when he was like that; I don't know why. My father spoke very softly and he never complained, although we knew he was suffering. My father's godson, Jose Kani Teigita, always looked at me whenever my father became silent. He would say, "Check my godfather." So I would go over and touch my father's hand. He would open his eyes and smile, and say, "I'm all right. Don't worry." Then he would say, "Why don't you sing a song so I can go to sleep?" But I didn't know how to sing Carolinian songs then. I could sing some Japanese school songs, but not Carolinian. I continued to help my father like this because I loved him. The day he died he asked me to put pillows on my lap so he could sleep. He rested like that for two or three minutes, then he moved to a box where we kept our clothes. He put his head down there and slept. I sat there and waited for him to talk to me. Then he fell down on the ground. I was very excited because he never laid down before. My mother knew that he was dead because he didn't move. We all prayed, then I was sent to tell all of our relatives that my dad died. I started walking along the railroad tracks into the village, but before I reached my destination I heard the air raid sirens and bells. Then I could see American planes, and plenty of ships all around the island. I stood there and watched; I saw Japanese planes get shot down. Then my stepbrother, Francisco, threw a rock at me and told me to get down. I could see the smoke and fire coming from the cannons on the ships. The hill in back of us is where the shells exploded, because they could see tanks moving around there.

There was nothing we could do; we just wrapped my father up, and some relatives took him to the Tanapag Cemetery and buried him. My mother was afraid; she was shaking. My sister, Rosiana, told my mother that we had to get out of there. So we did. We ran further up the hill above Tanapag. Some people were kind enough to share their cave with us. They gave us water and some ripe bananas. I don't remember their names, but they were a Chamorro family and they were very nice. They were in a cave, but there was not enough room in there for all of us, so some of us had to stay outside. There was a big tree outside of the cave, so if any planes flew over they couldn't see us. A small stream passed by this cave, so at night we could go down and get some water. We stayed there for about three weeks.

One of my brothers-in-law who ran away from Aslito Field came looking for his family. I don't know how he did it, but he found his family on the other side of the hill from where we were, on the east side of the island. My aunt was there and she asked my brother-in-law to look [for] my mother and the rest of us. He looked around for us until he came to the place where we were hiding. This was at night, around midnight. He told us to come with him. So we went out of the cave, and with him to the other side of the mountain. We stayed in that area until the U.S. Marines came and took us out.

After what happened to my father I became very afraid of Japanese soldiers. Then one night about four or five Japanese soldiers came to the cave where we were hiding. They asked if there were men among us. We said, "Yes." There were my brothers-in-law, my cousin, and two others. The soldiers told the men to go with them and they would show them where they could find some food. So, my brothers-in-law and the others went with the soldiers, and they took them to Tanapag Church. There was a hole there; I don't know who dug it. It was full of supplies like biscuits, canned goods, and sweet things, like candy. They brought these things back to us through the kindness and good heart of these Japanese soldiers. I was wondering why my father was killed by the Japanese, then these soldiers take some of my family to get food for the rest of us. Up to this day I cannot make sense of it.

We continued to stay in that cave, and at night we had to go out and look for water. That was the most crucial thing. I would go with my relatives. They made some rope out of banana leaves and hung two canteens around my neck. I liked to go because if I found sugar cane I would chew it, and that helped alleviate my thirst. And when we couldn't find water we had only the sugar cane.

Believe me, I enjoyed my stay in that cave there with my mother, my sisters, and other relatives. I liked it especially in the early morning when the sun was coming up. American planes, small ones— maybe they are taking pictures— they would be flying all around the island. They would turn off their engines so that you wouldn't hear them coming, and they would come lower and lower. I would wave to them. They didn't wave back; they just looked. Then they would start their engines back up and fly away. My mother would be so mad at me. She would say, "If we all die here because of your craziness I'm going to spank you!" I wanted to laugh, but I didn't. I just said, "Sorry, Mama."

One morning about seven o'clock, my cousin, Rosario Omar, saw somebody running towards our cave. He ran forward, then he threw himself down on the ground. Then she saw another one do the same. They would run forward, then throw themselves on the ground. Then they stayed down, because there were Japanese above our cave and they started shooting at these men. They were American Marines. We just kept watching. Then one of my brothers-in-law, Joaquin Taisague from Guam, told everybody to keep silent. He said, "Those people are Americans. They are going to save us." The Americans kept coming; there were about five of them. Then they started shooting over us at the Japanese. Then my brother-in-law, Joaquin, stood up and ran towards the Americans. Somebody from above us shot him in the leg, and he fell down and stayed down. Then a Japanese soldier threw a grenade and it landed just in front of our cave and exploded. Fortunately, none of us were killed, but some were wounded. One of my brothers-in-law, Joaquin Sarapou, was hit in the fleshy part of the chest and the back of his shoulder, near the neck. But because he was so scared, he didn't feel any pain. Then my brother-in-law, Joaquin Taisague, who had been shot in the leg, got up and ran to where the Americans were.

When the hand grenade exploded my sister, Rosiana, was hit just behind the right ear and she fell back. Blood and white stuff came out — her brains. Her son, my nephew, was about three years old, and he was hit in the right upper arm and his hand was broken. My cousin Florencia took him and ran to where the Americans were. I tried to run too, with my mother, but she didn't want to leave my sister, so I ran by myself. At the same time, the Americans were running toward us. Then they threw themselves on the ground again and signaled us to do the same. I did, and as soon as I lay down the Americans started shooting again. I was shaking all over because of all the guns shooting.

After the Americans killed all the Japanese that were above our cave they brought my mother, my aunt Josepa, my brother-in-law Jose Camacho and his son Simeon, and my sister who was wounded, out of the cave. They put my sister, Rosiana, on a stretcher. She couldn't talk; she couldn't move. Tears were coming down her face. They gave her medicine to save her life, but there was nothing they could do. Her brains were coming out. A priest prayed for her while we were waiting for transportation. About thirty minutes later two big trucks came and took us to Camp Susupe. My mother was crying because she thought the Americans were going to kill us. We never saw my sister again. We assumed that she died, and the Americans buried her on that hill. My nephew also died about a week later, and we buried him in Susupe.

# With Father Tardio and the Nuns

MARIE SOLEDAD CASTRO

*After World War II Marie Castro went to a Catholic girls' school in Pohnpei. While there she joined the Mercedarian Order of the Catholic Church. She was a nun from 1950 until 1971. During these years of service to the Church she went to St. Mary's College in Leavenworth, Kansas, and eventually completed a master's degree in education. In 1973 she started a new career as an elementary school teacher in Kansas City, Missouri. She is now retired and divides her time between Kansas City and Saipan.*

When I was going to school I stayed with my grandmother on my mother's side because my parents worked on our farm in Marpi. They came home only on the weekends. Our house in Garapan was built by the Germans. It was a big stone house. In fact, that is why I bought a stone house in Kansas City where I live now, because it reminded me of my early childhood.

I think one thing very special about my parents was that I never heard them argue. If they had a disagreement they waited until we children were in bed, then they quietly solved the problem. They always talked very softly to each other.

My father was very strict and religion played an important part in our upbringing. Whenever we had visitors the children were not allowed to sit and listen. That was considered very impolite. I never saw my father drink, and curse words were unknown in our family.

I started school when I was seven years old. I walked from my house in Garapan to the school, which took about fifteen minutes. Going to school during Japanese times—I was always scared because of the way we were treated. The teachers were very strict. What I remember most about school was the severe punishment that students received when they did something wrong. One time a classmate sitting next to me was caught whispering to me. The teacher punished her by cutting her eyelashes off. The name of that student was Ana Muna and when her mother saw what the teacher did she was very disgusted and went to the teacher's home and started arguing with her.

Once, I was late getting back to school with some other students because we were cutting tangantangan to use as fertilizer in the school garden. When we got back, the rest of the students were lined up and ready for dismissal. As punishment we had to sit on the porch of the school with our arms held above our heads. We had to sit that way for about a hour. Then Vicente Guerrero's father — we called him "Komoi"—came up on his bicycle. He was a police officer. He started arguing with the vice principal, Sugaruma-sensei, and that was the end of our punishment.

On another occasion when a group of us were late returning to class our fingers were burned with drops of acid. We were all crying and if we moved our fingers they would put more acid on them. So, we just had to sit there crying while the acid burned through our skin.

My nephew, Alejandro Cabrera, was punished inside the classroom by his teacher, Soijima-sensei. He was beaten, slapped, and kicked. Alejandro was crying and asking for pardon, but the teacher would not listen. When Alejandro fell down the teacher told him to stand up, then he kicked him in the stomach, then picked him up and threw him across the room. He did this several times until Alejandro couldn't get up any more. I had to stand there with the other students and watch this. The desks were all turned upside down, and when it was over Alejandro did not come to school. He died several days later. I remember going to Alejandro's house after he died. All of the relatives were there. His mother was very nervous after that, and very sad. She was always crying. I don't remember the teacher ever being punished.

Seeing things like this—I couldn't learn in that environment. I was scared to death all the time. I was so glad to leave school in the third grade because all I remember from those days is the punishment. What learning we had was memorization — nothing to stimulate the mind.

In 1943 the Kaigun — Japanese navy—came to Saipan. The sailors flooded the streets. All we could see in the streets of Garapan were white uniforms. Many of them were drunk and they came into the houses looking for women. I was in our house with my mother, father, and older sister, Rosalia, when three of them came into our house. They asked my father, "Are there any ladies here — young ladies?" When my father heard that he had us secretly go out the back door, and told us to go to my cousin's house. We ran because the Kaigun were coming from the south and my cousin's house was about three blocks to the north. We told my uncle that the sailors were coming and they were looking for young ladies. So he hid us in the attic along with our

*Marie Castro in 1998.*

two cousins. When the sailors came in and asked for women my uncle Vicente said, "No, there are no young ladies here, but I have my son. His name is Antonio and he is a policeman." So the sailors went away and we stayed in the attic until the sailors were gone from the streets.

These sailors had come from Guam, and I understand that they had prostitutes on Guam. Probably these Japanese sailors thought we also had prostitutes here on Saipan, but our Jesuit Priest always reminded us of our moral obligations. We knew about prostitutes; we called them "famalaun babui," meaning women of the pigs.

By 1943, I think it was, we were moved out of our house in Garapan by the Japanese. We moved to our farm at Marpi on the north end of the island. Sometime after that my father was forced to leave us to work for the Japanese at the docks. He left in the evening. The next morning we were surprised to see him back at the farm. I think he really missed us. I was at the house with my brothers Augustine, Frank, and my little sister, Rita. My father asked us where our mother was, and I told him that she went to the field to get some sweet potatoes. He didn't say anything after that. He just kissed all of us and left.

The first American air raids on Saipan hit the docks where my father was working. That area was all in flames because the Japanese had a lot of oil storage tanks there. When that happened my father and all the other men fled. After that he stayed on the farm with us.

There were some Japanese soldiers on the northern part of Saipan at that time. There was also a Japanese general. I remember the name Swaisan. Probably it is a fictitious name, but it is the one he gave us. Every day he would go past our farm and down to the beach. He would walk up and down that beach, sometimes until dark. Then he would go back to wherever he was staying. He did this many times. Then one morning he asked for my father. This was a Sunday morning, and he sat there by the door for many hours and talked to my father. They were speaking very softly, and up until that time I didn't know how much Japanese my father understood, but he was able to communicate with this Japanese general. He told my father, "Pedro, I will tell you where to go when the fighting comes, and not one bomb will touch that place." And he said, "Don't tell anybody else. This is only for you. Keep it a secret." On another visit he came with a bag full of money. He said to my father, "I'm going to show you where I'm going

*The parents of Marie Castro, Pedro DeLeon Castro and Virginia Camacho Castro. Date of photograph not known.*

to bury this money. If the Americans win the war all this money will be yours." After the war my father tried to locate that spot, but that part of the island had been bulldozed and he couldn't find it.

This Japanese general didn't look Japanese. He had a long nose like a Caucasian. When I related this story to my friend Ana Muna after the war she said, "You know, I think that is the same general that we saw during the war. He put bandages all over his head and put mercurochrome on them, pretending to be wounded. But he had earphones under the bandages. His tactic was to go from cave to cave looking for Japanese soldiers. And when he saw a place with lots of Japanese soldiers, the minute he left that place would be bombed. I think he was a spy for the Americans."

The Americans invaded Saipan on June 15, 1944. That morning one of our Japanese neighbors came and knocked on our door. He said, "Pedro, Pedro, wake up because the Americans are invading the southern part of the island. Take your children and go for safety." All my father could think of at that time was the water tank. There was no water in it, so we went inside and stayed there until about nine o'clock that morning. But when he heard planes flying low and close to our farm he thought we weren't safe there. We went farther south and my father found a canal that went under the road. We hid there for three days. During that time we could see the American ships. We could even hear the sound of the ammunition being loaded into the guns, then the guns being fired.

After those three days in that canal my father remembered what that Japanese general told him about where we would be safe during the fighting. So we went to that spot and my father found a little cave. We were there for about a week when the nuns and the priests came.* The cave was somewhat divided, so the priest and the brother stayed on one side and the nuns on the other. Sister Angelica had been wounded sometime before she arrived at our cave. Her wound was right under the left arm, in her side.

Remedios Castro, who had accompanied them all this time, had put some dressings inside Sister Angelica's wound to prevent bleeding. I remember one night Remedios had to remove the dressing from the hole in sister Angelica's side. Sister Angelica was really in pain. I had to go all the way down to the beach that night with my mother and some others to wash the dressings. We prayed all the way because we were afraid we might run into some Japanese soldiers, and we didn't want to be hit by bullets fired from the ships.

Every morning and night my father had to go out and look for food and water. We had run out of water and everyone was very thirsty. We prayed for rain but it never came, so my father went down to the ocean to fetch some sea water. When he came back everybody surrounded that bucket. Sister Mercedes put some to her lips but couldn't swallow it. It was too salty. She just looked up to heaven — she was in tears. Nobody could swallow it. I cried too, I was so thirsty. I tried to swallow it, but couldn't.

While we were in the cave Jose Matsumoto, a Korean, read a Japanese leaflet that said the Americans were going to kill all the men and take the women and children to the ships. When my father heard that he called my mother and said, "Take the children with you. I think you will be safe. I will go somewhere and look for my own safety." My mother said, "No, Pedro. We will stay together. If we are going to die, we will die together." That convinced my father, and we stayed together until we were taken by the Americans.

That morning my father came back with some sugar cane; it was somewhat burnt. He told us to take good care of it because it was the last he could find. About a hour later two American Marines came right up to our cave with their rifles and bayonets. Then one of them motioned for us to come out and put our hands up. They then led us up to Asuela† and gave us food and water. We felt so safe with those Americans. We felt we were in heaven high up there on the hill. The Marines were interviewing the sisters and the priest. Sister Angelica was speaking in Japanese to one of the Marines.

While we were up there the Marines asked us to lie on the ground for a few minutes. I noticed one of the Marines speaking on a phone, I believe to one of the ships off the coast. There were two trucks full of Japanese soldiers coming toward us. Then, while we were on the ground, we heard some explosions. I didn't see what happened, but we were allowed to stand up again after that.

After that we were put on trucks and taken to Camp Susupe. On the way we came to two little Japanese girls standing in the road. One was four years old and the other was eight. They were dressed in nice kimonos. One of the Marines told us that their mother had dressed them in their best clothes, given them some money, and told them to keep walking until somebody

**Mother Teresa Cortazar, Mercedes Gonzalez Quinata, Pia Goicoechea, Joaquina Revuelta, Angelica Salaberria, Aurora Garate, Father Jose Tardio and Brother Ermano Oroquieta. Sister Genoveva Garate was killed near Mt. Tapochau.*

*†Now the site of a radio station.*

*Marie Castro in 1971.*

found them. I think their parents committed suicide. They were crying and saying, "Please take care of us. We don't have our parents." The nuns were trying to comfort them.

On the way we saw a lot of bodies. All we saw were burned bodies and burned trees everywhere. It was smelly. Nothing was green any more.

When we got to Camp Susupe all the Chamorros came to greet us because they saw that the nuns and the priest were with us. They also wanted to see if their family members were on the trucks.

In Camp Susupe all we did was pray the rosaries and talk about the war. We prayed every night for the deceased, and prayed that the Americans would win the war. We were so thankful that the Americans came and saved our lives. There was a rumor at that time that the Japanese were going to throw all the Chamorros in a big hole and kill them. We felt that the Americans were God–sent.

Whenever there is a documentary on TV about World War II, especially about the Pacific, I never miss it. I remember when we surrendered to the Marines on Marpi there was a Marine taking movies of us. I'm always hoping I will see this in one of the documentaries, but I never do.

The war affected me in a positive way. I have always wanted to express my thankfulness to the Marines, because I felt we were so oppressed during Japanese times. When the Marines came, life came to us. I feel they saved our lives. When I was teaching school in Kansas City, Missouri, I felt in my own little way I was paying back America for the lives that were given to save ours.

# The Boy from Taegu

TAEKI LEE

*Taeki Lee was ten years old when he left Korea with his family to start a new life, first in Pohnpei, then Saipan. Mr. Lee was repatriated to Korea in 1946 along with the rest of his family. He, like so many others, struggled to survive in the early years after the war in a country newly liberated after forty years under Japanese rule.*

My father was a farmer in Taegu, Korea, but he liked to gamble and he lost everything because of it, including the house. My mother was so mad at him. He had seven children, plus my mother and grandmother to support and he lost everything. He had plans to go to Manchuria after that, but then some Japanese came to Korea to recruit farmers to go to Micronesia and work in the sugar cane industry. My father had little choice. We were so poor.

The sugar cane company sponsored our trip. They paid for our transportation and everything. Fortunately, after we left Korea, my father gave up gambling.

In 1938 we left Korea from the port of Pusan. We went first to Shemonoseki in Japan, then we took the *Yokohama-maru*, first to Truk, then to Pohnpei. That trip took us one month. We didn't have to work while we were on the ship. I was just a ten-year-old boy, so for me it was all very strange and exciting; like a cruise.

In Pohnpei my father, mother, and two older brothers worked in the sugar cane fields and I went to school for the first time. I went to the elementary school with Japanese even though the Japanese looked down on Koreans as second class citizens. The teachers taught Korean history as something inferior. That would make me mad and sometimes I wouldn't go to school, but mostly I got along with the Japanese I knew on Pohnpei. Sometimes the Pohnpei people also treated the Koreans like second class citizens. One time there was a big fight between Koreans and Pohnpeians. The Japanese authorities didn't do anything about it. They just watched, but nobody was killed.

In Pohnpei it rained too much and there was an

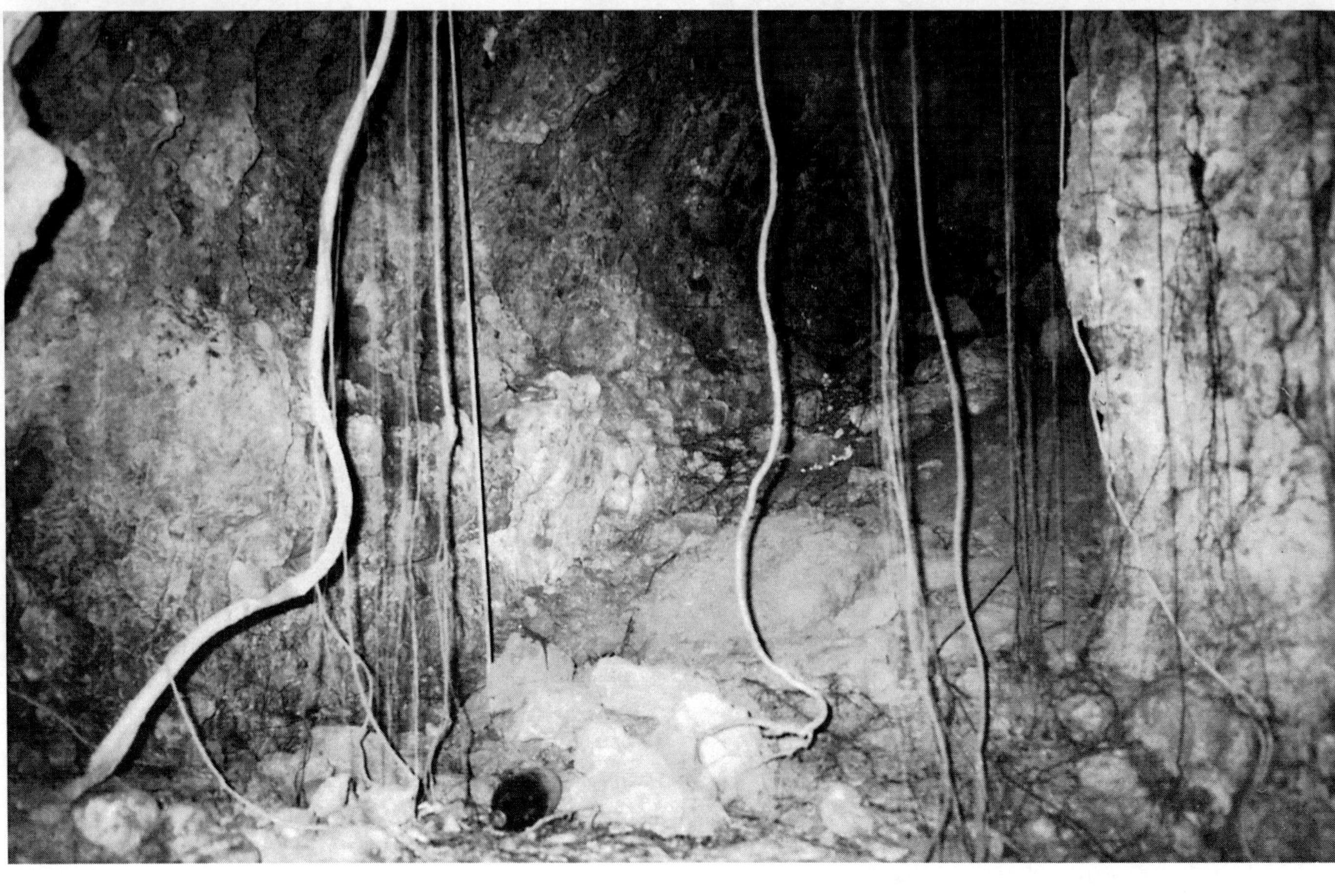

insect that attacked the sugar cane, so they couldn't produce much sugar. What they did produce they used to make alcohol. Plus, after the United States and Japan went to war it was difficult to get supplies.

We were in Pohnpei when the Japanese bombed Pearl Harbor. This was announced in our school by our teacher. She said the Americans started the war because they cut the oil supply to Japan, and oil was necessary for the survival of Japan. At the time I thought the Japanese would win, but after the Battle of Saipan I started thinking differently. We were all very scared because the Japanese Army told us that if the Americans come they would burn us, and attack us with bombs and tanks. Then, they decided to close down the sugar cane business in Pohnpei and move us to Saipan. That made us afraid too, because we had to move to Saipan by boat and we were afraid of American submarines. We had a destroyer escort but still we made life jackets out of bamboo, just in case.

We made it to Saipan without any problem. We had a house at the south end of the island near Aslito Field. We were not far from the beach and we could see Tinian from where we lived. My father worked at the sugar refinery and I continued to go to Japanese school. One of my best friends was the son of a Japanese doctor, but after the battle on Saipan I never saw him again. I didn't have any Chamorro friends, and my Japanese friends I only saw at school because they would go to their community and the Koreans would go to theirs.

When the Americans first bombed Saipan we didn't have any place to hide, but after that we dug some shelters. During the pre-invasion bombardment one of my friends was killed while playing near the beach. After the Americans landed on Saipan it was another seven days before we saw the first American troops and we were able to surrender. We had plenty of water, but we had enough food for only one day. So for six days we had nothing to eat.

We were about ten families hiding in the same area. The Japanese didn't put up much of a resistance in our area. That is to say, there wasn't much fighting. However, there was one detachment of Japanese soldiers who came to where we were hiding and told us to leave because they needed our shelters for their wounded. We found another place to hide but it was too small for all of us. After one night we went back to our original places of hiding and found the Japanese had left.

When the Americans arrived where we were hiding they came in firing their guns. Four Korean adults were killed before we could raise our hands and surrender. There was one Japanese civilian hiding in a cave near us. The cave had many twists and turns so when the Americans used their flame thrower on it he was not burned, but he surrendered right after that. After that the Americans took us to Camp Susupe. At that time there were only about twelve or fifteen Koreans in the camp, but by the time the battle was over the number was closer to 1,200.

While I was in camp somebody pointed out two Korean women to me and said that they had been "Comfort Women" for the Japanese military. That was the first time I heard of "Comfort Women." After we had been in camp for a while they allowed the men out during the day to work. The women and children remained in the camp. Some of the men worked at picking up dead bodies and burying them. I worked in the administrator's office for the camp. I was paid twenty-five cents a day.

For the first time as a Korean I felt superior to the Japanese. For example, Koreans could go to the Japanese camp, but the Japanese couldn't come to the Korean camp. Besides, the Japanese were losing the war.

On 6 February 1946 we were repatriated to Korea. On the way back to Korea from Saipan my grandmother died. They wouldn't let us take her to Korea for burial, so we had to bury her at sea. It was very cold in Korea at that time of year, so the Americans gave us all warm clothing; parkas, pants, socks, shoes, and blankets. But, when we arrived in Pusan the Americans there took it all away from us except for the children and women, because when the Americans in Saipan supplied us they didn't inform the Americans in Korea that they had given these things to us.

Our return to Korea was probably more difficult than anything we suffered during the war. We were cold. We had no money and no work. We returned to Taegu where we lived before going to Micronesia eight years before. We had to beg for food. Sometimes we starved. Sometimes we had nothing but raw grains of wheat to survive on. Our poor condition like this continued for the next four or five years. We received no assistance from the Americans. Not until the Korean

Opposite: *Examples of the many manmade and natural limestone caves on Saipan where Japanese civilians and soldiers hid during the fighting. If the occupants did not surrender, the usual routine was to blast the caves with flame throwers, then seal them with high explosives.*

War started did things improve. My father never worked again after we returned to Korea, not even during the Korean War. My older brother went into the army and was killed during the fighting. I found a job working on a farm and was able to send rice home to my family. After that I found a job working in a government office and was able to send money home. My brothers and sisters found work and life began to get better.

# 2 Yap and Tinian

## The Flemings from Yap

ALFRED FLORES AND ROSALIA ALDAN FLEMING

*Alfred Flores Fleming, born in 1922, and Rosalia Aldan Fleming, born in 1924, were third generation Chamorros living in Yap on the eve of the war between the United States and Japan. In 1948, at the request of the Yapese, the United States Naval Administration removed the Chamorros from Yap. Many settled on the island of Tinian, which had been virtually uninhabited since that island was taken from the Japanese in 1944.*

ROSALIA: My grandfather went to Yap during the German time to work as a carpenter. He died when I was six years old. My father, Joaquin Concepcion Aldan, was a fisherman most of his life except for a few years when he worked for the NBK (Nan'yo Boeki Kabushikigaisha — South Seas Trading Company) in Ulithi Atoll. My mother died on Saipan in 1950 from tuberculosis. She was forty-five years old.

When I was seven years old I started to school. Classes were small, maybe fifteen people. If you didn't understand something the teachers worked with you until you did. Children were well behaved. They listened to their parents and were respectful. Today, children don't listen. They talk back and do whatever they want.

After the fifth grade that was all; I just stayed home. I liked school; I always wanted to learn, but I did have one very cruel teacher. His name was Kanamori-sensei. One day I was tardy and he called me to the front of the class. He saw that I was wearing earrings, so he slapped me on the ear so hard that I spun around two times and my ear was ringing after that. He hit me so hard that he tore my earring out and I felt the blood running down. Since that day I don't wear earrings. Not all of the Japanese teachers were cruel like that. Some were very nice.

ALFRED: There was no higher education unless you left and were willing to pay for it. But, if you wanted to work there was always jobs.

ROSALIA: Yes, but jobs that were only for men, not for women. I had ten brothers and sisters, so I had to help around the house. I helped my mother on the farm, working in the taro patch, and making copra from the coconuts. My mother was always busy. She raised all of us children. She sewed, and she cooked very good food. She never had time to sit down and talk to us.

We had electricity from seven in the evening until midnight. During the weeks before Christmas my mother would continue to work by candlelight after midnight until three in the morning, sewing clothes for other people. She did the same thing before Easter. Then she had to get up at six every morning to get us children ready for school.

My father was always out fishing; sometimes at night; sometimes during the day. He knew how to build his own boat and make the sails. If the weather was nice he caught lots of fish. If we had bad weather for one week we had almost nothing to eat. That was what life was like then. The only recreation we had was going swimming in the lagoon. Today, the children watch television all day.

I had an auntie who was married to a Japanese. They owned a restaurant that only Japanese could go to. When I was very small; I think I was eight years old, I used to work there serving food to the customers. I couldn't understand anything; just served the food and took away the dishes when they were done. I didn't get paid, but if there was any food left over my auntie gave it to us, so I was very happy to get good food. After the war my auntie's husband was sent back to Japan, but she didn't want to go to Japan. They never saw each other again.

In Japanese times people always showed respect. In my twenty-four years in Yap I never heard of anybody raping little girls. Even during the war when we were living in the jungle we could walk one or two hours and meet many soldiers and they wouldn't do anything to you. They were very respectful.

ALFRED: My father came to Yap from the Marshall Islands when he was seventeen years old to work as a bookkeeper for "His Majesty" O'Keefe. When the Japanese took Yap from the Germans they took over the business. (David Dean O'Keefe was a late nineteenth-century trader and businessman on Yap.)

ROSALIA: When I was sixteen I married my first husband. He died in an accident during the war. He was working for the Navy Department at the time. Some Japanese officers were going to have a party, so my husband, my cousin Jesus Aldan, his friend Albert Fleming, and two Japanese soldiers went fishing with dynamite. Before they could catch any fish some American bombers came over and they threw everything away and reported what happened to their superiors. Their boss, a Japanese officer, said, "Let's go back and I will show you how to fish." My husband, his friend, and these three Japanese soldiers went. On the boat this Japanese officer tied the dynamite together and lit the fuse. Everybody told him to throw it before it exploded, but he said, "It's okay; I know what I'm doing." Then it exploded. Two people were killed, the Japanese officer and my husband. The Japanese had his stomach ripped open. My husband died after five days. I spent those five days in the hospital with him until he died. When he urinated red blood came out. When he coughed black blood came up. After the second day he developed a fever and chills. I think he knew he was going to die because he asked me to wash his body and put clean clothes on him. His name was Filipe Aguino and we had two children together. I was a widow for five years before I married Alfred here on Tinian.

ALFRED: During the war I was working for the Japanese Army Headquarters in the transport and distribution of military supplies. This was by boat. One morning I got up to go check the boat before going to breakfast. So when I crossed this river I saw the "Taisho" (general) wearing his pajamas. Everybody knew him as "The General." I don't know what his name was. But, he was holding a stick about six feet long with a string on it. It was very shallow water, and I wondered how anybody could catch a fish in it. The other end of the fishing line ran up the sleeve of his pajamas. I thought to myself, "This is a new kind of fishing." Anyway, I saluted him and he looked up and smiled.

The following month, on a full moon, the general wanted to take the boat out to go fishing. The only other people on board were myself and Ben Pangelinan. He was the chief engineer and I was the coxswain. While we were out at sea this general went to the stern and took out a piece of paper. What he wrote was not Japanese because he wrote from left to right. Ben saw this but he couldn't look too close because he might get punished. Then he rolled the paper up and put it in an empty whiskey bottle and dropped it over the side. This is when the Americans were bombing Yap every day, every day.

We all thought this general was a spy for the Americans because when the American planes came and bombed everybody would run and hide, but he would go to the top of a hill in his white pajamas. Then one week after the fighting stopped some Yapese people saw the general go to where the harbor is in Colonia. One night they saw two American officers and three sailors come ashore and walk into the general's house. The next morning we heard a rumor that the Americans had taken the Japanese general out to one of the ships. After breakfast some people went to his house, but nobody was there. His uniforms were hanging in there, but he was gone. Nobody ever heard or saw him again.

We suspect that he is the one who saved the people because during the war the Japanese dug a big tunnel in a mountain. The purpose was when the Americans came the Japanese were going to put all of the natives in there and kill them. When the tunnel was completed the Americans bombed it. Then the Japanese dug another one; not just one, but every time they completed one of these tunnels the Americans bombed it.

During the war Yap was divided between the Japanese Army and the Navy. The Navy wanted to kill all of the natives so there would be more food for the Japanese, but the general said, "No. Let the natives plant for us and we will fight the enemy, so don't kill them."

On Yap at this time was a family of White Russians. After the Russian Civil War they came down to Japan, then Yap. The father's name was Tretnoff; Alexander Tretnoff. The mother was Augusta. One of the sons, Alix, lives on Yap. There was also a Japanese soldier from Hawaii. He went to Japan on vacation, and while he was there he was drafted into the Japanese Army. His face was Japanese, but when he talked you could tell that he was American. He was a hospital corpsman. He told us that he had orders to give injections to all of the natives and kill them if the Americans landed. But he said he wasn't going to do it. Then he explained that he was going to inject water instead. He was in the Japanese Army but his heart was American.

ROSALIA: The war was very scary because the Japanese told us that if the Americans come, "They will rape you; they will kill you," things like that. The Americans first bombed us on March thirty-first. I cannot forget. You know why, because I was pregnant with my second child — my daughter. It came early in the morning just as it was getting light. We heard their engines from a distance. At first we thought they were Japanese airplanes, but then they slowed down and we could see them throw the bombs. We knew they were close to us because we could see the shock waves from the bombs. That is when we ran into the river bed. It was dry and had high banks. We just kept on running until we were almost on the other side of the island. The whole day we didn't drink water; we didn't eat. We had no desire to.

It was my father who carried my two-year-old daughter because my stomach was so big from being pregnant. We stopped at a wide place in the river where we could all stretch out. It was then that I felt the pain that I was going to deliver the baby. Right after I delivered, the Untalan family passed by and they heard the baby crying. They stopped to see and my father asked if anybody had some scissors to cut the cord with. Tomasa Untalan said she had a pair.

We stayed there about seven days because during Japanese times you weren't supposed to walk long distances after giving birth because you might get sick. We lived on coconut juice and bananas. After that we went back to my father's farm near Colonia. We didn't work during the day time. My mother and father were always scared, and my brothers and sisters were not with us because the Japanese took all of the strong men and the school children to work on the airstrips; one on the west side of Yap and one on the north. They carried stones in baskets to make the airstrip. The children were working on the field when the Americans bombed and shot machine guns at it. Everybody ran like ants. My brothers and sisters survived, but it was more than one week before we found them. I went with my mother, my father, and one sister to look for them. We went at night, and when we had to cross a river there were only two logs for a bridge. My father said everybody should cross over one at a time, and I should be last with the baby. When my turn came my father couldn't help me with a light because it was too dangerous. As soon as I took two steps the bridge broke and I fell to the rocks below. The baby was not hurt because I did not let go of her, but I landed on my side and I was all black and blue. I could not walk. I stayed in that place for another five days, and my family stayed with me. My father would get young coconut for me to eat.

When the airstrip was bombed by the Americans my brothers and sisters became separated. They all came to my father's farm after awhile. My sister, Grace, was the first but when we asked about the others she said she didn't know. Then the rest showed up one by one.

Nobody that I know of starved to death during that time. We had enough to eat but it was all local food. We were healthy, but five of the kids, we were ten families together, had some kind of skin disease. It was really ugly, all yellow around the mouth and dripping something where the skin was broken. If you had open skin you would get it. Right after the war the American doctors came and gave us penicillin, and after one shot the next day you could see it get better. They gave us that maybe three times. Then they treated us for worms. Everybody had plenty of worms. Every time I went to the bathroom there were plenty of worms, big like a pencil.

The Japanese knew the war was over before us because when the planes came over we all hid, but the Japanese just kept on walking. This went on for about a week and a half, then one of my brothers, Francisco Aldan, whispered, "I think the war is over because tomorrow we are going to take some Japanese officers to the American ships."

My future father-in-law was always scared and in

hiding because he doesn't look like a Chamorro. He had white skin and a long nose like an Englishman. If the Japanese thought you might be for the Americans they would kill you. Henry Hofschneider was part German and he was the only one who knew that my future father-in-law was part Scottish, but he never told anyone. He was a very good man. See, in World War II the Germans and Japanese were friends. The Scottish were not friends.

Then one day the American soldiers came into the jungle and found us. We were so happy. They were so friendly, so we were not afraid. I don't remember ever having any problems with American troops. But, some of the Japanese officers did commit suicide.

After the war two groups of Chamorros had left Yap already. One group went to Guam and the other went to Saipan. As the last group we thought we would stay in Yap forever because our grandparents had been there since German times; who knows, maybe since Spanish times. We owned the land and all of our trees were bearing fruit. We thought we would die there. Then in 1947 all the chiefs from all over Yap had a meeting and asked the U.S. Navy to take the Chamorros away. Captain Kenney then called a meeting with all of the Chamorros and said that Tinian is a very nice place and maybe you will be happy there because you belong to the Marianas. He said we don't belong in Yap because we are Chamorro. So seventeen Chamorro men from Yap went to Tinian to see if we should move there. After a week, or week and a half they came back and said it was a beautiful island, "the roads are nice, there are buildings, and there is lots of food."

We were told that we could take whatever we could carry. The people who first went to Tinian noticed that there were no tall trees so they decided to bring everything including cats, goats, chickens, cows, and many coconuts for planting. Also, bananas and some other trees.

I don't know, but later I heard two stories why the Yapese wanted us to leave. One story is that under the Japanese the policemen on Yap were Chamorros and that the Yapese were abused by these policemen. In those days if you were a policeman you could go to a village and say, "Give me coconuts, give me chickens, give me this, give me that." That is what I heard. Also during the Japanese times it was against the law for Yapese to drink alcohol, and if the police asked you if you had been drinking they would really hurt you if you said, "No." The police would beat you. Sometimes they would make you squat with a piece of bamboo between your thighs and calves, then they would roll it back and forth. That was really painful. If still you do not confess they laid you down and force water down your throat. So, even if you didn't do anything wrong you had to say you did to make them stop the torture. That was the Japanese system, and they did it to Chamorros too.

I am happy that we came to Tinian, but the first six months were difficult, because we were put in buildings originally meant for Japanese POWs. The house was too small, only about ten by twelve feet, with one community kitchen and one community shower. At that time my father had eleven children. I had two children; we slept like sardines in there. Then we found some old navy Quonset huts and moved up there, but that was too far away from the harbor. In those days there was only one boat a week that came over from Saipan, and only two trucks were operating on the island. For us it was a long walk there and back, especially if the boat didn't come, which sometimes happened. So, we moved into the village. There were so many fish in the harbor in those days, and they were so easy to catch, but not anymore. Also, the American military left big Quonsets full of food and lots of diesel fuel.

There were still old B-29s on North Field, but in 1950 two companies came to take them away. They melted down the aluminum right there and made them into blocks. Then once a month a big ship would come and take it away.

When I was young we worked hard; we had to. Today there is welfare and food stamps. People don't want to work.

# The White Russian from Yap

## Alex Tretnoff

*The father of Alex Tretnoff, Alex Sr. was born and raised in Russia. His mother, Augusta, was born in Vladivostok to parents who immigrated there from Germany. Alex's two older sisters, Olga and Ada, were also born in Vladivostok. The family sided with the Czarist armies during the Russian Civil War and was forced to flee to Japan as Bolshevik armies advanced east. The family settled on the island of Yap in 1925. Alex Jr. was born there in 1930.*

My father was born and raised in Moscow. He spoke many languages: German, Polish, Russian, and Italian. He was working as a radio operator for the Siberian Railroad at the time of the Russian Revolution. My mother's name was Augusta and she was German. Her family lived in Vladivostok where they owned and operated a business. That is where my father met and married my mother.

My father was on the losing side of the Russian Civil War. He didn't fight, but he helped tear up the railroad tracks to slow down the advance of the Bolsheviks. After that he fled to Japan to save his life and the lives of his family. From Vladivostok they took a ship to Japan. My father told me that everybody had to stand on the ship on the way to Japan because it was so overloaded. There was no place to lie down. While my family was in Japan my father bought a book about Micronesia and concluded that Yap was the best place to go because the people were nice and there were no dangerous animals that might harm the children. They arrived on Yap in 1925 and I was born there in 1930. My father opened a bakery and provided bread and other baked goods to the local population. At that time there were only civilians on Yap — Japanese, Okinawans, Koreans, and Chamorros. There were also a few Europeans.

Even though I wasn't Japanese I was allowed to go to the Japanese school. All of the other students were Japanese, Okinawan, and Korean. At that time my sisters were older and didn't go to school except at night, and that was so they could learn Japanese. Mr. Yamada was the principal, but he left before the war. He came back to Yap maybe fifteen years after the war with a group of Japanese school children. He looked me up and we went fishing together, but we never talked about the war. He died just two or three years ago in Japan.

One of the boys I went to school with was from Okinawa. His name was Oshiro and he later became governor of Okinawa. I think that was in 1969 or 1970, something like that. All of my teachers were pretty good. I never got beaten up, but sometimes if one student did something wrong the whole class had to stand up, face off in twos, and slap each other across the face. Then after school we would find the student who caused the trouble and beat him up. Once the war started getting close to Yap, the school was closed and most of the civilians were sent back to Japan. Some made it, but some were torpedoed and their ships sank.

Before the war life was very good. We had good times and plenty to eat. I didn't have to work after school. I played with my friends and went fishing. Even after the war came to Yap we had plenty to eat. We had good relations with the Japanese and Chamorros. My father was a good friend of the Japanese governor. The governor spoke German; that is why he and my father got along so well. However, my father never learned Japanese so one of my sisters acted as his interpreter.

Agapito Hondonero and his wife, Filomina Untalan, were good friends of my mother and father. Agapito was a Filipino weatherman. I remember him as a big man, but I never got to know him because when adults came to see my family they always chased the children outside. I used to play with Agapito's children, Baltazar and Caroline. They were about my age. I remember Agapito's wife, Filomina. I think she was the most beautiful girl in her family. Her two sisters, Tomasa and Ursula, are still alive and live on Guam. All the members of the Hondonero family were arrested later during the war. They were taken to Palau along with some Catholic fathers and killed. At this same time there were four Americans, two from a plane and two frog men,* who were captured by the Japanese on Yap and sent to Palau on the same ship. At least that is what somebody told me. My father asked the Japanese general on Yap if they were going to arrest him too, but the general said, "No! Don't worry." That was General Edo.† You see, the orders to arrest those people came

*The U.S. submarine* Burrfish *landed a beach reconnaissance party on Yap in lieu of a planned invasion of the island. Half the party failed to return, and to date no one knows what happened to them. The invasion of Yap was later canceled.*

†*According to Col. Hiroshi Shiraishi, chief of military history at the Staff College of Japan's Ground Self Defense Forces, his real name was Col. Daihachi Etou.*

from the Kempeitai (military police) on Palau. They were the only ones who had the authority to execute people. We didn't know they had been killed until after the war. The Untalan family came back to Yap sometime after the war, then went to Palau. They tried to find the graves of Filomina and her family but never did.

I was a young boy during the war and for about two or three months I worked for Taisho (General) Edo. He was a Japanese general, a big shot. This guy was always smoking Lucky Strikes, Chesterfield, Old Gold. I was thinking, "Where did he get these things; they're American cigarettes." He also had a stock of American canned food. General Edo could speak German and English. At night he would visit my parents and take them rice and corned beef. They were good friends. During the day he was carried around the island by Japanese soldiers on a chair with long poles. At night he would walk around dressed like a Yapese. I passed him one night dressed like this, and I said to myself, "Hey, that's my boss." I said to him, "Where are you going dressed like that?" He said, "I'm going to see your folks."

The Japanese started sending troops to Yap in 1943, or maybe it was 1944. The officer in charge of the navy had higher rank than General Edo, and he had a plan to kill all of the natives because there wasn't enough food. I don't remember the name of that admiral, but he was having tunnels dug in the sides of this mountain. When they were done he was going to have all of the Yapese and Chamorros taken in there and killed. I know this because a Japanese medical corpsman who spoke English told me this. His name was Ichki, Masumi. When the war was over he said he would write to me but I never heard from him after that. He came to my family and said the Japanese are going to kill all of the natives because the soldiers are starving. But when General Edo met with the other Japanese officers on this subject he said, "No! Put them to work growing food for all of us." The admiral said, "No, no, no! I am higher than you. We are going to kill them."

Lucky for us, before he could kill any of us, this admiral was killed by one of the American bombs. That left General Edo in charge and we were saved. After that the whole island was put to work planting sweet potatoes and other crops to feed both the Yapese and Japanese.

I was still working for General Edo when the Americans began bombing Yap. I remember one morning when the Americans were bombing he said to me, "You're not going into the bomb shelter; don't worry about it." He told me they weren't going to bomb where we were. His house was out in the open, in the middle of a taro field. During the whole war the Americans never bombed his house; they never shot at it with machine guns. Then, after Yap had been bombed for about two months, the general said, "I think we should go into the bomb shelter today." That day the Americans dropped bombs all down the valley where we were.

The general's laundry was another thing. He never hung it from a line, and he never tried to hide it from the planes flying over head. He had us lay it flat on the taro patch where the planes could see it, and he made us lay it in patterns that looked like letters. One day we would wash his laundry and lay it out to dry. The next day he would have us take the same set of laundry, even though it wasn't dirty, and lay it out again but in a different way. You know, at that time I was very young and I didn't think too much about why we did things like that — why the General had us hang his laundry this way one day, then that way the next. But after the war I started thinking, "Maybe he was sending a message to the planes."* They bombed all over Colonia, and even in the jungle, but they never even came close to the general's house.

After the bombing stopped and the war was over General Edo disappeared. An American boat came in at night and he was gone, just disappeared. This happened even before the Marines landed. His second in command, I think his name was Colonel Ito, was left in charge. He ran Yap until all of the Japanese were sent back to Japan. The Americans left him there to run things. Even the American troops then on Yap were under Colonel Ito. I think that lasted maybe three months.

All of the Chamorros who were living on Yap were sent back to the Marianas after the war. They weren't sent away because they were bad people, but I think the chiefs on Yap wanted their land. A Commander Kenney was in charge of Yap for a while after the war. I think he was afraid of the chiefs; that is what one of the chiefs told me. He said Commander Kenney was afraid of the chief's magic.

After the war lots of Yapese were killed, probably more than during the war. We had all of this dynamite that the Japanese had left and people were using it to get fish in the lagoon. But the fuses were old and sometimes the dynamite would explode before they could

**Col. Shiraishi believes there is no evidence to support the idea that Col. Etou was a spy for the Americans.*

Above and left: *A Japanese airplane destroyed on the ground during an American air raid on Yap.*

throw it. My friend Francis Tikihn was with four others trying to remove the fuses from a mine to use in fishing when it blew up. Francis was thrown twenty-five feet away, but he lived. The other four were in small pieces. What was left of them wouldn't fit in a small basket.

# 3 Rota

## Digging Tunnels on Rota

Antonio Shimabukuro Borja

*Antonio Shimabukuro Borja was born on Tinian in 1927. His father, Kancho Shimabukuro, was Okinawan and his mother, Maria Borja, was Chamorro. Mr. Borja was separated from his parents and two brothers when he went to Rota to visit an aunt in 1943. The war prevented his return to Tinian until the end of hostilities, and it would be another nine years before he saw any of them again. After the war Mr. Borja was elected three times the mayor of Tinian.*

My father came to Tinian in 1917 when he was twenty-three years old. In those days Tinian had a lot of wild pigs and cows, so he was authorized to have two shotguns to shoot the animals with. This was before the sugar cane industry got going, but he continued with the same line of work even then and right up until he was repatriated to Okinawa in 1946.

My mother was born on Tinian in 1903 and married my father in 1926. She had three children by my father. Since my father was not Catholic the church would not recognize her marriage to my father. I was the oldest of three boys. I had one brother, Jose, five years younger than me who was killed during the war. He was about nineteen years old and was killed when American planes were strafing Tinian. My mother and father never talked much about it to me afterwards. I was on Rota at the time and didn't find out about it until after the war. My other brother, Joaquin, survived and still lives on Tinian.

Because my father was from Okinawa I was recognized as being Japanese and was allowed to go to a Japanese school on Tinian. I finished sixth grade in 1938, then went to navigator school on Saipan for almost two years. Navigator school was a four-year program, but because of the war I never graduated. I would see my family on Tinian as often as once a week. The last time I would see them until after the war was September 1942.

After I left navigator school I was stationed on a ship. We transported troops and supplies to Rota and other islands. In 1943, when I was nineteen years old, I went to Rota to visit my aunt on my mother's side. I was there for one week when the Japanese military police came to my aunt's house. I don't know who gave them my name, but they had it on a list. I was told to report to an artillery company the following morning at 8:00 A.M. That morning they took my civilian clothes and gave me a uniform. I was a Japanese soldier. I couldn't say anything or they would have beaten me. I was also issued a rifle, bullets, and hand grenades. I was given a book on Japanese military policy and told I had one week to learn it. I spent all day digging tunnels for cannons, then at night I had to study that book. After the first week the Japanese started to beat us with their fists. This was military policy to make us hard and strong, or something like that. They didn't hit me much because I was young, but the older Okinawans had their eyes swollen and their mouths were bleeding. As Okinawans we were Japanese, but treated differently than Japanese from the northern islands of Japan. We were

*Antonio Shimabukuro Borja as he looks today. Photograph taken at his home on Tinian.*

forbidden to speak our own language, only Japanese. We weren't supposed to see or know anything. It wasn't safe to ask questions. We didn't even know about the invasion of Saipan and Tinian until after the war.

It was like that for almost eighteen months. From seven in the morning until midnight, six days a week, we were digging tunnels for cannons. We breathed in lots of smoke from the candles they used in the tunnels. We were all black by the end of the day.

Some Chamorros were killed when B-29s bombed Rota. One was my cousin, Crispen Manglona. He was planting sweet potatoes when that happened. But I don't know much about what happened to the Chamorros on Rota because they were kept on a separate part of the island.

I had an uncle on Rota, his name was Ignacio Dela Cruz and he was arrested by the Japanese on suspicion of spying for the Americans. Then one day when the Americans were bombing Rota I heard part of the jail was destroyed and some of the prisoners escaped. My uncle and a Catholic brother were among them. After about two weeks they were recaptured. I had a friend, Ramon Blanco Barcinas, who told me that after they were captured the Japanese killed them. Ramon was working for the Japanese in laying down communication lines. He was hiding nearby and saw it all happen. He told me the prisoners had to dig their own graves, then their hands were tied behind their backs. My uncle took only one shot in the back of the head. The brother was shot eight times, but he was still alive, so they cut his head off.* I know others were killed on Rota but I don't know about them. I think there were three others.

In September 1945 we found out that the war was over and we were told to collect all of the ammunition and take it to the harbor before the Americans arrived. I was scared because I didn't speak English and I didn't know what the Americans would do to us. However, when the Marines arrive they were very nice.† They gave us clothes, food, and cigarettes. They started schools for the children. They even had movies for us, and they didn't beat us. The Americans did question some people on Rota about crimes committed by the Japanese. They had a list of names but they never questioned me.

Sometime after the Americans came to Rota a wealthy Guamanian by the name of Jose Torres, who was married to a Chamorro from Rota, arrived. He came to Rota and he asked me and three others if we would like to go to Guam and study English. If we didn't want to study English he said we could work for him in one of his businesses. I took the offer along with the other three to go and study English. So in November of 1945 I went to Guam. We all stayed with the Torres family. There was a barracks for us, and he also provided us with food and money. He gave us $100 every fifteen days.

I had relatives on Guam, and on weekends I would visit with them. My cousin, Pedro Santos, was a captain on the Guam police force. Once they asked me about my mother on Tinian, but I told them I didn't know what happened to her. We never talked about it after that, and nobody in my family made any attempt to find out for me. I never knew any Americans while I was on Guam, and didn't know how to go about finding out what happened to my family on Tinian. Plus, I didn't go out much. I was still scared and

**Dr. William Peck in his book,* Tidy Universe of Islands, *provides the following information on these executions from a Rotanese by the name of Emilio Inos he interviewed in the 1980s: Hecho' Koyama returned from the execution he had just performed and the ritual of purification that cleansed his soul. "A number of hecho's, were there and we all volunteered to kill him for we all hate spies. But I was the one who was chosen and honored to do it. So we stood the first spy, who was some kind of priest, up front of the grave we had dug for him, and I aimed my gun at his heart and pulled the trigger but nothing happened. The damned gun wouldn't shoot. So I aimed it at the sky and pulled the trigger and it shot like it was supposed to. So I aimed it again at the spy, pulled the trigger and once again nothing happened. By that time everybody was laughing at me and I got mad and threw the gun on the ground, grabbed my sword and ran with it and jabbed it into his chest. But that didn't kill him either. He just sank down on his knees and looked up at me and said in the funny way he tried to talk Japanese, 'My friend, it hurts.' By that time everyone was laughing and making me feel ashamed, so I grabbed his face, threw him on the ground, put my foot on his head and chopped it off with one, clean blow. Then everyone clapped and shouted respect for the way I had done it."*

*†Ninth Marine AAA Battalion.*

Guamanians didn't like Chamorros from Rota and Saipan because of the things they did on Guam during the Japanese occupation. Once when I did go out some Guamanians asked me where I was from. I said, "From Tinian." There were very few Chamorros living on Tinian during Japanese times and none were sent to Guam. They said, "You are lucky you are from Tinian. If you were from Rota or Saipan we would kill you." I told them I was sorry because I don't know anything about that. After that I didn't want to go out because I was so scared. I never told anybody I was on Rota. I always said I was from Tinian.

In 1946 the U.S. military ordered all Japanese nationals repatriated. My father was sent back to Okinawa. My mother and younger brother went with him. It was 1953 before I saw any of them again. Until that year none of them had any idea that I was still alive. I didn't know if they were alive or dead either. I thought maybe they were all dead but I didn't know for sure and I made no attempt to find out for a long time.

When I returned to Saipan in 1947 I was recruited by Juan Pangelinan to join a unit called Army Security. He was then the chief of Army Security. Then in 1948 there was an announcement that the Americans were recruiting for something called the "Constabulary Force." There was a difference between the "native police" and the Constabulary Force. The native police couldn't arrest Americans and they weren't allowed to carry guns. I had to go through three months of training where they taught us how to use American weapons, even .50-caliber machine guns. We had rank just like the Marines. After the three months of training we were all promoted to Pfc. Life was pretty peaceful in those days. We didn't have too much crime like murders, mostly things like accidents.

It took me a long time even then to get the courage to seek help in finding out what happened to my family. At first I only had contact with low-ranking American personnel. Then in 1952 an American told me that all of the Okinawans from Tinian were sent back to Okinawa in June of 1946. That is when I went to the head of the Naval Administration and talked to the Navy Commander and asked him to help me find out what happened to my family on Tinian. I knew that all of the Okinawans had been repatriated to Okinawa, but I still didn't know if my family had survived. It took six months for the army in Okinawa to find them. Then I received orders to go there and pick them up. My mother was so happy when she saw me, she cried. I saw my father, mother, and younger brother, but when I asked my mother about my other brother, Jose — that is when she told me how he was killed by an American fighter plane. We never talked about it again after that.

After one week I had to come back to Saipan. My mother and brother came back with me, but not my father. I wasn't able to bring my father back until 1966. It was very hard to get permission to bring my father back. My mother passed away in 1995. She was ninety-two years old. My father died two years before that. He stayed on Tinian for only two years, then went back to Okinawa. He said he wanted to die in his own country.

## Hungry and Thirsty on Rota

### Jose King

*Jose King was born on the island of Rota in 1931. His father, Jose King, Sr., was born in Korea and came to the Mariana Islands sometime between 1914 and 1920. His mother was Juana Borja King. Jose, Jr., moved to Tinian in 1947 where we worked as a farmer and fisherman most of his life.*

My father moved to Saipan from Korea but I'm not sure when. He was the only one from his family to come to the Marianas and he never returned to Korea after that. When the Japanese decided to expand the sugar cane industry to Rota he moved there. My father's real name was Kim, but the Japanese changed it to King. He became a Catholic when he married my mother, Juana Borja, in 1925. The church gave my father the Christian first name of Jose.

During Japanese times, before the war, the Japanese were very kind and life was peaceful. Because my father was Korean we were allowed to live in Songsong Village with the Japanese. The Chamorros lived maybe two or three miles away in a small village.

After the war started we were told that if the Americans landed on Rota we should not take any prisoners, but kill them or they would kill us.

When I was still going to school there was a big

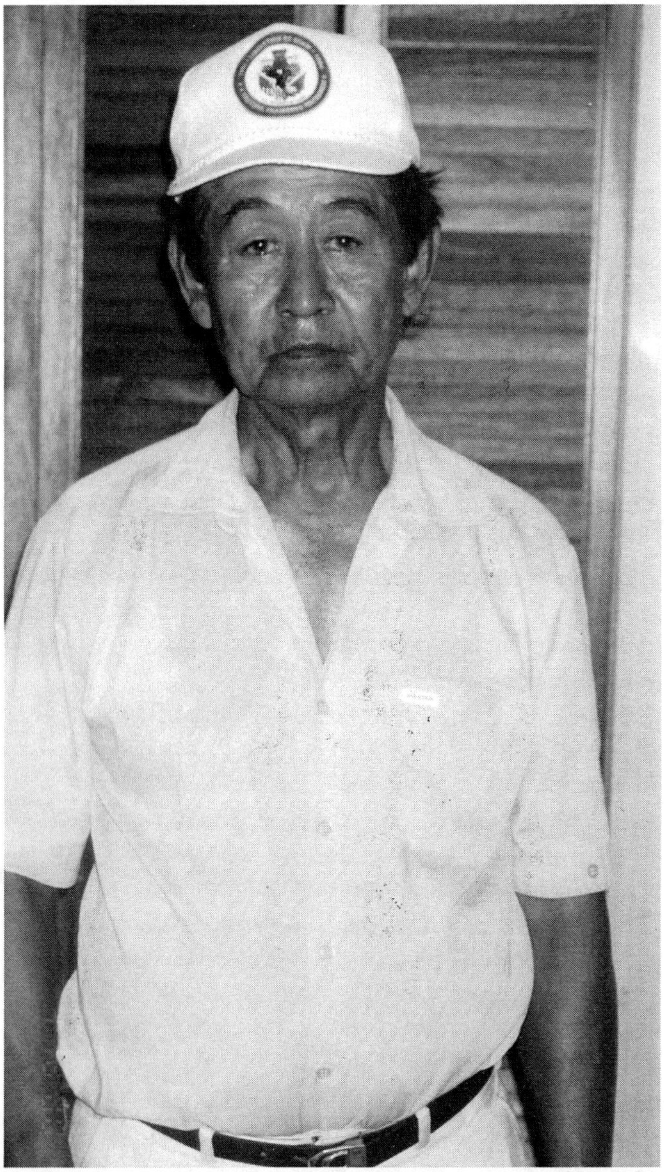

*Jose King was born and raised on the island of Rota, in the Marianas. His father was from Korea, and his mother a native Chamorro. Jose moved to the island of Tinian after the war and has lived there ever since. This photograph was taken of him by his wife at their modest home on Tinian.*

ship come into the harbor at Sansanlagu* (west of Songsong Village), and that night the Americans blew up that ship by submarine. Many people died, and many were wounded. I think they were mostly Japanese soldiers. Everybody from the village and all of the school children lined the road to the hospital and bowed when they brought the dead and wounded from the ship.

When the Americans started bombing Rota there was no more school. They burned all of the houses, so we went to the jungle and we farmed. There was no more job for my father so he started growing vegetables and raising cows, pigs, and chickens. Then more Japanese soldiers came to Rota, but after a while no more ships came from Japan so we didn't have rice to eat. The soldiers would come to our farm and take the chickens and pigs. If we refused they threatened to kill us. We had to go into the jungle to find food. We made slingshots to hunt birds. We grew sweet potatoes but the Japanese soldiers would take those too. They left the little ones, the size of your finger, for us. We would also eat the leaves of the sweet potato. Everything else we had to get from the jungle.

My father would go out at three in the morning because when the sun came up the American fighter planes would come and it wasn't safe to be out. In the dry season we didn't have enough water. My father, brother, and me would go to the beach and collect rain water from the rocks and put it in metal containers. One time an American plane saw us on the way back from collecting water and he started shooting at us. It was early morning — maybe two miles to walk. The bullets hit the ground right beside me. Thank God, none of us were hurt.

We were always hungry and thirsty. When it rained we put our blankets and clothing on the ground, then squeezed out the water to drink. At times I thought it would be better to die than live like that. Every day we didn't know if we would eat. My father would sit and think where to get food to feed the family. My mother was very skinny because if she had food she wouldn't eat. She always gave it to the children. We lived like this for maybe eighteen months.

There were other Chamorros living south of us. Our camp was farther north, and high up at a place called Sakaya. The people in the south had water that came down from the mountain. That same water they use today in Songsong Village. They could also catch fresh water shrimp.

My older brother, Ignacio, was sixteen years old. He was good with the slingshot, so a Japanese officer took him to be his house boy. The Japanese were hungry too, so during the day my brother would hunt birds for the Japanese officer. We were not allowed to visit him, and he was not allowed to visit us. He was gone for eight months. Our home was a cave. It wasn't safe to build a house because of the planes. One morning a Japanese soldier came to our cave very early after my father had come back from looking for food. He said to my father, "Mr. King, I am sorry about this, but my officer told me to tell you about your son. He was killed

*Probably the* Shoun Maru.

this morning." My father was told to come and get my brother's body. I told my father I wanted to go with him. We had to walk very far. We went over a mountain to make a short cut. When we arrived the Japanese were praying and we sat down together. Ignacio was covered with leaves. We uncovered him and I saw his face. He had a hole in his chest. The Japanese officer said to my father, "Mr. King, I am sorry about your son. He was a very good boy. You can take your son to your place." We were going to take him to our cave by truck, but it was very dangerous because of the planes, so he was put in a box and four Japanese soldiers carried him back to our cave for us. My mother was almost crazy. She kept on crying and crying. She said, "I wanted to see you before you died." We buried him outside of our cave. When I say outside our cave I mean about a thousand feet away. We planted two bamboo by his grave and put flowers in the bamboo. Now those bamboo are very big. The bamboo is still there, but ten or fifteen years ago the church transferred his bones to the cemetery in Songsong Village.

Ignacio Dela Cruz, my mother's cousin, was arrested by the Japanese because they said he was a spy. He had white skin and many hairs on his chest and arms. He also had a lot of tattoos. He worked on whaling ships before Japanese times. Because of that they said he was a spy.*

One time I saw Japanese soldiers digging holes near the beach. I asked them what they were doing. They said they were going to hide there and shoot the enemy when they came. They also dug holes maybe ten feet wide and ten feet deep and covered them with tangantangan and coconut leaves. That was for enemy tanks to fall in, they said. They also cut long, straight coconut trees and painted them black to look like cannons. They said the American planes would spend all of their ammunition on these coconut cannons and not have enough to attack the Japanese.

One night the American planes dropped bombs that spread fire all over the island. I don't know what they called it. They also dropped tiny time bombs. I was in a sweet potato field at the time with one old Japanese man. There was a tank of water near us in the ground that had maybe one foot of water in it. There was fire all around us and there was nowhere to run, so we jumped in this water tank, but the fire came into the tank. We used the water to wash the fire off of us, otherwise we would have been burned to death. We stayed there until the next morning. When we came out the fire was gone except for these little bombs. They had blue fire coming out of them. There was one Chamorro, Manuel Manglona, who took a piece of wood and tried to move one of the bombs. That is when it blew up. He didn't die, but almost. The hand that was holding the wood was all cut up and he had many holes in the body and face. Everybody ran away after that, but when Manuel kept calling for help they came back. We put him on a board and took him to the hospital cave in Songsong Village.

One problem we had was no bandages and no medicine. For bandages they used dry banana leaves. At the hospital they cut the skin on his wrist back and cut the hand off, then put the skin back. There was no medicine for pain. They cut his hand off like that. I was at the hospital with him because that guy was my cousin. Every night he moaned like he was going to die. He survived and for a long time lived here on Tinian. He lives on Saipan now.

One more thing I remember. The Japanese said they were going to dig a hole to look for water — a well. For one month, two months— they kept on digging with hammer and chisel in the rock. About twenty feet down — no water, keep on digging, forty feet — no water, hundred feet — no water. Then, they stop digging. I went there and dropped down rocks in the hole, but I hear nothing because it is very, very deep. I asked my dad how come there is no water in that hole. We are very thirsty. My father said, "I am going to tell you a secret. Don't tell anyone. This well is not for water. The Japanese are going to put all the Chamorro people down there. They are going to kill all the people." I asked why. "Because," my father said, "Not enough food for the soldiers, so it better to kill all the Chamorros." The hole was about twenty feet around, big enough to put all the Chamorro people down there. He knows, because he has a Japanese friend. He told my father that all the Japanese officers had a meeting about killing the Chamorros because there was not enough food for the soldiers. According to my father this old Japanese man said, "Wait a minute. I'm going to say don't kill the people. Instead of kill them why don't we use the people to plant all kinds of vegetables. The soldiers no need to plant food; they can work to plant mines on the beach and on the reef. Better we use the Chamorros to plant for us," and they agreed.

This old man was a very close friend of my father. Before that meeting he told my father, "You better run deep into the mountains, because tomorrow they going to kill all the Chamorros; maybe not you because your

**The son of Ignacio Dela Cruz lives on Saipan. He told me that his father was held in a cave with a Catholic missionary, and that he was responsible for taking food to his father every day, until one day his mother told him that the Japanese had killed his father along with the missionary. According to the son, they were both decapitated.*

family is on the side of the Japanese." My mother was Chamorro, and we had many Chamorro relatives; we had to help them. Nobody ran away because we didn't know for sure what was going to happen. Then because of that meeting they decided not to kill all the Chamorros; nobody had to run away. From that time everybody — men, women, and children — were put to work planting.

There was one time the B-29s kept coming and dropping bombs. There were Chamorros working in a sweet potato field and three of them were killed by the bombs. One was Crispin Manglona, my uncle. One of the other guys I didn't recognize because his face was all burned. The next morning the dead bodies were brought to our village — not village but our jungle camp high up called Sakaya. I saw one Chamorro, his stomach was going outside. His hand was nothing. One nurse, an Okinawan lady around seventeen years old, came and cleaned the bodies. She put the intestines back and sewed up the stomach.

That lady, I still remember her name. It was Higa, Kachuk. She was very pretty. The next day, she was going to the hospital to serve the wounded there — not a hospital, but a cave where they had many wounded. An American plane saw her — I think because she was wearing a white dress and white hat she was very easy to see. The plane had a small bomb. He didn't use his machine gun, but dropped the bomb. Part of the bomb hit her on the left hip, but she didn't die yet. After one hour, maybe two hours, some people passed by that road and found her. She was still alive, but I think no more blood. When they took her to the hospital she was no more red, but white like a vinegar color. She died after one or two hours.

She was a very beautiful lady. If anybody needed help, even a Chamorro, she would go there. But, she didn't have any medicines, only clean the wounds and tie them up with dried banana leaves. Her cave was very near our cave, maybe two hundred feet away. Her mother and my mother were close friends because they planted crops together outside our caves.

I was there when they brought her body back to her family's cave. Everybody was crying, crying. They buried the body outside their cave. There were maybe ten or fifteen bodies buried like that outside of the caves, because people were afraid to go out too far.

Also, many babies died because the mothers didn't have milk in their breasts. There were many small kids, naked, very dirty, very skinny. We had nothing to wash our bodies. When the American bombing started we had only the clothes on our bodies and a few we could take before we started running.

About three months before the Americans came, but after my brother was killed, my mother lay down in our cave like she was dead; not dead, but cannot move. Nobody could wake her up, but we knew she wasn't dead because her pulse was still moving. Even when we shook her she didn't wake up. She was like that for maybe one night and half a day — maybe sixteen hours. Later she told us she could hear us. She could feel the rats touching her body, and hear them running by, but she could not move. When she woke up she said, "I see my brother, I see my sister. They are still alive on Saipan. If we are still alive after this war is over, we go back to Saipan to see my brother and sister." Because of this vision or dream, my father accepted that we should go back to Saipan after the war. So when we went back to Saipan in 1947 we saw that my mother's brother and sister were still there, alive. My mother told her sister and brother about her dream. She said to her brother, "When I see you, you were sitting in that chair over there." She pointed to the chair. She said she saw her sister in the kitchen washing something. That's true.

Before we were told the war was over the planes kept coming over, but no more bombs; no more shooting, but still we were running and hiding. One day the planes dropped cigarettes— Chesterfield, Lucky Strike, Camel. But we were afraid to use them because we heard from the Japanese that they were time bombs. But some kids got the cigarettes and opened them — no blow up. That is when we all got the cigarettes. I brought them to my mother and father. Then the Americans dropped papers, and the papers said the war is over.

We were outside our cave; it was early morning. All my family was there, my mother, father, brother, and sister. We knew the war was over, but we were still hiding. Somebody said, "Hey! Look behind you! Somebody is there." We turned around and there were some very big guys; some are black and some are white. I never saw blue eyes before. We thought maybe these people came from the heaven, something like that. Their shirts were like green leaves. They were carrying small guns— the carbines. There were many dry leaves all around at that time, but no one heard the noise from them coming. They were all around us. They pointed their guns at us. Then they said, "You Japanese, you Spanish?" But nobody talked. My mother knew German and little bit of Spanish. Together with the Marines was one who spoke Spanish. He asked if anybody spoke Spanish. My mother said she understood.

*A B-29 "Bone yard" just off North Field, Tinian. When B-29s crashed and burned on take-offs or landings, what was left was bulldozed off to the side of the field. In this photograph are the barrels of .50-caliber machine guns sticking out of their melted Plexiglas turrets.*

There were also some Hawaii-Japanese there. They asked if there were Japanese hiding here, but we said, "No. They are all on other side. This is all Chamorro people here." After that they were giving us biscuits, bread, canned goods, but still we were afraid to eat it—maybe poison. The Spanish-speaking Marine—he was the one who first started eating to show us it wasn't poison. But when we ate we got a pain in the stomach. We ate a lot, but our intestines were so dry. That is why we got sick. It was three or four days before we could eat without getting sick.

The Americans put us in a camp. It was a very nice place. They took our old dirty clothes and gave us very nice, clean clothes. They also cleaned our bodies with fire hoses—just that first time because the camp was not yet finished. There were five other Koreans on Rota that were married to Chamorros that I remember. After the war the Americans wanted to send all of the Koreans back to Korea, but the wives cried because they all had children and they didn't want their husbands to be sent away, so the Americans said, "Okay, you can stay because you have families."

We stayed on Rota for another two years. My father started again to work on our farm. Then in 1947 we moved to Saipan. When went back to Saipan my mother took me to the school in Chalan Kanoa. I was anxious to learn the American language. You know the sound we speak on Rota is different than the Chamorro they speak on Saipan—different pronunciation, so the other students kept teasing me. "Oh, you came from Rota." They called me names, and sometimes they pushed me. I went back home and told my mother, "These boys give me hard time, so I don't want to go back to school." So I only went to school on Saipan for two days.

While we were on Saipan I worked for a short time for Jesus Matsumoto. He was a Korean like my father.*

**The Japanese forced most Koreans to take Japanese names in an effort to assimilate the Koreans into Japanese culture while at the same time wipe out Korean culture.*

He and my father tried to make a business by making miso and soy sauce, but after they sent all the Japanese back to Japan there was no market. The Chamorros don't like miso and soy sauce much. Then Mr. Matsumoto decided to make another business, so that is the time he was thinking about the American military. He tells me to go buy handkerchiefs. I ask him how many. He says, "Two hundred." I don't know what he is going to do with the handkerchiefs. I watch, first he draws the body of a woman, then he paints it — naked body. I was the one selling them. I went to the barracks of the military. No problem selling. American soldiers think they are very nice. I sell them for two dollars each. I did that for around two months, then my father decided to go to Tinian.

First, he went to Tinian to see the place. He found many military houses, and cars like trucks and Jeeps. Everything they had on Tinian, even military clothes still in the boxes. The military just left it. Everything they left, even the guns— they left many guns. There was one warehouse — very big house full of food. We didn't have to worry about food on Tinian. We took plywood and tin roofing and built houses in the Marpo area. Everybody was a farmer then. We sent vegetables to Guam. In those days there were many fish, many coconut crabs, but not now. Now, no more. All of my life on Tinian I was a farmer and fisherman. I married and have one dozen children.

## Chicken and Corn

### Jose Hocog Mundo

*Jose Hocog Mundo was born in 1931 on the island of Rota to Rudolfo Atalig Mundo and Beda Hocog Mundo. In 1948 he moved to Guam where he attended high school. He then worked at various jobs until his return to Rota in 1984, where he now lives.*

Even before I was old enough to go to school I worked on my father's farm. The Chamorro school was in Tatachauq. The Japanese lived in Songsong Village. I went to first, second, and third grades. I don't remember how the war began, but I was on our farm with a friend catching coconut crabs. When we came out of the jungle where we were hunting for crabs I saw these American planes. They were very high in the sky. I remember the sound of their aircraft was very different from the sound of the Japanese aircraft. I could see the stars on the American airplanes. We started running in the direction of our ranch. Then we met this guy — I think he was a Japanese or Korean farmer. He was going in the opposite direction. We asked him what was going on, and he said there was a war coming up. I could hear the sound of machine guns coming from the direction of Sinapalo, no bombs yet. I saw some planes circling then go toward Songsong Village. All of the commercial buildings were down there. That is when I heard bombs. I ran into one of my uncles. He was an Okinawan. It was funny, he was coming with his spear gun. The spear gun was for fishing, but he said if the Americans came he was going to shoot them with it.

That evening I noticed that a rosary was being held at the church in Tatachauq. It was almost sundown. I noticed a guy standing on the hillside looking down. There was a road there. He was smoking, and I was facing uphill on the other side of the road. While I was talking to him some more planes flew overhead. Like I said, this guy was smoking when all of a sudden this Japanese appeared. He walked up to this guy and pulled the cigarette out of his mouth and smashed it on the ground. While I stood there he grabbed this guy by the neck and took him away. The next day I heard the Japanese killed him — cut his head off. His name was Bonifacio Estabes.

After that first bombing everybody moved in different directions to hide. My mother and father and I went to the highest mountain area where there was a cave. The area I am talking about is above Songsong Village. We were worried about how to get food and other supplies. There was no water supply there.

One day I went to a farming area to find some things to eat. It was mango season, but they were hard to carry because it was uphill back to our cave and the planes were still bombing, and all the time I heard the machine guns. Then I ran into another guy about my age. His name was Sebastian San Nicolas. Instead of going back to where my mother and father were, we went in another direction. Again we didn't have anything to eat, no water — nothing. We slept that night where we were, but when we woke up the next morning we were worried because we don't see nobody. Then we saw some wild papayas and these loose cows. We were pretty hungry. This guy Sebastian was funny — he went to this cow and started to suck the milk out. Me, instead of doing that, I took a big round leaf and made it like a funnel, and squeezed the milk into that. Then I drank it.

Later the Japanese military ordered us out of where we were to some other area where they could find us. So from there the Japanese moved us to the Sakaja area, and As Apulu. When we got there we found a lot of other people. There were some Chamorros with one Japanese civilian in charge of us. The name of the Japanese was Yamamoto. This was to be our new village, and every time the planes came we had a place to hide because there were a lot of caves around. With Yamamoto watching us, if we wanted to leave that area we had to have a pass. He checked us going in and out.

There were projects for all of us. Some people were assigned to plant sweet potatoes, corn, or anything that can be eaten. They set up teams to do that. I was assigned to work with another fellow about my age. His name was Antonio Manglona. He was my cousin. Every day we had to clear an area for planting. We were the smallest and the youngest, and the others in our group felt we weren't very efficient. We didn't do a very good job. So, our group decided to give us a different assignment. They sent us to hunt coconut crabs. We went into some jungle areas where we could find some. Everybody was very happy. Tony and I did that for three or four months, then they made us security guards. We had to watch the corn, to see if anyone was coming in and taking the corn. What we did was very interesting. We didn't have any shelter, but there was a big mango tree that wasn't very far from the cornfield. We climbed up there with some wood and made like a play house. One time we found somebody taking some corn. This is a sad story for me because I didn't know it was my grandfather's brother, Juan Charfauros. I think they punished him, but I didn't see it.

The next day Tony and I went to my grandfather's farm to pick some mangos. This was a sad time, a very bad part. We threw stones at the mangos to knock them down so that we could sack them. On the tree there was a sign in Japanese, but I couldn't read it because it was in kanji. I was taught takakana and irakana. Then some Japanese soldiers came in the direction where we were — some Navy people. One of them was holding a cane. "What are you guys doing here?" He said something like that. I told him I was picking mangos. "This is my grandfather's farm," I said. He said, "This is Japanese mango." I said, "Oh, I'm sorry. This is our farm." He said, "No more. This is Japanese. You have to ask permission." Then he made us stand at attention as an American plane passed over head. When the Japanese tell you to stand straight they don't like you to move or look around. I didn't look at the plane, but Tony, maybe he was worried the plane might shoot its machine gun or throw a bomb. He looked around for the plane. You're not supposed to scratch yourself or anything. Then another Japanese came over. He walked around Tony and checked him out like he suspected he was maybe a spy. He asked Tony if he was Spanish. Then he said, "Lets take him and kill him." After they took Tony I asked them what they were going to do to me. The Japanese told me to drop the mangos and go home.

I ran until I was exhausted and I had to stop for breath. Then I would continue again. When I got home I went to Antonio's mother and said, "The Japanese have taken your son and I think they are going to kill him." I don't remember everything that happened after that, but I think Tony's mother, another woman, and that Japanese who was in charge of our village, Yamamoto, went to find Tony. As it turned out, he was still very much alive. I don't know what happened, but Tony was released. He later told me that if I hadn't rushed home and told somebody the Japanese would have killed him, probably the next day. Why they thought a young guy like that might have been a spy, I don't know.

Again we were put to work clearing ground for planting. One night an American plane dropped lights over our field — flares. I ran and tried to hide in a pile of dead grass so the plane would not see us. I didn't know there were Japanese soldiers out there watching the Chamorros — watching what we were doing. After the airplane passed, and there was no more light one of the soldiers came over and asked me what I was doing there. I told him I was hiding because I was scared. Then he put his arm around my head and said, "Are you scared?" "Yes sir," I said. "I'm scared." Then he said, "Let's go." Tony was not taken that time, so we were separated. Maybe it was my turn to be killed. I think there were six soldiers altogether. They took me to some head guy. I called him "taisho." That means general. I don't remember his name, but the name of the battalion was singkantai. The soldier holding me told me not to be scared. Yeah, but I don't know what they are gonna do to me.

His headquarters was a little house in the jungle under some trees, a place called As Funta. They had dug a tunnel underneath the house. The next day the taisho said, "I want you to stay with us, and all you have to do is show us where the Chamorros are. You don't go anywhere. You gonna stay with us." I said, "Yes sir." The next day he told me to take him where my parents were staying. When we go there the first person I saw was my aunt, Beata Mendiola. A Japanese by the name of Sasakura was her husband. Duenas was her maiden name. She was shocked to see me with these Japanese, but she came out and bowed. She was the first person to point out that I was with a high-ranking official. He always carried a sword. The other Japanese with him only had guns.

We went to another place east of Songsong Village called As Maloti. I heard somebody whistling. When we followed where the whistling came from, it turned out that it was my uncle, the youngest brother of my mother. From there we went back to As Funta. He seemed satisfied that I had shown him where Chamorros were staying. I stayed with him for the rest of the war. I took him wherever he wanted to go. He just wanted to see where the Chamorros were and what they were doing. He seemed satisfied that they weren't doing anything wrong.

During this time with the taisho I couldn't see my mother and father unless I asked permission. Sometimes when I asked and he said, "Okay. You can go tomorrow, but you have to come back." Before leaving I would gather up a sack full of sweet potatoes for my family. One time the Japanese let me stay with my family for one week. It was like a vacation.

I had three younger brothers but they all died at the beginning of the war. I don't know how they died — maybe starvation. I don't know because we were moving all around. My parents never talked about it to me.

The first Americans I saw when the war was over came driving down the road in Songsong in green trucks. One of the Americans had his feet on the top with the windshield down. Then I saw this American come down from his Jeep. I don't know if he is a general or what. He met with some high ranking Japanese. They sat at a small table near the road. The American had a piece of paper. The Japanese took out a flag and handed it to the American. The American took out his knife and cut it to pieces and threw it on the ground.

More Americans came to Rota, but none of us spoke English. One American called to me, "Hey Joe, puss-puss!" Puss-puss in Chamorro means a type of food we make with chicken and corn, so I took him to my uncle's house. I told my aunt this American was my friend and he wants something to eat. Already I am calling him my friend. I told my aunt to hurry up and make my friend some puss-puss. My aunt serves us, and I eat mine, but the American never ate his. He is chewing his gum and looks at my cousin. My cousin was very young at that time, maybe seventeen. The American keeps pointing at me and saying, "Hey Joe, puss-puss." My aunt was the one who discovered what he wanted. She says, "Son, I think he wants your cousin. You better take him down to those Japanese or Korean ladies." Near the shrine area was where the comfort women were. I took him there and he was very happy.

After the war in 1948 my father sent me to Guam to stay with my grandfather's sister. There were no schools on Rota after the war and my father said if I like it on Guam I can stay and go to school, but I came right back because I had never left my mother and father like that. My father tried to convince me to go back to Guam — to go back to school. He said, "I need you here on the farm, but I think it better if you go to school and learn. Here on the farm I can teach you things, but I cannot teach you English and things like that." So I went back to Guam that same year and stayed a little bit longer, maybe six months. Then again I still wanted to come back to Rota, because I still don't like being away from home. I don't see my mother, my relatives, my friends. It was like I was a stranger to the place. Then my father's sister moved over there and I went back and stayed and went to school. I finished high school then found a job. I moved back to Rota in 1984.

# Palau Islands

4

## I Worked for the Kempeitai

ROMAN TMETUCHL

*Roman Tmetuchl was born in Palau in 1926. During the Japanese period in Palau he worked for the local newspaper, Nanyo Shimbun. He was later recruited to work for the Kempeitai (Japanese Military Police). After World War II he was sent to Guam to study English. He attended the Pacific Islands Teacher Training School in Guam, and in 1951 he graduated from George Washington High School, making him the first Palauan to earn a high school diploma. He continued his education in the Philippines with funds provided by the United Nations. Returning to his native Palau, he served as assistant public defender and administrative officer of the Palau Trust Territory High Court, organized the first labor strike in the history of Palau, served as a District Court judge, and was an elected member of the Congress of Micronesia.*

When I was old enough to go to school I began to hate God. I was maybe ten years old; I thought if there is a God he must be an unfair person. Palau was dominated by foreigners. That is what made me think, "If there is a God, he must be unfair." Of course, later on in my life I went looking for God and discovered that he was fair.

When I started to school I saw that the Japanese went to one school and we went to another school, and I didn't like that. I wasn't a very good student. I did well academically, but I hated the Japanese. I didn't like any foreigners. We had many Chamorros from the Mariana Islands living here during Japanese times but I didn't appreciate having them here either. I would ask myself, "What are they doing here?" We went to school together but I didn't have any close Chamorros friends. I always caused trouble. I started a gang of local boys and we would get in fights with the Japanese children. I was a revolutionary even in those days. I was punished a lot. The Japanese didn't hit us too much, but they made us do things like clean the toilets, clean the classrooms—things like that.

I know there are some on Palau today who claim that life was better under the Japanese and that it was easier to make a living, but I don't think that is true. The Japanese dominated us. My father grew up during German times; he liked the Germans better than the Japanese. A lot of my thinking came from what I learned from my father. We didn't have any radios, no television. A ship might stop in Palau once every three months, maybe six months.

We had Koreans in Palau. The Japanese treated them lower than Palauans. I thought we were the lower class of people under the Japanese, but the Japanese were not nice to the Koreans at all.

I remember when the Japanese bombed Pearl Harbor. They made a big deal about it. The Japanese were always parading down the street when they had a big victory. They said the Americans were devils and that they should all be killed. They also said that if the Americans came to Palau they would rape all of the women and kill all of the men, but I didn't believe that. My father told me some stories that I believed, and they turned out to be real. He said that Japan couldn't beat

*Roman Tmetuchl*

America; America is too big. He said, "In Japan they eat rice. In America they feed rice to the chickens."

I can't say that life changed for me after the war started because I always had enough to eat. It wasn't that way for everybody. Many people starved to death after the Americans started bombing — both Japanese and Palauans. But I was working for the Kempeitai and I had three meals a day. I can't say that I was ever really scared. I found it rather exciting. My sister thought I was crazy. She once told me, "You are the only person on Palau who enjoyed the war."

When I was still quite young the Japanese advertised for people to go to Indonesia to learn how to work on steamships. All of the candidates had to take an exam. I got the highest grade of all the people who took it, but before I could go I was drafted to work for the Kempeitai. I had no choice. I received a summons on red paper just like when they drafted people into the army. It said I had to be at a certain place at a certain time. My boss was Col. Miyazaki. He was an old man.*

**He later committed suicide at his home in Japan before he could be sent to Guam, where he was to be tried for the murders of six Catholic missionaries and four members of the Hondonero family from Yap.*

I didn't want to work for the Kempeitai but I knew I could not refuse. When I first started to work for the Kempeitai they had me cleaning bicycles. I did that for two days. Then I was put to work washing dishes and cleaning the office. After I don't know how much time, they told me that I would be going upstairs to work directly for Col. Miyazaki. I was just supposed to take care of his needs, and if he was out of the office I was supposed to watch over things. Sometimes late in the afternoon he would ask me to take him out in the lagoon in a row boat. I guess it was a form of relaxation for him. He would take a book and read. Sometimes he would talk to me, ask me questions. Then he got a speed boat, very fast — the fastest one in Palau. He trusted me, and sometimes he let me take the speedboat out by myself. I wasn't supposed to do this, but sometimes I even took that boat out with the Colonel's pennant flying, and when I went past other boats everybody saluted me. I had a really good time doing that.

Colonel Miyazaki made me a deputy Kempeitai. He trusted me that much. I had twenty Japanese soldiers working under me, and a pass that allowed me to go anywhere. I was sent out to the villages to ask questions and look for spies. I never found any. I think the Americans used Japanese-Americans as spies. On more than one occasion I came across cigarette butts with Lucky Strike on them. Sometimes I came in contact with Japanese soldiers who had strange accents, but they were always with a group of others and I couldn't prove whether they were Americans or not.

The Japanese had comfort women for the soldiers. They were everywhere. All of the Japanese officers had one for themselves, mostly Japanese women. The others were Korean and Taiwanese; all very young.

When the Americans started bombing Palau in 1944, some American pilots were shot down and captured. The Americans didn't like Japanese food. It was just a soup with rice. So what I would do was put some biscuits in my pocket and when I took them to wash I would slip them the biscuits. I kept guard on some of them, but the Japanese didn't keep them prisoners for long. They took them out and killed them. I don't know if they were shot or decapitated. I never saw how they were killed.

While I was working for the Kempeitai there was also talk about what to do with the native population. There were some high ranking officers in the Japanese military who wanted to do away with the native population so there would be more food for the Japanese. Plus, they were afraid that the natives might aid the Americans. Their plan was to bring all of the natives to one area and shoot them. They trusted me and I overheard these conversations. Of course, I spoke out against this sort of thing. I told them that we Palauans were pro–Japanese, that we would fight for the Emperor. There was a lower ranking Japanese officer by the name of Yoshiyasu Morikawa who was actively involved in working with the local population and he also had a lot to do with preventing any slaughter of native peoples.

At the same time there were six Catholic missionaries and a Chamorro family from Yap who were shot and killed by the Japanese. Three of the missionaries were from Palau (Father Elias Fernandez, Father Marino Dehoaz, and Brother Emilio Villar). I knew them. The others were from Yap (Father Bernardo de la Espriella, Father Luis Blanco y Suares, Brother Francisco Hernandez, Agapito Hondonero, his wife Filomena Untalan, and their two children — Baltazar and Caroline).* I never talked to them and I didn't see them, but I was at the headquarters when their executions were being discussed, and the officer in charge sent the detachment out to do the killings. When they came back to headquarters after the executions there was very little talk.

When the fighting was over and the Americans landed on the rest of the islands in Palau we were happy; we knew the fighting was over. The Americans were very nice. Nobody was mistreated. They spoiled us. The Americans somehow knew that I had worked for the Kempeitai because they had my name on a list and they interrogated me about what happened to the American pilots that were shot down and captured, the Catholic missionaries, and the Hondonero family. In 1946, I think it was, the Americans took me to Guam to testify in the War Crimes Trials being held there. My testimony lasted only half a day. When I got up to testify I was so scared I couldn't talk. There were all of these American soldiers with weapons and they were covered with decorations. When I saw those Japanese prisoners sitting there, I felt sorry for them. I know some of them did bad things, but in the Japanese Army you had to follow orders or you would be killed. The judge called a recess because I was too scared to talk. That gave me some time to calm down. The American who interrogated me spoke fluent Japanese. He asked me questions in Japanese and translated my answers into English for the court. Anyway, they thought it would be best if I testified in Japanese so that the defendants could understand my testimony. I was asked a lot of general questions, but my impression was that they already knew the answers. They had already done a lot of investigation before they asked me any questions.

After the war I knew one thing — I had to learn English. The Americans started schools here on Palau, but I was selected to go to Guam and study for two years. I lived in a barracks with other Micronesians and was the first Palauan ever to graduate from high school. In 1954 I went to study in the Philippines with money provided by a United Nations scholarship. When I came back I worked for the Palauan Trust Territory Government.

I was not always liked by the American authorities because I was always causing trouble. Under the Japanese we Palauans received lower salaries than what the Japanese received for the same work. Under the Americans there were three salary levels. The Americans received the highest salaries, Europeans received the next highest salaries, and the Palauans received the lowest. I heard locals complaining about this so I organized a strike and we won. The Americans understood why we were unhappy so the strike didn't have to last long.

In 1994 Palau became independent for the first time. This is what I always wanted for Palau, but now I think that was a mistake. I don't think Palau is capable of being an independent nation. I think we should have stayed with the United States in any form possible; a commonwealth, a state, even as a colony. If the United States pulls out of the Pacific completely we will become like the American Indian — like the Maoris in New Zealand. Even worse, we could be taken over by the Chinese.

**Jose Untalan Diaz and Alfonso Untalan Diaz were nephews of Filomena Untalan Hondonero. Alfonso was a policeman for the Japanese. Alfonso is no longer living, but Jose lives on Guam. He told me the following: "My auntie was held in a shack along with her husband two small children, and the six Catholic missionaries. My brother explained to her that he had been authorized to take her and her children. (The Japanese didn't consider her to be a spy, only her Filipino husband.) She started to cry, then she told us loud and clear, 'I know what is going to happen to my husband, and I am not going to go with you. We are going to go with him, and we are going to die together.' She didn't want to go with us. She wouldn't even let us take the children, so we left."*

# The Sailor from Angaur

MANUEL S. SABLAN

*Manuel S. Sablan was born on the island of Angaur in Palau in the year 1917. His father, Benino St. Nicholas Sablan, moved to Angaur to work in the phosphate mines during the German occupation of those islands. The surviving members of the family did not return to Saipan until 1946.*

I was born in Angaur* and did not see Saipan until I was fourteen years old. My father worked in the phosphate mines for the Germans. Before I was born my family returned to Saipan, but after the Japanese took over in 1914 they returned to Angaur. My father continued to work in the phosphate mines on Angaur for awhile, then moved to the big island of Babeldaop where he worked in a bauxite mine.

I wanted to visit my family in Saipan — my grandparents. I lived with my aunt in Tanapag, and while I was there I worked for a paper company, not a newspaper company but something like that. After four years I returned to Angaur and worked for the Yamada Company. It was a private store owned by a Japanese. I worked there for almost two years. The pay was very low, maybe fifteen yen a month. Then I worked for a Palauan by the name of Era Dbemel. He was a wealthy man from Peleliu. He built a boat that went around to the different islands in Palau to buy dried coconuts— you know, copra. When we had enough copra we sold it to the Nambo Company and they sent it to Japan. That is where I learned how to work on engines. I did that for about five years, then went to work for the Nanyo Aluminum Company on Babeldaop with my older brother. They paid good money, maybe 300 yen a month, but even with money you couldn't buy anything, not even clothes. I was single then; food was not a problem, but it was local food.

As the war got closer we were forced to work from six o'clock in the morning until six o'clock at night, seven days a week. That is when I decided to work for the Japanese Navy. I thought the work would be easier and I had training as a mechanic. There was a Japanese lieutenant who came from New Guinea. His name was Kuwada. He was looking for people to work on these wood dive boats to take supplies to New Guinea. Eight of us volunteered, five Chamorros and three Yapese. Lieutenant Kuwada gave us all Japanese names because for him they were easier to remember. The name he gave me was Minami Tetsutaro.

I boarded my boat just before the Americans bombed Palau the first time. They bombed for two days [March 1944]. We hid from the bombing at different places, then about four days after the bombing stopped we left Palau and headed for Tobi Island, which was to the southeast. It took four days and four nights to get there.

Tobi is a small island and the Japanese only had a few soldiers there. Just before we reached Tobi Island an American submarine sank us with its deck gun. They hit my boat twice. The first shell went through the hull without exploding and hit just in front of one of the other boats. The engine on our boat died when the engineer tried to make it go faster. I could see the submarine getting closer. There were two Yapese on the boat and I told them to throw two pieces of wood into the water. Then we jumped in. We were in the water between the submarine and our boat when they fired the second shot. I could see the American sailors on the submarine. I heard them say things like, "God damn Japanese!"

Lieutenant Kuwada was on the same boat with me, but he didn't survive. The captains of each boat had their wives with them. They were supposed to go with us to Papua New Guinea, then take a ship back to Japan, but they didn't survive either. Only one boat survived, but it was damaged. We spent eighteen hours in the water. The submarine sank us in the early evening. The next morning we could see the surviving boat, but it was very far from us. We only had a piece of wood to keep us afloat. There were ten of us in a group. Altogether there were fifty people on the four boats, but only twenty-five survived.

We started swimming towards the one surviving boat. It was not moving because the engine was damaged when it was hit by the submarine. When we started swimming toward the boat sharks started coming to us but nobody was bitten. They just circled us.

We reached the boat in the afternoon. The engineer on that boat was killed when one of the shells hit inside the engine room. We wrapped him up in a blanket, put weights around his legs, and dropped him in

*Palau group of islands, approximately 500 miles east of Mindanao.*

*Manuel S. Sablan, the Sailor from Angaur, as he looks today.*

the sea. Then I was the one who worked on the engine to make it run. The air compressor was damaged so I used two guys to turn the flywheel to get the engine running. It took me four hours to get it going. Then we waited for more survivors to reach us. Two Chamorros were among the men we picked up, David and Enrici Borja. We had twenty-four people on board that one boat out of a total of fifty who started out. The twenty-fifth survivor, a Korean, was found after forty days when he washed up on Halmahera Island. He spent almost three months in the hospital.

We had six months' supply of food on each boat when we started out, so that was no problem, but the water tank was full of holes from the shelling. We had only about ten inches of water in the tank to last us until we found land. Our compass was broken, but the captain pointed us in the right direction by looking at the stars. Once he thought he knew which was the correct direction we started up the engine and two hours later we found Tobi Island. We stayed there for twenty-seven days.

From Tobi Island we returned to Palau on a tuna boat that was used to bring supplies to the soldiers. From Palau we took a destroyer to Sorong in western Papua New Guinea. The next day we went to Kasim Island off the coast of New Guinea. From Kasim we watched Japanese planes take off to bomb the Solomon Islands. At least somebody told us that. We would always count the number of planes that took off. The Japanese were lucky if one or two came back out of fifty.

We were in Sorong for three months. After that we were sent to Ambon Island. After seven days on Ambon we went to the Celebes—Makassar Island. After two days and two nights there we went to Balikpapan in Borneo. The next day they sent us to Sangasanga, and stayed there for several months. It was while in Sangasanga that I learned that Saipan had been invaded.

Samarinda was the Japanese naval headquarters on Borneo, and that is where they sent us next. So from there they sent two of us who were from Palau to Tarakan Island—Ben Benito Reyes and me. Tarakan is a small island off the coast of Borneo and there were oil wells there.* We were there for ten months with no bombing. Then the Australians took Halmahera Island. From then on we got bombed every day. If they didn't bomb us during the day, they bombed that night. Then the Japanese started to make an air base there on Tarakan. When the Japanese started making the air base the Australians didn't bomb it. They waited until the air base was finished, then they started to bomb it. I only saw one plane get shot down while I was on Tarakan Island. It had two engines. The pilot died — everyone died.

One day the Australians dropped leaflets on the island. The leaflets said what month, what day, what time they were going to make landings on Tarakan. The Japanese tried to hide the leaflets from us. They didn't want anyone to know what they said. Then one morning I started to work. There was an air raid warning so I jumped into a foxhole. One plane passed over but he didn't drop any bombs. Then a Japanese officer came by and he told me that the Australians were already landing and that I should stand by to go into the jungle. After that I went back to my room to get everything I needed and headed for the jungle. I didn't have a gun, but I was given a hand grenade and told that if I see the enemy I should throw it. I never threw it. I hid in the jungle for three months.

There was one group of us. We were eight people and at one point decided to go see where the enemy was. When we came to a jungle road we divided up into groups of three, two, and three and made sure that there was a large gap between each group as we walked down the road in case something happened. I was in the second group. When the first three reached a crossroads, there were some Australians there. They fired their machine gun. My group and the group behind me laid down in the road. The ones in the first group were all killed. When we got up to run the Australians started to shoot again, so we had to lie down again. After that we went back to where we came from and hid in the jungle some more.

The day I was captured was in the evening after we had cooked some rice over a fire. Some Australians saw the smoke and came in looking for us. They just started shooting and we all ran away. I jumped onto a road and two Australians stopped me. They said, "Come over here. Are you Japanese?" I said, "No! I'm Chamorro." They said, "What is a Chamorro?" I said, "I'm from Saipan," but they had never heard of Saipan.

When we got back to their base they gave me two packs of cigarettes and some matches. Then they put me with fifteen Japanese they had recently captured. They gave us Australian khakis and some new shoes. Our first meal was one loaf of bread cut in half, and one can of corned beef for each man. One Japanese said, "What they gonna do with us?" I said, "We lost the fight; what can we do. If they are going to kill us, what can we do?"

We had to hold hands as they marched us to their headquarters. There they interrogated us one by one. When it came my turn they gave me the number 227. Of all the prisoners on Tarakan at that time I was number 227. More surrendered later. I guess it was about five days after they captured me that the war was over.

From Tarakan they sent us to the island of Morotai (north of Halmahera). I was there about ten months. While I was there the Australians brought in around 100 Taiwanese and their Japanese officer. These Taiwanese and their Japanese officer had had 600 Indian POWs that they marched across Borneo in forty days. They called it the "Bloody Walking," because if the prisoners got sick, or couldn't walk anymore during the march they cut their heads off. Only 60 of the 600 survived. The Australians held an investigation, then took the Taiwanese and their Japanese officer and executed them. I was working in the galley then, and we prepared a last meal for them, and some beer.

After ten months in the POW camp one ship was sent to take all the Japanese from my camp back to Japan. They took the Japanese from Halmahera and those of us who were held on Morotai — 4,000 people — and put us on that one ship. It took us five days to get to Japan. Only one person died on the way. He had malaria. The ship took us to Tanabe. That's a town in Wakayama Prefecture. I think it is south of Yokohama. The next day they gave us 300 yen each and a train ticket home.

When it came my turn I said I want to go to Saipan. They told me there was no ship to Saipan. They had to call Gen. MacArthur's headquarters in Tokyo to get instructions, so I had to stay there another week while they waited for instructions. After that they sent me by train to Kurihama. I had to wait there another three months. I didn't have any money because the Japanese never paid me for the work I did for them.

When I got back to Saipan it was no longer a green island — no trees. I had to wait on that ship for eleven days off of Garapan because there were so many ships. They were all lined up to get into the harbor. When I finally got off the ship I found my brother, Jose Sablan. He was on the police force. He was a policeman under

**The Japanese Navy started importing oil from Tarakan in 1915, a few years after they switched from coal to oil.*

the Japanese and he was still a policeman. My sister, Soledad Cepeda, had come back to Saipan from Yap and she had a house in Susupe already, so I stayed with her. Her husband was killed in Yap by a bomb. I got a job with the U.S. Navy as a mechanic — Jeeps and things like that. After one or two months my mother and father returned from Palau. They were surprised when they found me on Saipan.

While my family was on Palau some Chamorros and some Palauans escaped to the American ships offshore, and the American ships took them to Angaur. After that the Japanese watched the other Chamorros day and night to make sure they didn't contact the Americans. My mother and father were interrogated many times.

In 1951 there were still some Japanese hiding on Anatahan, an island north of Saipan. Commander Johnson, who was the naval administrator of Saipan, wanted to take them off Anatahan. He sent a fishing boat that had a two cylinder engine on it and I was asked to go along. For two days and two nights I didn't sleep. We circled the island. That is when we saw five Japanese. We put up a Japanese flag and called to them, but they ran away. We had some of the Japanese from Saipan with us and we put them ashore with some food and drink. Then we circled the island one more time. When we got back to the beach where we had left the Japanese from Saipan there was one of the Japanese from Anatahan with them. That was Kazuko Higa, the only woman in the group. When they brought Kazuko back to the ship they told the captain that there was a machine gun set up near the beach. So the captain told me to get the engine going and we left without the other Japanese.

The other Japanese surrendered sometime later, but I wasn't there when that happened. Kazuko told me that the others were afraid to come out because they thought the war was still going. They saw planes fly over, and when old bombs were destroyed on Saipan they could hear the explosions. They thought the war was still going on and that the Japanese were still fighting on Saipan.

# 5 Guam

## The Interpreter

HENRY S. PANGELINAN

*Henry Sablan "Tochan" Pangelinan was born in 1917 on Saipan. In 1942 he was recruited by the Japanese to serve as an "Interpreter" and worked at the civil jail on Guam. He was captured in August 1944 by U.S. Marines. In May 1945 he was tried and convicted by a War Crimes Tribunal for "assault and mistreatment" of named Guamanian prisoners. Mr. Pangelinan lives on Saipan and is the father of sixteen children.*

My father's name was Mariano Duenas Pangelinan. He was a farmer all of his life. Before the war he was also a district commissioner under the late Juan Ada, who was the chief commissioner of all Saipan under the Japanese. These were not elected positions, but positions appointed by the Japanese. My father's duties were just to pass out information and orders—whatever the Japanese wanted to relay to the people. The easiest way was to gather them at some meeting area and give the message out. We didn't have newspapers, radios, or other means of communication in those days. Someone would go out into the street and yell, "We are having a meeting tonight. Everybody come!" My father would then give out information or orders. Information to the local people was restricted.

We had to work hard on the farm. Every member of the family had their own duties during the day. I had to look after the chickens and pigs. I checked the horses to see if they needed any grass. I had to do this before eight o'clock, then I went to school.

My teachers were very strict. The Chamorro people at this time were still, you know, under their original customs and these teachers were trying to convert us to the Japanese way of doing things. They gave us a basic education, limited to five grades. They gave me a good comprehension of the Japanese language — good enough to be a messenger. Beatings were common. Every mistake resulted in a punishment. Some teachers were really brutal.

My older brother, Jose, went to Japan in 1922. He went to Sophia University as a special student — only to observe. He was included in the classes but was not allowed to graduate. He was repatriated back to Saipan in 1923 because of the big earthquake that shook Japan that year.

I went to Japan in 1932. I had finished the fifth grade on Saipan, so in Japan I entered the sixth grade. At first it was so hard — I just couldn't catch up with the other students. But they gave me special attention and after that I could line up with the rest of the students. I then went to middle school and eventually to university. At the university there was a woman from England who taught English. It was only two hours a week of lecture but that is where I first learned the language. Also, I did my best to find foreigners who spoke English. I would even spend money buying coffee for people I met in order to have conversations.

I had to work my way through school but I could not find a good job at first because the Japanese had most of the good jobs. There were days when I had nothing to eat. Then I met this group of Filipino entertainers. They took me in and fed me and taught me how to sing. I found that the Japanese loved American music. It didn't matter if you were good or no good, if you could sing American songs they loved it. That is when I started to get a little money.

After that I got a job with the Helms Corporation in Yokohama. It was a German company. They had a six-story hotel. At the time they didn't have anybody for English-speaking people who came to the hotel, so they hired me for that purpose. That is when I met my wife, Hideko Koyama. She was a telephone operator at the hotel. By then I had dropped out of school. I had one year left to graduate, but I had a problem with transportation and then the war started in Manchukuo [Manchuria]. Hideko and I knew each other for about six months before we got married. Her parents protested at first, but I think they realized that nothing could be done about it and they accepted. She gave me twelve children and she was a great mother. In our family I was the provider and she was the administrator.

In those days, for a Chamorro man to marry a Japanese woman was something the Japanese tried to prevent. The Japanese authorities did not recognize our marriage for about four or five years. In Japan we just lived together. The Japanese authorities never allowed Hideko to change her name to Pangelinan. We returned to Saipan in 1937. Except for the weather my wife had no problem adapting to Saipan. As far as other Japanese on Saipan, we suffered no discrimination from them. It was just the Japanese authorities that we had problems with.

When we arrived back on Saipan my application for employment with the NKK, the sugar company, was accepted because of my knowledge of Japanese. I worked in Lands Registration where they negotiated the leasing of land for the sugar company. I had no great responsibilities—I would describe myself as a messenger. My salary was probably thirty to fifty percent lower than that of Japanese employees.

The Koreans on Saipan were concentrated in one area of Garapan. They didn't associate with the local people. They stuck together. They didn't seem to like Chamorro people. I didn't know any of them personally except for Jose Matsumoto and that is because he was married to a Chamorro and was pretty well integrated into the community. Most of the Koreans did manual labor. I didn't see any of them that had a good job. Some of them opened up a whore house using Korean ladies. They entertained Japanese nationals only. Local people were not allowed.

As far as health problems before the war—tuberculosis was common, so was dysentery. Infant mortality was high. Typhoid was not curable—it killed.

When Japan invaded Guam certain Chamorros from Saipan and Rota were selected to be "Interpreters" since they could speak Japanese. I was not very much interested in going, but there was a rumor that if you refused to go the Japanese would kill your whole family. That was not confirmed—just a rumor.

On January 13, 1942, I was with a group of Chamorros who were given twenty-four hours' notice that we were going to Guam. We were put on a fishing boat escorted by a destroyer. For some reason the destroyer left us before we reached Guam. Right after this a submarine popped up in front of us but nothing happened. I don't know if it was American or Japanese. We arrived on Guam the next day. I was assigned to the civil jail as a warden and interpreter. The Japanese were trying very hard to convert the Guamanians to the Japanese system, but it was very hard because these Guamanians were real believers in America. They had lived together with the Americans for quite a long time. If they were suspected of being pro-American their names were written down and they were closely watched by the Kempeitai (Japanese military police). The Japanese way was hard—they delivered quite a lot of punishment to the people on Guam. I could do nothing about it. I had to follow what instructions they gave me.

When the Japanese investigated someone, they would beat him before they asked him any questions. So many people on Guam did nothing, but being a suspect in Japanese custody was the same as being guilty. When they were beaten they had to agree with the questions to avoid further punishment. One of the tortures the Japanese used was to lie somebody down and put a wet towel over his face so they couldn't breathe. I witnessed this many times. I remember Antonio Guerrero being ordered to do this to a person and he cried the whole time.

Another way they had of punishing people was to tie them to a chair and beat them with anything hard enough to cause pain. They also tied your thumbs together with string and hung you from the ceiling so that your toes barely touched the floor.

One of my jobs was to take care of the food for the prisoners and lead the prison detail for picking up firewood so that the prisoners could cook their food. There was one American by the name of Brown who was in that jail. I took care of him. He was a civilian. He was a calm old man—never complained. He had decided to just take whatever came. He was later killed in the pre-invasion bombardment when the Americans retook the island.

Once, this Japanese officer came up to me at the jail and put his pistol to my forehead. I said to myself, "This is it—finished." The Japanese office said to me, "You are a spy!" That surprised me. I don't know why but I remembered a word I had learned someplace, "Tenno Heika." It means "Hail to the Emperor." I said, "Before you kill me let me tell you this, 'Hail to the Emperor!' I work for him and I try never to let him down. He is my superior. He is my Lord. He is my God." Finally, he calmed down. My insides were cold. I thought I was gone already. He was still very, very suspicious of me after that.

We also had a female prisoner. Her name was Luisa Campos. She was the only female prisoner we had at that jail but I don't know why she was there. The Japanese officers raped her repeatedly. I think she was there for more than one year before she was able to escape. This was during the pre-invasion bombardment in 1944. A lot of prisoners escaped then.

Many Guamanians suffered before the Americans came back. B. J. Bordallo, who was my cousin from my father's side, was beaten nearly to death by the Kempeitai. He was a wealthy Guamanian. His son later became the governor of Guam. I tried to talk to him while he was in jail but it was very difficult. They were trying to get him to admit that he was concealing an American sailor by the name of George Tweed. They also accused him of being a spy.

There was also a Juan Acosta who was arrested for stealing a cow. He didn't do it but he had to admit that he did because of the punishment he was getting. I witnessed his execution in the cemetery. That poor fellow was tied to a pole and six Japanese sailors were selected for his execution. "Can I see the priest?" Acosta said. His request was denied. Then he was executed.

During the pre-invasion bombardment of Guam, an American plane was shot down. The pilot crash landed in the Machanao area. It so happened that a Guamanian by the name of Jose "Papa" went to the crash site and tried to help out the pilot. The first thing the pilot said to him was, "Do you have a dentist?" He broke some of his teeth when he crashed. The pilot left the area before the Japanese arrived. Nobody saw "Papa" help the pilot but he did make one mistake—he kept one of the pilot's gloves. When the Japanese saw that they took him to the jail. I took care of him. They tried to make him talk, but he was a patriotic man, loyal to the U.S. He was taken to Naval Headquarters for interrogation many times. After that Pedro S. Deleon Guerrero and I escorted "Papa" up the hill. The Japanese made him dig his own grave, then they asked him what he wanted. "Papa" said to Pedro, "This is my ring. Can you give it to my wife?" Then one of the Japanese took out his sword and cut off his head. We were warned not to tell anybody what happened. We didn't because we feared for our families.

The American pilot was also captured. The Japanese cut off his cock and made him chew it like a cigar, then they killed him.

When the Americans invaded Guam I was hiding in the cemetery. The cemetery was right in front of where the Americans landed. A gravestone saved me from an American bullet. I ran and hid in the jungle after that. Fortunately, I found one of my prisoners by the name of Jamora. We went together because he knew the jungle better than I did. We were walking and we didn't know that there was a gadget in the jungle that would alert all the soldiers. They put out a lot of tin cans on a string and when we stepped on them they made a lot of noise. At the same time I bumped my head on a wasp nest and they started stinging us. We dropped down to the ground, hoping the wasps would calm down and leave us alone. That is when a machine guns started firing in our direction. The bullets went just over our heads. If I had been standing I wouldn't be here today. Two or three minutes later the Marines were all around us pointing their guns at us. Jamora said, "I am a native. I am a Chamorro." I said the same thing, but they didn't trust us right away. They continued to point their guns at us.

That was a terrible period in our lives. We didn't know what would happen to us. We didn't know if we were going to live or die. We were put in a concrete building with some other people. The first person I saw was Bishop Komatsu. He was a Catholic priest—a Japanese Catholic priest. We were detained there for three days. I hadn't eaten in a week, so they fed us. Chocolate and Spam. We ate heartily, believe me. Then we got dysentery.

I was put in the stockade. There was a Lt. Savage who was interrogating the Japanese prisoners. They discovered that I spoke some English so they took me to the interrogation center to do some interpretation. Then they took me to dig Japanese stragglers out of the caves. I did that for about a month—hunting for the stragglers.

I cannot remember everything from those days. The little things I can forget easily, but those crimes against humanity I can never forget. My fellow

Chamorros who were executed on Guam — I cannot forgive that.

I was classified as a War Criminal by the Americans. Some of my fellow Chamorros from Saipan were sentenced to life in prison. Some got ten years. I was lucky; I got two years. I received the lightest sentence of all.

My family did not suffer while I was in prison. The American military provided them with food and shelter. You can see the result of that today. The Chamorro people cannot go without Spam. It is more than an addiction — they love it. I love it too.

When I got out of prison there were still about 23,000 U.S. military personnel on Saipan. I got a job working in the Subsistence Office. I cut provisions for all of the units on the island. I cannot remember why I quit, but after that I worked for the Civil Administration as a land appraiser. I had one Japanese helper who spoke English fluently. Kan Akatani was his name.

I had good Japanese friends before the war but I lost contact with them. I'm not interested in seeing any of the ones I knew on Guam. Many times I was slapped by Japanese officers. I am eighty years old now. I am subject to go any time. I am just glad that this is behind me.

## The Interpreter's Wife

### "Marikita" Palacios Crisostomo

*"Marikita" Palacios Crisostomo was born in 1923 to Juan Fausto Palacios and Juana Tudela. In 1943 she married Luis Crisostomo and moved to Guam, then under Japanese occupation, where her husband served as an "Interpreter" for the Japanese military. After World War II Mr. Crisostomo was tried and convicted of war crimes by a United States military court and sentenced to life in prison. He was released in 1953. "Marikita" lives today in a small cement house squeezed between two hotels near the beach on the northern part of Saipan.*

My father was a farmer. He raised cows, pigs, chickens, goats, and fish. We had a pond where he raised the fish, just a few for our use. He also raised shrimp. We had a big house — a cement house in Garapan, but during the war the Japanese military took it. The house we had here on the farm was made of wood and tin.

We had Japanese friends and they were really nice. They were always respectful, but the Japanese government discriminated against us. I didn't like the Japanese government because they paid the Japanese a high salary and the Chamorros a low salary, and they only allowed us Chamorros to go to school until the fifth grade. I was not allowed to get more education. Anyway, Japanese was not my language and I had trouble in school. Because of that my mother sent me to the Catholic Mission School. At the Catholic school I had a very good education. We learned how to use the typewriter. We were also taught music and piano, and things like art and drafting.

There was a Japanese teacher who came to the mission school because she wanted the sisters to teach her how to play the piano. The sisters agreed to teach her, but only if she would teach Japanese two days a week to us students in exchange. That way we had a class in Japanese, also. We were lucky because that was only for girls— no men.

Every day my father would go to the farm in Achugao and my mother would stay at home and watch us children, but sometimes we would go to the farm when we were not in school. The Japanese asked my father to lease his land to them so they could plant sugar cane on it, but my father didn't want to. He wanted to use the land to feed his family. We had coconuts, breadfruit, oranges, lemons, pineapples, bananas. We even raised a little rice. And he made money from the farm by selling to the Japanese. My father also made good money by selling cows to the sugar cane company. The cows would sell for 600 or 700 yen a piece. My father made very good money during the Japanese time. That is why we had a cement house. After the war my father continued to farm because people who worked for the U.S. military were only paid thirty-five cents a day. My father made ten times that amount from farming.

When my father went fishing in the lagoon with a net, sometimes he would take me with him and I would go swimming, but he was very busy most of the time. My mother would play with me too, but like my father she was very busy. My mom was a good educator. At night before going to bed she would say, "You have to be respectful. You have to be responsible." If we didn't listen to our parents we were punished. And we prayed every morning when we got up, and every night before we went to bed. That is why people my age never cause trouble. Today things are different. America gives this island protection, opportunities, and equal rights but we don't know how to use these liberties, and we don't understand the meaning of justice. The Japanese did not allow the people to drink whiskey and beer. Maybe the Japanese knew that if the Chamorros drank they would make trouble. The people of the Northern Marianas were very peaceful then. Now, there is corruption. I don't mean just the government; I mean the young people. The parents are trying to make money. They don't raise their children anymore. A Filipina maid raises the children, so they are not educated by the family.

One of my grandmothers died in 1978, I think it was. She was ninety-eight years old. She went to school during Spanish times. She said there used to be much fighting between the Chamorros and Spanish, and many Chamorros died. She had to learn Spanish in school when she was growing up. My father had to learn German, and my generation had to learn Japanese. We were not allowed to speak Chamorro in school.

Before the war we had another farm in Chalan Kiya. That was only for growing coconuts to make copra, but the Japanese wanted to kill all of the coconut trees to have more land to raise sugar cane. I think that was 1933 — they brought in an insect bigger than an ant that killed the trees. This was very sad for the Chamorros, so our leaders went to the Japanese and said this was abusing us. After that the Japanese gave the farmers a chemical to kill the insects. Maybe because of that some of the coconut trees survived. The coconut was very important to the islands. You can eat it, make oil from it, and vinegar. It is even good for babies. The war destroyed most farming on Saipan. After the war people were sent to the northern islands to get coconuts to plant here on Saipan.

I knew Luis, my husband, for eight years before we got married. I was close to twenty-one when we got married in 1943. Before we got married Luis was recruited by the Japanese military to go to Guam as an "Interpreter." Not recruited — forced! At first I didn't even know where he was. They just took him. The Japanese don't give you a choice. If the United States say you have to go to the army and you say, "No," they throw you in jail, but if you say no to the Japanese they beat you to death. But after that he came home often. The third time he came back he married me. First he

*Mrs. Marikita Palacios Crisostomo*

asked my mother and father. My father told him to go back and think about it because we were in war time. My father said, "I cannot say yes now; maybe next year. You come back next year." In those days I couldn't make a decision like that on my own. I had to get permission from my parents. When he came back my father was mad because Luis came back in January. My father said, "You came so early; it's January and you are ready? You're so fast." So Luis asked my father when he could marry me, and my father said, "Next May." When Luis came back in May he only had one week. We had a big wedding in the church, then five days later we went to Guam.

Before we got married the Japanese started recruiting Chamorro women to be trained as firefighters and stretcher-bearers in case the war came to Saipan. We had to learn how to carry ladders and stretchers, and how to put out fires with buckets of water. But then I got married and moved to Guam. And of course when the war did come to Saipan, none of that worked. Everybody ran away when the fighting started.

When our ship arrived at Guam, staff from the Japanese Chief of Police were there to meet us. They were there to help us move into our quarters. On Guam we stayed in Agana for three months, then we moved to Agat. I didn't need any orientation when I got to Guam; I already knew not to ask questions, or talk about things that were happening. When I got together with my family or friends we just talked about the family, nothing else. It was a bad situation there. Guamanian Chamorros would come to the chief of police and say that other Chamorros were hiding weapons or they were doing this or they were doing that. Sometimes they lied. Maybe they were jealous of somebody, or they were enemies for this reason or that. My husband worked for the chief of police. His name was Takibana. If Luis was told to beat somebody ten times he had to do it. Our house was next to the police station and sometimes I could hear the tortures and the beatings.

I had family members from Saipan who were married to Guamanian Chamorros, so even while my husband was away from our house in Agat I never had to be alone. The fact that Luis was an "Interpreter" for the Japanese never had a bad effect on my relationship with them. Even after the war, when Luis was in prison, I would go to Guam every year around Christmas time for two or three weeks and visit my husband in the stockade. I would stay with my relatives on Guam and they were always very helpful. They never complained of having any problems from other Guamanians because of Luis' position with the Japanese on Guam during the war.

Luis had a cousin on Guam whose son was chief of police. He would drive me to the prison when I wanted to visit my husband. His name was Candido St. Augustin. He was a policeman under the Americans, the Japanese, and again when the Americans came back.

We were in Agat when the Americans first started bombing in February 1944. We were hiding in the "boonies" and a Chamorro came out from hiding. The Japanese were looking for this man because he was accused of hiding a pistol. His name was Pedro Dumanal and the Japanese had been looking for him for a long time. The story that I heard was that this Dumanal tried to get his brother-in-law to go with him to kill Japanese, and when he said no, Dumanal beat him up. This was reported to the Japanese Chief of Police by other Guamanians. My husband's boss, Mr. Takibana, told Luis to go into the jungle and find this Dumanal. Dumanal's wife was taken in by the police and beaten because they suspected her of taking food to him in the jungle. I don't know what happened to her after that. Some Japanese troops were also sent over to help look for him. My husband was afraid that if Dumanal saw him first, Dumanal might kill him. So he took a shortcut through the jungle. Luis ran into Dumanal, who was with two young boys. Dumanal asked Luis if he was an "Interpreter." When my husband didn't answer Dumanal took out a pistol and my husband jumped at him and knocked it out of his hand. They fought on the ground and my husband took out a big knife and stabbed Dumanal. Dumanal didn't move after that, so my husband ran to where the road was. A truck with Japanese soldiers drove up and some of the soldiers went into the jungle where Dumanal was and shot him. I don't know if he would have lived if they had not shot him, but after the war all of the Guamanians said, "Crisostomo killed him. Crisostomo killed him." So he was tried by a military court and sentenced to life in prison. I don't know what happened to the two boys who were with Dumanal.

I couldn't go to his trial because the Americans said I had to go back to Saipan. I was not allowed to stay on Guam after the war even though I felt in no danger from the Guamanians.

After the bombing started my husband took me where we could hide in caves near Agat. We were in a cave with some Japanese soldiers and civilians. Takibana gave my husband a bottle with poison in it. He said we should take the poison if the Americans came to where we were hiding, but after Takibana left Luis threw the bottle away. Mr. Takibana sent his wife and two children back to Japan before the bombing, but I don't know if they made it or not because I heard that many of those ships were sunk before they made it back to Japan. Mr. Takibana went into the jungle with the other Japanese soldiers and I never saw him again. I don't know if he survived the war or not.

I had a four-month-old baby by that time and she was sick. Luis left me and went to hide in the jungle. Some Japanese told me I should go to a camp in the jungle set up for Chamorros. It was a place called Manengon, near Talofofo. For six months I didn't see my husband. I was so sad. I cried because I didn't know what had happened to my husband and, and I didn't know about my family on Saipan. Then, on January 1st 1945 my husband surrendered along with Antonio Camacho, another "Interpreter." Luis later told me that they were hiding from both the American and Japanese soldiers while he was in the jungle.

I was in a refugee camp on Guam after the fighting, and Luis was in the stockade. That is when my baby died. That was 14 January 1945. The doctors said she had pneumonia. The MPs brought my husband from the stockade to go to the hospital with me and the baby. While my baby was in the hospital a Japanese priest by the name of Father Komatsu came and prayed, and when she died he helped me take her to the cemetery. I knew Father Komatsu from when I was going to the mission school on Saipan.

My husband told me that while he was in prison they were taken out on work details and Guamanians would come up to them and say, "You are monkeys now. You beat the Chamorros, and now you are monkeys." Some would say, "Come here so I can kill you," but the American MP would tell them, "Get out of here!"

While my husband was in prison on Guam I lived with my family in Chalan Kanoa on Saipan, and worked as a housekeeper for the wives of American Navy officers. That is how I learned English, by working in the homes of American officers and listening.

After eight years the United Nations came to Saipan and asked us what we wanted. One lady was crying and when they asked what was wrong, she said that her son was in jail on Guam for things he had done on orders from the Japanese. She told the United Nations people that it wasn't his fault because the Japanese forced him. I don't know what the people from the United Nations said to the American authorities on Guam, but six months later all of the Chamorros from Saipan were back home. After my husband came home we made six children.

At that time I was working in the tailor shop for the Naval Technical Training Unit [a pseudonym for a Central Intelligence Agency operation in the 1950s and early 1960s on Saipan]. I asked Francisco Tudela, who was head of security for the NTTU, if he could find a job for my husband as a security guard. He said, "Sure, we always need security guards." My husband was only making forty dollars a month at that job and I was pregnant and couldn't work anymore. I helped out by doing sewing at home, and after the baby was born I opened a beauty shop. I made very good money making wedding dresses, and my husband helped me with the cooking and cleaning.

The Japanese when they were here made lots of money from these islands. They grew sugar cane, cotton, coffee, tapioca. They had many factories on Saipan. They made money from the ocean and the land. This island is God's gift to us, but we are going to be sad. There is not enough land for our growing population and we are damaging it. Outside people are coming in and taking over from the Chamorros. They build golf courses and other properties, and there will be nothing left for the Chamorros. I blame our local government for this. My father wanted to preserve this land for us, but my brother and sister leased the land north of my house for a hotel. My aunt leased some more on the other side of my house to another hotel. Just ten years ago we could catch many fish right here by my house. Then they built these hotels and now there are no more fish. They don't come anymore. I don't think life is better now than before. I worry about this, I worry about that — alcohol, drugs, crime.

## From Sumay to Santa Rita

GREGORIO BORJA

*Gregorio Borja was born in the village of Sumay on Guam, which is now part of the U.S. Naval Supply Depot. He served in the U.S. Army from 1952 to 1954. He worked as a civil servant for the U.S. Navy for thirty years, retiring in 1986. Following retirement, he was elected mayor of Santa Rita for two terms. He is now retired completely and lives in Santa Rita, Guam, with his family.*

My father's name was Francisco Santos Borja and he was born in 1892 and died in 1977. He was a cabinetmaker by trade. Before World War II he worked for the U.S. Marine Corps for ten years, from 1921 to 1931. They had a squadron of sea planes in Sumay. All of the buildings were wood then, and he helped build them and maintain them. Sometime in the 1930s the Marine Corps squadron pulled out of Guam and he didn't have to work much after that because we owned a large amount of property and he did some farming. Most of what he produced he marketed to Pan American Airways and the Marine Barracks. He worked for Pan American Airways for a while and they sent him to Midway Island for a year. That was 1940 to 1941. There

*Sumay Village, Guam, as it looked in the 1930s. After Guam was liberated from the Japanese it was made into a U.S. Naval base. The residents were relocated to the nearby village of Santa Rita.*

were many, many Guamanians who worked for Pan American. Some were taken to Midway Island and Wake Island. On Wake Island, some were killed during the fighting for that island during World War II and the rest were sent to China as POWs. After the war they were given veterans' status by an act of the United States Congress.

Before the war Guam was a pretty tranquil place. We only had a population of about 22,000 then. My town of Sumay had a population of about 2,000. My oldest brother, Vicente, was out of school and working for the J. H. Pomroy Company, improving the harbor for the U.S. Navy. His salary was less than what an American would make, but we didn't have to pay any income tax either. We were under U.S. military rule, but we had a lot of freedom. There was also a lot of regimentation by the military. Most of the police then were U.S. Marine Corps enlisted men — very few were Guamanians. The chief of police was always a Marine Corps officer, and the governor of Guam was a Navy captain. There weren't that many military personnel on Guam before the war — maybe an undermanned Marine battalion and a few naval personnel. They also had what they called the Insular Guard — Chamorros that were inducted into military service. They did the work, and they were considered military. However, they got only half of the pay of regular U.S. service personnel. Later in 1938, Chamorros were allowed to enlist in the Navy but only in the steward service, along with blacks and Filipinos. However, they did receive regular pay.

There were some Japanese living on Guam before the war. Some of them even married into the local communities, and some of them were big business people. They were pretty well integrated into the community. Practically all of them learned how to speak Chamorro. My godfather was Japanese. His name was Juan Datsun. He came here when he was a very young man, and he never married. He was very close to my father and my grandfather. That is how he became my godfather.

I remember when I was a little boy his home was almost like a store. He had jars with all different kinds of Japanese candies. Not too many kids had access to candy before the war, you know. I would go there to get my normal supply — me and my cousin — but we had to work for it. As far as I recall, and what I heard from the adults, none of the local Japanese turned on the community after the Japanese Imperial forces took over Guam in 1941. Some of them had to cooperate with the Japanese or they would have opened themselves up for punishment, just like the local population.

My father's younger sister, Dolores, was married to a Marine Corps first sergeant, Otto Cox, who had retired from the Marine Corps in 1921. He was first out here in 1911 and again in 1916. They resided here on Guam until the war broke out. Mr. Cox was then taken prisoner to Japan. He was interned in Kobe, then returned to Guam after the war. He was over forty years old when he was sent to Japan. My uncle Otto talked a lot about his experiences after the war. He said they were not treated badly while they were in Japan. Some of their guards even spoke English. Kobe was like an international city. The Scandinavian Red Cross was bringing in items to the prisoners, so they didn't go hungry. Occasionally, they were allowed to go downtown and do some shopping.

When the Japanese troops landed on Guam on the 10th of December 1941, they didn't expect a friendly environment. There were about 4,000 or 5,000 troops that landed on Guam. Remember, the Chamorros had been under American rule for about forty years, so naturally nobody was welcoming the Japanese with open arms and there was always the belief that America would be sending troops back to recapture Guam. After the Japanese started bombarding the island we moved inland to where the Naval Ammunition Depot is now. The Japanese troops came ashore near the village of Agat. We were up in the hills when they came through our area, some on foot, some in trucks. We were told to just act friendly to them. The troops didn't stay long, three or four months at the most, then they pulled out. They left behind civil affairs types. It wasn't until later in the war that they started bring in troops again.

My mother, Isabel Munoz Cepeda, was born in 1899 and died in 1995. She was mostly in the background, taking care of the cooking, taking care of the chores, and other things. In pre-war Guam women were pretty much housewives except those who were school teachers. There were eight of us children in the family. I was number five of the boys and there were three sisters. My oldest brother, Vicente, was conscripted to work for the Japanese during the war hauling supplies and ammunition. Then toward the end of the war when the American forces were invading Guam, the Japanese were afraid that he and the others working with him would revolt against the Japanese. So they put them in a cave and told them that they would have a party for them because of all the hard work they had been doing. That night they threw grenades into the cave and fired machine guns. There were both men and women in there. Not all of them died. Many were wounded, but then the Japanese went in and started poking them with bayonets to see if some of them were still alive.

Still, some survived and lived to tell what happened. My brother was one of those wounded and was able to leave the cave, but he was seriously wounded in the leg and died later. We recovered his bones a year later. We found him in a sitting position leaning against a coconut tree. Maybe he bled to death or starved — I don't know. His remains were still intact. His clothes were still there. His belt was identifiable because it had his initials on the buckle. Also, he had some fillings in his teeth because he had planned to join the U.S. Navy before the war and he had some dental work done.

There was a second group in another cave about a half a mile away and when they heard that the first group was being killed they moved out — ran away. You probably read about that; it was called the Fena Massacre. My brother was the only family member I lost during the war.

The Japanese put a lot of restrictions on our movement. You had to have pretty good reasons for going to another village. I spent most of the war years right here in Sumay. We also had to wear a badge made of cloth with Japanese characters written on it. You had to wear this to show that you had been registered. If you didn't salute or bow down to the Japanese you got a slap on the face.

Then the Japanese introduced their school system. It was six days a week and we started out early in the morning 'til about two or three o'clock in the afternoon. They shaved our heads— the boys that is. The original group of teachers were Navy people, then they brought in civilians. You had to learn or you got punished.

Shortly after the Japanese arrived they invited us all to the former U.S. Marine barracks to show us a propaganda movie about when they were bombing the American fleet in Pearl Harbor. The film showed their aircraft strafing and coming down low over the battleships and whatever ships were in the harbor. Then it showed one of the planes going over a ship that had the American flag waving. At that point we started clapping and yelling. After that the projector was turned off and the lights came on. They told us that the projector was broken and we quietly left. If they had shown that film later in the war when all of the soldiers came back — my God, they probably would have killed us because the soldiers were very different from the Japanese civilians.

*The Sumary cemetery on Guam where Rosalia Dumanal and several other Guamanian Chamorros were decapitated by the Japanese in 1944.*

The troops—you had to avoid them, stay out of their way.

I remember Luis Crisostomo. He was an "Interpreter" from Saipan. Sometimes he was in the classroom assisting the teachers. He enforced the rules for the Japanese. I knew him, but not in the sense that I would strike up a conversation with him. For the most part, everybody tried to avoid him because we knew that he was more regimented than some of the others. He would not hesitate to inflict punishment. He didn't have to be ordered by the Japanese.

Luis is the one who killed Pedro Dumanal. Pedro was a retired U.S. Navy man, and he and his family were from Sumay. He also had a brother, Jose Dumanal. When the Japanese invaded Guam, being a retired Navy type, Pedro was very pro-American. He started avoiding the Japanese after he had a confrontation with one of the "Interpreters." I don't remember which one. He tried to enlist several other Guamanians who had been in the Navy with him for some kind of guerrilla activity, but maybe because they had families they didn't want to endanger their lives. Plus, there was no indication that the Americans were coming back soon, so they didn't join up with him, and he resented that.

After he went into hiding the Japanese took his brother, Jose, in a couple of times and beat him up. Then Jose went into hiding, too. He came out after a while and the Japanese arrested him and tried to make him tell where his brother was, but he told them that he was hiding by himself. The Japanese let him go but arrested him again later and killed him. Pedro's wife, Maria Rosalia, and one of her older daughters were also taken in by the Japanese and tortured. The daughter was about seventeen years old. She survived but her mother was killed.*

Everything was controlled. Everything you did you

**According to Juan Dumanal, the son of Jose Dumanal, his mother told him that his father (Jose), Rosalia Dumanal (the wife of Pedro Dumanal), Ignacio Qeintanilla, Joaquin Mafnas, and Juan Toves were all decapitated by the Japanese in the Sumay cemetery while family members were forced to watch. Juan still lives in Santa Rita, but has declined to be interviewed for this book.*

had to think first because the Japanese had to agree with it. They even took inventory of our livestock. Our two-story house was occupied and it was about a year before we could move back. Then in 1944 we had to move out again. That is when we moved inland — maybe a mile to Fena. That is also when the American bombardment started getting heavy. We were there for a short while, then the Japanese moved us to the concentration camp in Manengon.

I think the Americans began bombing and shelling Guam about four months before they invaded. We were in Manengon at the time. It was the Seventy-seventh Army Division that liberated us. I heard that the Japanese were planing to kill all of us but the Americans moved so fast that they didn't have time. We had problems with food at Manengon, but we got water from the streams. They were not contaminated in those days.

After the fighting we were moved back down to Agat. Some of the men found employment with the Fifth Marine Service Depot and the Naval Supply Center. We were there from September-October 1944 until April 1945, when we were relocated because they were going to clean up all that area and build Quonset huts for supplies for the planned invasion of Japan and for other continuing war efforts. That is when the new village of Santa Rita was established. The people of Sumay were moved to Santa Rita.

In 1949 the U.S. Congress authorized the military to take possession of properties on Guam they needed. My family lost approximately 80,000 square meters of land. The initial payment was just $800. About six years ago, because of our congressional delegate, the U.S. Congress passed a bill to compensate us. My father had already passed away, but I think my mother received around $50,000. But you know that was prime property. What are you going to do? Even if the military moves out the land is not in its original state. They back-filled the land and there is about five feet of coral fill in places.

There have been a lot of improvements made on Guam since before the war. There is more employment available for the locals. And like I said, practically everybody had to work because the land that they were farming was taken from them by the U.S. military. The Naval Air Station in Agana was prime farming land. There is some farming going on today on other parts of Guam, but its limited — not as much as before the war. There is not much profit in it, and like I said, the fertile lands are not there anymore.

# PART II

## American Voices: Oral Histories of U.S. Military Veterans and Their Families

# The Marines

## 6

## The First Armored Amphibian Battalion

DALE L. BARKER

*Dale L. Barker was born in Pensacola, Florida, in 1919. He grew up in several Southern states and graduated from high school in 1936. During the Depression he couldn't find work, so he joined a federal work program called the Civilian Conservation Corps (CCC), and for the next two and a half years worked in Northern California in the Modoc National Forest. In May 1942 he enlisted in the U.S. Marine Corps. After boot camp at Parris Island, South Carolina, he was sent to radio operator and materiel schools in New York, North Carolina, and Washington, D.C. He was then sent to Camp Pendleton, California, where he was assigned to the First Armored Amphibian Battalion. Mr. Barker has a Ph.D. in library science and has worked at numerous university libraries. He is now retired and lives with his wife in Atlanta, Georgia.*

At Camp Pendleton I was made communications chief of D Company. At first I didn't know what armored amphibians were, but neither did anyone else recruited into that outfit. As we all learned, armored amphibians were amphibious tanks, also called amtanks or LVTAs. There was another important tracked vehicle, the amphibious tractor, otherwise called an amtrac. The two vehicles, amtanks and amtracs, should not be confused with each other. Both were designed for assault from the sea, across coral reefs, and onto hostile beaches. The amtanks had turrets and more fire power. Their purpose was to blast the beaches. The amtrac's job was to transport troops and materiel across reefs and deposit them on shore. Both of these tracked vehicles were needed because Pacific islands were usually ringed with coral reefs extending a half mile or more from the shore. Except at very high tides, boats could not deliver assault troops all the way to the beach. They could bring them no closer than the edge of the reef.

The first model amtank was equipped with a 37mm cannon and four thirty-caliber machine guns. It required a crew of seven men. Because each tank had a radio, one of those seven men was to coordinate radio and other communications. It was my job as communications chief to coordinate communications for D Company in the battalion.

The primary mission of armored amphibians was beach assault. At sea we were usually transported on LSTs (landing ship, tank). For a landing, our tanks would debark before dawn through the bow doors of the LSTs from as far out as two miles from the beach. While we were forming up at a line of departure, the Navy would be bombarding shore targets, and planes would be bombing and strafing the beaches. The last naval vessels to fire on the beaches were little LCIs (landing craft, infantry) located near the edge of the reef, and armed with cannons and rockets. We would pass between the LCIs, climb onto the reef and take up firing where the LCIs left off. We would then proceed towards the beach, firing at whatever targets presented themselves.

Behind us would come the first and succeeding waves of amtracs loaded with marine infantry. We would continue our fire in an effort to keep the Japs' heads down until the amtracs could deposit their troops on the beach.

The First Armored Amphibian Battalion was activated at Camp Pendleton in August 1943, less than three months before we were to ship out for the Pacific Theater of war. Training was intense. We were the first battalion of our kind. The Marine Corps actually had only three amtank battalions throughout the entire war. Neither the Marine Corps nor the Navy knew just quite what to do with this new weapon, the amtank. Our Battalion Commander, Maj. Louis Metzger, worked hard to prepare us and our untried vehicles for combat in the short time available.

In January 1944 we loaded on LSTs in San Diego and did practice landings on San Clemente Island off the coast of California. These maneuvers were a disaster. The weather turned bad, the seas were rough, and the LST skippers didn't know what to do with our strange vehicles. Several amtanks sank and one man, Sgt. Strothers, was lost at sea when his amtank went down.

We made repairs, and received replacements. Then on January 6 we sailed for our first taste of combat, the islands of Roi and Namur, two islands of the Kwajalein atoll in the Marshall Islands. That operation began on January 31 and was soon over. During four days of landings we led troops of the Fourth Marine Division according to plan. On the first day, however, the surf was fierce. Several of our 16-ton amtanks flipped over. We lost more men to drowning than to enemy action. Kwajalein was considered a light operation, and the casualties were light.

The battalion and its surviving amtanks boarded LSTs and were taken by way of Funafuti to Guadalcanal. There we built a camp in the jungle at Tetere Beach, and spent four months training for our next operation.

In May 1944, we began rehearsal landings on Guadalcanal beaches with the Third Marine Division and the First Provisional Marine Brigade. This went on almost constantly for two weeks. What was lacking to make these maneuvers realistic was a coral reef. There were no reefs on Guadalcanal.

We stood out to sea on May 31 and soon learned that the next invasions would be Saipan, Tinian, and Guam in the Marianas. The invasion of Saipan was set for June 15 with the Second and Fourth Marine Divisions. We were to serve as Floating Reserves for the Saipan operation, then land on Guam three days later. We didn't know how much the Japanese would upset that schedule.

*Dale L. Barker, U.S. Marine, First Armored Amphibian Battalion. Photograph taken in 1943.*

For staging we laid over for three days at Kwajalein, already a major American military base. Thousands of men and hundreds of ships gathered there from Guadalcanal, Hawaii, California, and other parts of the Pacific.

By June 15 we were in waters south of Saipan. Twice on June 15 and 17 our convoys were attacked by Jap torpedo bombers. Several Jap planes were shot down, but the only loss in our convoys was an LCI damaged so severely it had to be sunk.

We didn't keep our date to land on Guam. The Japanese fleet came out of the Philippines in an effort to break up the Saipan invasion. What happened was a disaster for the Japanese at the hands of Adm. Marc Mitscher's carrier planes. The downing of 243 Jap planes on June 19 came to be known as the Great Marianas Turkey Shoot. But our schedule had been disrupted. The Japanese naval challenge and the stiff resistance on Saipan kept us on tap as reserves. We weren't relieved of that assignment until the end of June. Our LSTs were running low on water, fuel, and food. The men had been aboard crowded ships for more than a month and it was hard not to get restless.

The LSTs were not designed as troop carriers, and there were no quarters for our people, only for the ship's crew. We slept where we could; most of us topside on the weather deck, or down on the tank deck.

We were ordered back to Enewetak in the Marshalls for restaging. There the ships refueled and reprovisioned, and we were allowed to go ashore briefly for exercise. On July 15 we left Enewetok on our way back to the Marianas.

On July 20, the day before the landings on Guam, we were allowed fresh water showers. Two simultaneous assaults were to be made on Guam, including one on the beaches near Asan by the Third Marine Division. The other was near the village of Agat by the First Provisional Marine Brigade. The Army's Seventy-seventh Division was assigned initially to act as Floating Reserve. Amtanks from our C and D Companies, plus three amtanks from Headquarters and Service Company, led the attack on the Asan beaches. Amtanks from our A and B Companies led the attack on the Agat beaches.

Friday, July 21 was officially called "L" Day, or Love Day. Reveille was at 0200 hours whether you had slept or not. On *LST 220*, where I was, breakfast was at 0345h, and the cooks served us steak and eggs. Not all ships did that, and we were glad to get a hearty, hot meal since it might be our last for some time.

The LST bow doors opened, and at 0730h our amtanks lumbered forward, eased down the ramp, and plunged into the water. As our amtanks slowly moved toward the line of departure we could see the battleships and cruisers launching huge shells at targets on shore. Planes were already bombing and strafing the beaches.

I was assigned to act as radio operator on D Company's maintenance tractor. We had mechanics, medical corpsmen, and spare parts on board. Our job was to repair stalled amtanks, pull amtanks out of traps, and rescue troops from damaged amtanks. I was to do radio maintenance if it was needed.

At 0800h the Navy gave the signal and all of our armored amphibians churned toward the reef. We passed between the LCIs with their cannons booming and their rockets whooshing! Shells from our big

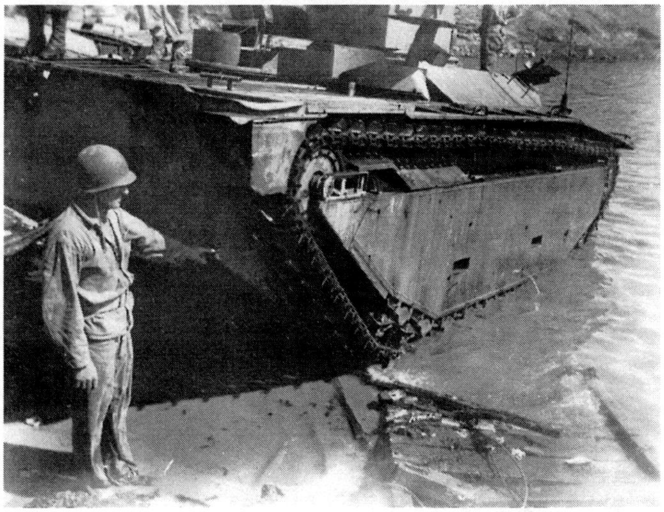

Top right: *Company C amtank after being hit by mortar fire during the Asan landing on Guam, 21 July 1944.* Left: *Assessing the damage to a Company C amtank after the Asan landing on Guam.* Bottom right: *LVTA-4, showing a 75mm howitzer and an additional armor plate in front.*

warships passed over our heads. D Company amtanks were on the left, heading for beaches designated Red One and Red Two, near Adelup Point. C Company, on the right, targeted Green Beach and Blue Beach, near Asan Point. Our D Company, Second and Third Platoons, advanced straight ahead. First Platoon took up positions on the left to fire at Adelup Point. Similarly, C Company deployed one platoon to the right to fire on Asan Point.

In our maintenance tractor we followed the amtanks, but pulled off to one side. The first wave of amphibious tractors, loaded with Marine infantry, followed behind us. The Third Marines were behind B Company. The Ninth and Twenty-second Marine Regiments were behind C Company. Right away, everybody came under fire. Most of our Second and Third Platoon amtanks made it to the beach and moved inland, firing at snipers and other targets. Those amtracs that made it ashore unloaded their men and headed back out to sea for more troops. However, not all of the amtracs made it. Some were hit from fire from Adelup Point and were knocked out or destroyed. The men in them were either killed or wounded.

Our First Platoon, covering our left flank, was hard hit by Jap 75mm guns firing down on them from Adelup Point. Amtanks D-2, D-3, and D-5 were knocked out. We evacuated the crews of D-2 and D-5, but only some of the D-3 men got out. That amtank burned all day with the bodies of three men in it — Lybarger, King, and Zitnik. Two other First Platoon men, Manfred and Christopoulos, also died in the landing. Seven wounded men were evacuated to hospital ships; six of those never came back to our outfit.

In my amtrac, we made several trips to the beach to retrieve disabled amtanks, and I had to repair the radio on Lt. McDowell's tank, D-16. He was our company commander.

Very soon the reef was strewn with wrecked amtanks, amtracs, and dead Marines. C Company, on our right flank, was catching hell. Ten days later we learned that in the assault on beaches down in Agat A and B Companies, especially A Company, lost more men and amtanks than we did. This was mostly from devastating fire from Gaan Point, Bangi Point, and Yoni Island. Capt. Lillie, the A Company commander, was one of those killed.

Once the amphibious assault was completed our main mission was over. From that time on we would make minor follow-up landings, but for the most part we would do beach defense against counterattack and infiltration from the sea.

Throughout much of that first day of the landings we sat in our vehicles out on the reef, watching the Marine infantrymen do the bloody business of trying to take the Chonito Cliffs behind the beach. At about 1500h my amtrac moved on to the beach, into the area occupied by the Second Platoon where they had deployed their amtanks for beach defense. We dug foxholes right in front of our vehicles. A very strange night followed. The enemy laid down artillery and mortar fire all around us. Our big ships at sea fired 16-inch rounds over our heads to targets inland. They sounded like freight cars passing over. Other ships fired flares to light up the whole beach area and the high ground behind it.

Mortar rounds falling in the Second Platoon area killed Murphy, a machine gunner, and wounded six others, all from amtanks D-9 and D-10.

On the second day our Third Platoon joined C Company to lead an assault on Cabras Island, near Piti. My amtrac and most of the amtanks moved out to the reef where we could watch the desperate efforts of the marines still trying to seize the high ground on Chonito Cliffs. That night a Marine artillery unit set up their guns near us on the beach, and the Jap mortar barrage seemed lighter than the night before.

Over the next several days we did beach defense at night and repaired our tanks, radios, and weapons during the day. Lt. McDowell went out on one amtank to retrieve the three bodies on amtank D-3.

For the rest of the operation our amtanks were used to haul cargo and support minor infantry advances even though our armor was not really adequate for that sort of operation. After about six days hostilities had moved inland and northward, away from the Asan beaches. Also, Orote Peninsula was sealed off and secured, and the Asan and Agat beachheads were joined. Some of our amtanks operated with the infantry in a push toward Agana.

On July 27 I moved south with most of C and D Companies to a location near Piti. There we rejoined A and B Companies and set up a temporary battalion camp. We cannibalized amtank and radio parts from wrecked tanks to keep our surviving vehicles in as near combat condition as we could. Between the Piti camp and the Agana area we maintained radio contact with our amtank crews working with the infantry. We learned on July 31 that Agana had been taken without much opposition, and our amtank units had set up a forward base on a baseball diamond there.

On August 1 two other Marines and I took a Jeep ride to Agana and were astonished, not to say aghast, at the incredible wreckage there. A Seabee camp was near ours at Piti. Always ingenious, those fellows were. They had rigged showers with cans with holes punched in the bottoms. We got our first fresh water showers there since the landings. Until then we had washed and shaved only in sea water, or in muddy rain water from shell holes.

Civilians began to gather at our camp near Piti. They were very friendly and seemed glad to see U.S. forces back on Guam. Two teenage Chamorro boys named Ramon and Cecil spent time in our camp eating field rations we offered them and sharing some of their experiences. One of them told us that prior to the Japanese invasion of Guam, Chamorros usually gave their children Spanish names. But during the Japanese occupation they began to bestow English names. They also told us that if a husband and wife were both American the Japanese would ship them both to Japan as internees. If an American civilian was married to a Chamorra, only the husband went. But if an American woman was married to a Chamorro, both were allowed to remain on Guam. In spite of extensive reading, I have never read any confirmation of that story, but I thought it interesting.

On August 6 the whole battalion moved and set up a new camp near Agat. I remember the Agat camp vividly for its rain and mud, the many wrecked amtanks and amtracs, a huge cemetery for war dead, and the persistent stench of dead bodies. Half of the battalion, it seemed, fell victim to dengue fever and dysentery.

While at the Agat camp John Evans and I hitched a ride out to Orote Peninsula to look for copper wire for our radio antennas. We were told that some concrete foundations we saw there were all that remained of prewar Marine barracks. We also saw children and other civilians gathered there. Later that day, Lt. McDowell told us we would be leaving Guam the next day.

On August 12, 1944, the battalion broke camp and boarded LSTs, along with the amtanks and other vehicles that were still operational. I remember how sick some of our men still were. All of D Company, plus some vehicles and crews from an amtrac battalion, were loaded onto *LST 24*, manned by a U.S. Coast Guard crew. We left Guam at 1730h that day. The total American casualties for the Guam operation came to more than 1,700 killed, and about 6,000 wounded. In our amtank battalion we lost 31 killed, and over 60 wounded.

The return to Guadalcanal took 15 days. For the able-bodied men on board it was a rather pleasant trip on an uncrowded, well-provisioned ship. The sick bays were full of men afflicted with dengue fever. They recovered gradually, however, and felt reasonably good by the time we reached Guadalcanal.

Our second stay on Guadalcanal lasted about five months, during which time we received a new amtank model, the LVTA-4. This replaced the old LVTA-1. Instead of the 37mm cannon, it had a 75mm howitzer mounted in an open turret. This not only gave us more fire power, but made possible a new mission. Beach assault would remain our primary mission, but we would also be able to operate as artillery.

Even before the new tanks arrived in November 1944, we were in classes learning about engines, armor, weapons, radios, and everything else on the new amtank. I was sent with several other radio maintenance men from Guadalcanal to Banika, an island in the Russell Group of the Solomons, to learn about the new radios.

We left Guadalcanal for the last time on March 12, 1945, bound for Okinawa. The Japanese general on Okinawa elected not to defend the beaches, and our landings were unopposed. We were used first in the northern part of the island, then in the south. We moved often, digging new foxholes, under fire much of the time, and living in rain and mud. Okinawa lasted three months. For us, that was from April 1 to July 4, 1945.

From Okinawa we had a new rear area to go to, Saipan. It was very different from Guadalcanal. The First Armored Amphibian Battalion arrived on Saipan from Okinawa in mid–July. I remember I was aboard *LST 530* as it stood off shore a little north of Tanapag Harbor when I saw a B-29 in flight for the first time. From the ship I couldn't fully appreciate how huge they really were. The LSTs opened their bow doors and disgorged their amtanks and their crews, and we chugged ashore. There we found a tent camp already in place, if not quite finished.

Saipan was quite a change after Guadalcanal. We were still in tents and on a beach, but no jungle; in fact there were no trees. The tents had wood floors, not bare dirt. We soon set in to improve the camp. Men brought in crushed coral to pave the company streets. We built mess halls, a recreation tent, an outdoor theater with a real screen, a baseball diamond, volleyball court, showers, and toilets.

The big B-29 bombers flying to and from Japan were a fascinating sight to us. A lot of the men, when they had liberty, made trips to Isley Field just to see them take off and land. Saipan, by that time, was a major military base, bustling with activity in preparation for the invasion of Japan.

Immediately adjacent to our camp was a powerful

*Dale L. Barker and wife, Carolina. Photograph taken in 1999 in Atlanta, Georgia.*

radio transmitting station devoted full-time to Japanese language propaganda broadcasts to Japan. In our radio tent we were startled to discover that we could put on a set of earphones and hear the voices of the announcers even when the earphones weren't plugged into any radio receiving equipment. When we went to the battalion theater the Japanese language broadcasts could be heard on the speakers until the movie started and the movie sound track overrode that signal.

We soon went back to work, training for combat, and maintaining the amtanks and other equipment. Some new tanks came in to replace our losses on Okinawa. We were also allowed more liberty time for rest and recovery from the Okinawa campaign. There was more recreation and entertainment to be found on Saipan than we ever had on Guadalcanal. If the movie in our camp didn't suit us there were movies and stage shows at other units not far away. Hollywood stars and other entertainers came to Saipan. One time Peggy Ryan and Eddy Bracken, two young popular movie stars, visited our camp.

We were still training for the planned invasion of Japan in early August when we heard of the first, then the second atomic bombs that were dropped on Japanese cities we had never heard of. We couldn't really believe it, but some of us hoped that maybe the war would end soon. At midnight on August 10 I heard voices outside my tent. Right away we turned on all the radio sets in the battalion to hear that the Japanese wanted to surrender, provided the Emperor could be saved. Absolutely no one regarded that as an obstacle if it meant the end of the war. Most of us opened bottles of beer or Coca Cola, and sat up for a long time talking.

On August 15, 1945, the Battalion commander announced the surrender of Japan, and said that the next day would be a holiday. We had no real perception of the terrible effects that the atomic bombs had on Hiroshima and Nagasaki. We did know that there would be no bloody invasion of Japan and that we could go home.

For about two and a half months after V.J. Day we marked time on Saipan, waiting for ships to take us back to the States. On October 5 a typhoon struck Saipan, destroying our recreation tent and theater, and killing a B Company man.

Through the rest of October we gradually dismantled the battalion, transferring amtanks and other service materials to service units. On November 2, most of us boarded the troop ship USS *Griggs* and left Saipan bound for home. The First Armored Amphibian Battalion was deactivated on November 30, 1945, and ceased to exist.

The First Armored was on active service for 27 months and 12 days, between August 1943 through November 1945. We had operated overseas for over 22 months of that time, six months of that time afloat, and 16 months ashore on islands. We led landings in three invasions. In many ways we were very fortunate in having a light casualty rate. The Guam landings gave us our heaviest losses. The Japanese decision not to defend against the initial beach assault saved us from heavy losses on Okinawa. Of the Marine Corps' three armored amphibian battalions, we probably suffered the fewest casualties. The Second Armored was hit hard at Iwo Jima, the Third Armored at Peleliu. The Marine infantry always had it worse than amphibious units like ours.

# The Bastard Battalion

## Frank Borta

*Frank Borta was born in 1927 in Chicago, Illinois. He was a scout and runner for the Second Platoon, Company A, First Battalion, Twenty-ninth Marine Regiment, on Saipan. It was a polyglot outfit and suffered the highest casualty rate of any Marine Corps unit on Saipan during World War II. The Twenty-ninth took and held Mt. Tapochau, the highest point on the island. Mr. Borta was later wounded while leading a patrol on Saipan and received a medical discharge from the Marine Corps. After receiving his discharge he returned home and went to high school. All of this happened before his eighteenth birthday.*

I grew up in a rough, tough neighborhood in Chicago, Illinois. We used to have gang fights for control of the local park. My gang fought against an Italian gang which was on Milwaukee and Chicago avenues. I joined the Boy Scouts and sold newspapers in order to make enough money to buy a uniform. We never wore our uniforms until we got to our meeting place because you never knew if you would get in a fight on the way to the meeting. In the Boy Scouts I met fellows I would serve in the Marine Corps with. One was Tillio Pompeo and the other one was Joe Sipka. They both fought in different Marine Corps divisions in the Pacific but survived. Pompeo cracked up and ended up in a padded cell.

In May 1943 we decided to join the Marine Corps. I was sixteen years old but lied about my age. In Hawaii I joined up with the Second Marine Division at Camp Tarawa on the big island. After a week I was pulled out and assigned to a new battalion called the Second Separate Infantry Battalion Reinforced. Rumor had it that this battalion was being put together to be sent back to the Mainland to make up part of the new Sixth Marine Division. However, after we boarded ship and headed out to sea we were informed that we would be part of the force to attack Saipan in the Mariana Islands. We had never heard of Saipan before, but we were on the way.

Aboard ship we were informed that our battalion was now the First Battalion, Twenty-ninth Marines. I belonged to the Second Platoon, A Company. We were attached to the Eighth Marine Regiment of the Second Marine Division.

On D-Day we participated in a fake landing on the northern part of Saipan which, as I understand, tied down a regiment of Japanese soldiers. We headed toward the beach, then swung out, and came back to the ship. We made a real landing on that same day at 1450h on Green Beach Two, which was the tail end of the Chalan Kanoa airstrip. The beach was supposed to be secured when we landed but the Japanese artillery coming in hit a couple of our amtracs and there was still some fighting when we landed. Sometime that afternoon our outfit was ordered to move south toward the sugar factory to help the Eighth Regiment.

My assignment in the platoon was that of scout

*Frank Borta lied about his age and enlisted in the U.S. Marine Corps at age sixteen. He fought on Saipan and was part of the team that took and held Mt. Tapochau, the highest point on the island. He was later wounded and received a medical discharge. Nine days before his eighteenth birthday he returned home and went back to high school to finish his education while the war still raged in the Pacific.*

and runner for our platoon sergeant, John Rachitsky. He was a Regular Marine — pre-war. He served in China and fought at Guadalcanal and Tarawa.

We moved up, heading towards the sugar factory, when all hell broke loose. The Japanese artillery fire was tremendous. We were out in the open when the shells came in. I was running south when I heard this shell coming in. Sergeant Rachitsky and I dove for the ground, and the shell landed between us. I thought I had been wounded. It felt like I had been hit in the rear with a wet towel. Then I felt what I thought was blood running between my legs. Sergeant Rachitsky jumped up and said, "Come on!" I said, "I can't — my legs!" He said, "Look." I looked to where he pointed and I saw that my canteen was hit by shrapnel and the water was running between my legs. I jumped up but the shells kept coming in. Twice I got spun around and later found two pieces of shrapnel went through my backpack.

*Frank Borta (center) is pictured with two fellow members of the 1st Battalion, 29th Regiment, called the "Bastard Battalion" because they were neither part of the Second nor Fourth Marine Divisions, but temporarily attached to the Second Marine Division for the invasion of Saipan. During the Okinawa campaign they were an element of the new Sixth Marine Division. At left is Milton Lemon, wounded in Saipan and killed on Okinawa. At right is Richard Carney, who was also killed in action.*

We ended up in a ditch right by the sugar factory. There were about six or eight of us. It turned out we had run through the lines of the Eighth Regiment and were in "No Man's Land," between the Japanese on one side and the Marines on the other. All night long tracer bullets from machine guns on both sides went over our heads. Nobody seemed to know we were there.

Flares lit up the night and I was wondering what the hell I was doing there. My mother had sent me a cross that she had blessed. I tied it to the end of one of my dog tags with telephone wire. While I was lying there that night I reached down to grab the cross and it was gone. I thought for sure I was a dead man.

As dawn approached the sergeant said, "Fix bayonets!" He said the Japs usually attack before dawn and they would overrun us. We fixed bayonets, and as soon as the sun started to come up we crawled back to our own lines. The Japs never did attack, and we got back to our lines, but as we went back we saw American bodies— arms, legs, heads— all caused by the Japanese artillery. When we got back to the beach there must have been between fifty and seventy-five Marines laying there, waiting to be evacuated — either dead or wounded. There wasn't a sound from them. Some of them were from my platoon. I heard thirty-two were killed or wounded from my company. Our executive officer had lost an arm. My buddy, Corporal Richard T. Carney, had his head blown off. The other scout/runner in our platoon, William L. Larson from Wisconsin, was cut in half.

I found out later that our platoon leader, Lieutenant Henderson, ended up behind the Japanese lines along with Gillespie of our platoon. It took them two days to get back to our lines. They hid during the day, and traveled only at night. They finally caught up with the company on the morning of June 17. A couple of days later I saw Gillespie on his way back to the first aid station. He had his little finger and ring finger blown off, but he said he didn't mind because his injury would get him out of this "Hell hole."

It took Platoon Sergeant Rachitsky all day to get the platoon back together, but half the men were already dead, wounded, or missing. Sergeant Rachitsky was killed by a sniper two nights later. He is buried in Punch Bowl Cemetery in Hawaii and I have gone there several times to pay my respects.

By the time we got ourselves back together as a platoon we were in some rice paddies near Lake Susupe.

We couldn't dig deep foxholes because of the water level. We were lying in water all during the night and we could hear enemy tanks coming in our direction along with a lot of firing. Our artillery was getting knocked off at the beach. The Japanese had the entire beach area zeroed in with their artillery and mortars. Our artillery would fire a few shots, then get blown away by the enemy.

We were getting ready for a big Japanese counterattack. We could hear the tanks coming. They hit us just before dawn. At that time our ships opened up on the advancing Japanese. It sounded like sixteen-inch shells roaring in. One shell hit a cave and there was a big explosion that followed. There was even lightning shooting up from the explosion, reaching up to the sky. After that everything stopped — all the fighting. Marines started stumbling back toward us— their ear drums punctured and bleeding. That explosion also stopped the Jap counterattack. The shock wave from the explosion knocked down farmhouses near us, and shattered my wristwatch which was supposed to be shockproof. It even knocked our helmets off.

I think it was also on the second day that an army unit landed and put their air panels out in front of their positions. However, we were out in front of them. These panels would show our planes where our lines ended. My platoon sergeant sent me back to tell that army unit to take those air panels out so our planes wouldn't strafe us. I went back, found an officer from that unit, and told him to pick those panels up. He said, "Do you know who you're talking to?" I said, "Yes, and if you don't take those panels down my sergeant is going to come back here and shoot you." He removed the panels.

The next day, D-plus three, we gathered to take the ridge in front of us. To get there we had to wade through part of Lake Susupe. The water was up to our chest in places and snipers were shooting at us. We couldn't move very fast and some of the guys got hit. Once we crossed the lake we moved up to a coconut grove when machine guns and rifles opened up on us. It got pretty hot and heavy. My sergeant pulled me aside and sent me back to the beach to get more hand grenades. He sent along Glenn Brem, a BAR (Browning Automatic Rifle) man, to go with me. We waded back across the lake, got to the beach, got the boxes of hand grenades, then waded back across the lake. When we got to the other side we laid against an embankment. A Jap sniper fired at us and the bullet struck between our two heads. The sniper was in a shack on the other side of the road. Glenn told me to go around to the back of the shack and throw in a grenade. If the sniper ran out the back way I was to shoot him. If he ran out the front, Glenn would shoot him. I went to the back of the shack and could see that the rear window had been shattered. I pulled the pin on the grenade and let the spoon go. I counted, "One-thousand-one, one-thousand-two, one-thousand-three." I jumped up from behind some bushes and threw the grenade. I missed the window and threw it over the roof. Glenn yelled and swore at me. He then went into the shack and sprayed the place with his BAR and got him.

When we got back to the coconut grove half of what was left of our platoon was dead or wounded. My platoon sergeant, Sergeant Rachitsky, was dead. I knelt beside him and said a prayer. Lt. Henderson, who had finally made it back to our unit early that morning, was badly wounded. Our battalion commander, Lt. Col. Guy Tannyhill, was also wounded. The remaining men were assigned to other platoons. I, as scout/runner, was sent to company headquarters.

We finally took the ridge although we took a lot of artillery fire in doing so. Some of the artillery fire was friendly. We could see a destroyer on the east side of the island firing their five-inch guns at us. They finally stopped, but we did take some casualties before they did.

We stayed on that ridge (Fina Sisu) — I think it was two days. We took more artillery fire, but no counterattacks. After that I lost count of the days. It was just a process of continuous fighting on ridges and hills— and taking casualties.

A new commander took over our battalion after Lt. Col. Tannyhill was wounded. His name was Lt. Col. Rathvon Tompkins. Replacements kept coming up from the beach and I ended up one night with a cook who had been sent up. He said he was hungry and wanted to get something to eat. I said, "If you leave this foxhole you are going to get killed by your own men, or by the Japs." But he crawled out anyway and returned sometime during the night with a five gallon can of fruit salad. We opened it up with our trench knives and ate it. During the night I started to vomit — it was too sweet. I never saw that cook again after that.

During the day the fighting was pretty rough. At night there were three different types of Japs. There were the ones who were behind our lines and trying to get back to theirs. Then there were the ones trying to get through our lines to hit our patrols bringing up ammunition and food. The third type were the ones trying to get us in our foxholes. Our flares went up about every eight minutes to illuminate the area. The Japs sent up flares too, but theirs gave off a yellow light, while ours gave off a bright white.

We had two men to a foxhole. It seemed every night I shared my foxhole with a different Marine. I had to ask every night if the Marine sharing my foxhole had to have a cigarette, because some of them couldn't go without a smoke. You couldn't light a cigarette at night unless you put a poncho over your head, and then there was the coughing. I wouldn't share a foxhole with anybody who couldn't get through the night without a smoke because the smoking and coughing made it easier for the Japs to find our foxhole.

One night a Jap jumped into my foxhole. I saw that he had a knife in his hand and I was able to get my knife and stick him in the guts. Then I dumped his body out of the hole. I don't remember who my foxhole buddy was, but he slept through it all.

On another night we had a Jap slide into our foxhole from the side, and both of us stuck him at the same time. My foxhole buddy stuck him in the throat and I stuck him in the stomach.

We finally started to get what they called the "thousand yard stare." We were so tired we couldn't see clear. Our boots were wearing out from the coral, and our uniforms were all torn. Yet the fighting continued.

I don't know what day it was, but we finally made it to the bottom of Mt. Tapochau. We tried all day to advance and could not because of machine gun fire and snipers. Then as evening approached our new battalion commander, Lt. Col. Tompkins, pulled A and C Company off the line and we moved single file very quietly around the mountain. We were on the west side of the mountain, moving south, then east and came up behind the Japs on top of the mountain from the east side.

Boy, that was a night to remember. My company was dug in just north of the peak on a plateau. We were on the furthest edge of Mt. Tapochau when the Japs hit us once they found we were up there above them. There was a lot of night fighting. The attack started when two Marines were scraping out a foxhole when a flare lit up the sky. One of the Marines was silhouetted against the sky. A Jap stabbed him in the back with a bayonet tied to a long pole. He screamed and fell over the cliff. His friend looked down for him and was shot in the head. It was a sad sight the following morning. The one stabbed was spread-eagle on his back and his buddy was lying on top of him.

A company usually has about 215 men. By this time there were only 40 of us in A Company and 42 in C Company. It was a tough night. One of the fellows, a captain I didn't particularly care for, sent me out to C Company to get more hand grenades, as if anybody had carried a surplus of hand grenades up there. I crawled from one hole to another, shouting my name. Then I crawled back and told the captain that nobody had any extra hand grenades. When I got back to my foxhole one of the fellows from my company was in my foxhole; an American Indian we called "Chief," of course. His foxhole had been overrun by some Japs. His foxhole buddy had been killed and he was bayonetted. I couldn't see, so I felt around for the wound and came up with my hand sticky with blood. I heard later that he survived the war, but drank himself to death somewhere in New Mexico.

I then crawled back to where the captain was and told him that someone was in my foxhole, so he told me to go out on the flank. There was a BAR man out there — a replacement. We always put replacements on the flank, and if they survived the first few days they became part of the platoon's inner circle.

We were taught never to open up at night unless it was a full-out charge by the enemy because the firing would give away our position. Well, sometime during the night this replacement opened up with his BAR. We thought it was a full-out attack by the Japs. As it turned out he fired because he thought he heard something. In the morning we found four dead Japs. One burst from that BAR got all four. So I guess he saved our lives.

The Japs would mortar us from time to time during the day while we were up on the mountain. We took more casualties from that. I was in a foxhole with a fellow from my company. He was laying down and I was sitting at the edge. I got up and took about four steps when a mortar shell came in and landed right in his foxhole — blew him apart.

After that I found a place between some rocks where it would be pretty hard for mortar shells to come in. I went to sleep for about half an hour, which was lucky for me. Then the captain came up and chewed me out — wanted to know where I had been. He told me Lt. Roach wanted me to lead a patrol but sent someone else because he couldn't find me. Then he told me to go after the patrol and tell Lt. Roach to hold the next mountain if there was no fighting, which I thought was ridiculous. I put my gear on and started off the mountain, and down into the valley. I saw three people coming in my direction, but I couldn't tell who they were. The only way you could really distinguish between us and the Japs was by their helmets. Two of the three people coming at me didn't have helmets. I went down to fire when one of them yelled, "Don't fire — Marines!"

*One of the four "Pimples," small hills just to the north of Mt. Tapochau, where the "Bastard Battalion" took such heavy losses before being pulled from the lines.*

That was the tail end of the patrol I was trying to catch up with. The patrol got ambushed. The lieutenant, the scout/runner, and the others were killed. We got another patrol together, which I led, and headed back. We found their bodies scattered along the trail. When I came back I never did see that captain again. I don't know if he got wounded, killed, or replaced, but I was glad to see him gone.

A day later we got a new captain from the beach. His name was Atrick G. Leonard. He wanted to see what our position was because we were going to attack the next day. We were walking for about a half hour on this ridge. We stopped. I sat down against a rock. He kneeled down next to me and took off his helmet. I was taking a drink of water when he was shot through the throat and killed. I guess the Japs spotted him because he had on fresh clothes and didn't look like the raggedy bunch that we were.

This captain was replaced by First Lt. Bradford Chaffin. He was a good guy. On one of our attacks a couple days later I was stunned and blackened by a Jap knee mortar and Lt. Chaffin crawled out and pulled me behind some rocks.

While we were trying to take the four hills just to the north of Mt. Tapochau called the "Pimples," our battalion commander, Lt. Col. Tompkins, got machine gunned in the legs and was being carried out when Gen. Edson from the Second Marine Division came up. I heard Lt. Col. Tompkins tell the general, "Hey Red, this battalion has had it. They should be relieved — they're burned out." Edson nodded, but we weren't relieved.

A major came up and took over the battalion. He kept pushing us to take the "Pimples." Then he got machine gunned in the legs too.

It was a continuous meat grinder. On a good day we would take 10 percent casualties. On a bad day we would take anywhere from 15 to 20 percent casualties. I lost track of the fellows left in my platoon. I would hear so-and-so got killed; so-and-so was wounded. Replacements would come in and be killed or wounded before I could learn their names.

One day when we weren't getting too much

*Casualties of a war fought over fifty years ago. Skeletal remains can still be found on almost any Pacific island where battles were fought. Several individuals, all believed to be the remains of Japanese soldiers, were found by the author and his wife on one of the "Pimples"—four hills just to the north of Mt. Tapochau.*

resistance Lt. Chaffin sent me out on the flank to make contact with the outfit on our left. I must have gone about 200 yards into the jungle without making contact with anyone when I came across a Japanese bivouac area. The fires were still smoldering. I spotted a Jap between some rocks. I went down on one knee to fire but he wasn't moving. I went up to him. He was in a sitting position with a piece of shrapnel between his eyes. He looked like a high ranking officer and he had a map on his lap. I grabbed that and came back. I told the lieutenant there was nothing out there—no Japs, no Marines—nothing. "We are out here by ourselves."

Again, I don't know what day it was when some major from the beach came up and was congratulating our battalion on the kills we were credited with. I think he said it was around 1,200. But he said it looked bad that we hadn't taken even one prisoner. Well, the Japs didn't surrender. They killed themselves, or tried to kill us. We did find one Jap in a cave and were pulling him out. As he raised his arms hand grenades came out from under his arms, and of course we killed him.

On another occasion a Jap sniper had killed one of our men and wounded another during the fighting. We finally shot him out of the tree where he was hiding. He was wounded and crying. He was a member of the Home Guard and no more than 14 or 15 years of age. The Marines dragged him to our command post. Once these Japs surrendered they talked. They would tell you their gun positions and everything. It was tough to get prisoners, but when you did they told you everything. At the command post there was a chaplain. He gave the prisoner some water. When the chaplain left the prisoner went crawling after him and grabbed his leg. He was afraid of us. The chaplain said, "Don't worry. You'll be all right." The chaplain left and we took the prisoner into the bush and killed him.

When we landed on Saipan on 15 June 1944 we had roughly 1,200 men in our battalion. After the fighting for the four "Pimples" we came down from the mountains into Garapan and were relieved. There were less than 200 of us left, not counting replacements.

## Farm Boy from Oklahoma

### Paul E. Cooper

*Paul E. Cooper was born in 1923 in Oklahoma. He graduated from high school in May 1943 and left that same day to join the United States Marine Corps. He was in L Battery, Fourth Battalion, Fourteenth Regiment, of the Fourth Marine Division. He is the only Marine I ever talked to who "enjoyed" boot camp. Mr. Cooper is a retired elementary school principal.*

I was raised on a farm and worked long hard hours, so I was in pretty good shape. I didn't have any problems adjusting to military life. I registered for the draft when I was eighteen and wanted to join the military right away but my folks wouldn't sign for me until I finished high school. My father also had to register for the draft, but was told that he probably wouldn't be called because he was more important to the war effort by raising crops and livestock.

I volunteered for the military before I was drafted so I could choose the branch of service I wanted to serve in. I would have been drafted very shortly anyway. I was very angry when the Japanese bombed Pearl Harbor and wanted to go to the Pacific area. I knew that the majority of Marines went to the Pacific and that is why I joined the Marines. I have never been sorry for doing so. Another reason I wanted to go to the Pacific is because that is where my father served at the end of World War I. He was there from 1918 until 1922 and served in Hawaii, the Philippines, and Siberia.

The sergeant who met us at the train and ordered us on buses was a huge, burly man who called us names I had never heard before. He told us to get on the bus and keep our mouths shut. If we didn't, he said he would close them by knocking a few teeth down our throats. I had never been spoken to like that in all my life. Fortunately, we never saw him again after that.

I was assigned to platoon 382. Sergeant L. E. Williamson, Corporal O. F. McMullen, and Pfc. H. J. Segelken were our drill instructors. There were on average about sixty men in each platoon. I came to love boot camp after the first few days, but it was an adjustment being away from home and friends. After boot camp I was transferred to Camp Pendleton, California, and assigned to the Twenty-ninth Replacement Battalion. This was an artillery school where we trained on 75mm pack-howitzers, 105mm, and 155mm howitzers.

In October 1943 we heard rumors that we would soon be going to the Pacific. We made practice landings on San Clemente Island off the California coast in November and December. In January we boarded LSTs in San Diego and headed for Hawaii.

Before leaving Hawaii for the invasion of Saipan in May 1944 we were tied up in West Lock, Pearl Harbor. There was a terrific explosion on *LST 69*, which was directly ahead of ours. At the time I was on "gangway watch" with Bill Dunlap. Bill was on the starboard side and I was on the port side. Bill and I were checking the passes of men going ashore on liberty. This was around 1500h. There were 34 LSTs tied up close to each other and each of them had fifty-five gallon drums of high octane gasoline secured on their bow decks. This explosion caused fires on several other LSTs. The explosion sent men flying through the air and into the water. Other men started jumping overboard to get away from the fire. I lost my helmet with the first explosion. When I got up a sergeant handed me another helmet to pro-

*Paul E. Cooper as a young Marine during World War II.*

tect my head from falling objects. A Marine captain ordered me to keep all the men below decks to protect them from falling debris, but then a second explosion occurred. All these men I was trying to keep below decks came running through the door at the same time. I got knocked down again as they went over the side and into the water. By this time the smoke was so thick you couldn't see much in any direction. The water around the LSTs became covered in diesel fuel and it was beginning to burn. Small boats came in to pick men out of the water, but visibility was so poor that some men were run over by the boats trying to rescue them.

On each LST there is a pipe guard rail around the screws. From where I was standing I could see six men in the water hanging on to one of these guard rails. I positioned myself in order to throw them a line. Five of the men caught the line and pulled themselves to safety just as the ship's engine started up to move the ship out of the way. The sixth man was pulled into the screws and killed.

The army was in the process of off-loading rockets from *LST 69* when the explosion took place. These exploded too, and started more fires. Before the fires were contained we lost seven fully loaded LSTs, two LCTs, 162 men killed, and 396 were injured.

On May 22, 1944, we were transferred to the USS *Leon*, and on the 25th left for the Marshall Islands. In the Marshalls we transferred on to *LST 340* for the invasion of Saipan, known as Operation Forager. As we were coming in we could see some of our landing craft turned upside down on the reef. On the beach itself we could see all sorts of vehicles and equipment on fire. The dead and wounded were lying everywhere. Doctors and corpsmen were treating the wounded on the beach, and as soon as landing craft were emptied of men and supplies the wounded were put on board and sent to hospital ships. We went ashore near the village of Chalan Kanoa on Blue Beach One. We had lots of trouble getting our 105mm howitzers unloaded on the beach due to heavy Japanese artillery fire coming at us. It was heavy and accurate. We later discovered that the Japanese had an observer in a smoke stack of the sugar mill near the beach. This was discovered and destroyed but we were still receiving artillery fire, and had people getting hit by small arms fire. Behind our position we discovered a well-camouflaged Japanese observation post. It was buried in the ground and had a heavy round metal cover that could be lifted from the inside so that the Japanese officer inside could observe what adjustments were needed to be made for more effective results. This was also discovered and destroyed. After that enemy artillery fire subsided considerably.

The next thing was to do something about the small arms fire. After awhile we discovered that some of the fire was coming from the top of a coconut tree about 200 yards in front of our position. One of our men stopped one of our tanks and told the crew what was needed. The tank then went down the road about 50 yards in front of our guns, made a ninety degree turn to the left, leveled its 37mm gun at the top of the coconut tree and fired one round. A Japanese fell out of the tree along with his weapon.

Each of our gun sections posted a guard out in front of each gun when we weren't firing, which was only at night. The guards had to be changed every hour because of the pressure, stress, and the fact that we went for days at a time without sleep. Some of the guards had their throats cut by Japs sneaking up on them, but none were from our battery.

On that first night ashore we heard something come through the brush across the road in front of our guns. The guard shouted "halt!" three times. When the noise didn't stop he opened up with several rounds. The next morning about thirty feet in front of our gun was a huge ox lying on his back with all four feet sticking up in the air.

Our second night on the island we were strafed by a Jap Zero. He was down so low you could see the face of the pilot when he came by. That afternoon Lt. Faulkner came by and got two other men and me to go forward to survey for another artillery position. We went about two miles and were looking over towards Tinian where we saw four fighter planes coming towards us. We were remarking on how beautiful it was to have those Navy planes for protection when all of a sudden they opened fire on us. We were close to an embankment so we dropped behind it and the bullets went over our heads. We were laying on our backs when four of our Navy planes came into view. They were right above us and engaged these planes that we had thought were ours. The dog fight lasted maybe four or five minutes. One Jap plane went down in a trail of smoke and fire. Then one of our planes went down, and no one got out that we could see. Then another one of the Jap planes went down. The other two high-tailed it out of there.

It was getting late so Lt. Faulkner suggested that we had better get back to our positions as it wasn't safe to be out after dark. We didn't want to get shot by our own people. We had just made it back to our positions when another Jap Zero came over and strafed us.

On the morning of June 18 the Japanese tried to counterattack by boat from Tinian. Part of the Twenty-seventh Army Division had just landed that morning and were in our area. At that time, we were given orders to turn our guns toward Tinian. This required turning our guns 90 degrees to the right, and this was difficult since our guns were dug in. The army guys jumped in our gun pits and helped us. After getting the guns turned towards Tinian we heard that the Navy had come to the rescue and we didn't have to fire a single round.

June 20 we moved forward to our new positions just north and east of Aslito Field. That night we put out our guards in front of each gun, as well as on the right and left flanks. On the morning of June 21, about 200 yards forward of our position, three men were seen walking in a stooped position towards one of our guard posts. As it turned out these men were from one of our Communications Sections. They were checking phone lines to see if the Japs had tapped into them during the night. Two of our guards opened fire on them and the communications men returned fire. We saw what was happening and started running towards them, trying to get them to stop. Both of our guards were hit. One was Private George A. Eisten. I don't remember the name of the other one. They were both fresh out of boot camp and this was their first taste of combat. They were taken aboard one of our hospital ships where they both died a few days later.

Every night since we had been on Saipan we had been bombed around midnight. We called this Jap plane "Midnight Charlie." Around June 26, near midnight, this plane made a run over Aslito Field. But what he didn't know was that the army had put up 90mm anti-aircraft batteries. On his third trip over that night they hit him and all the guys started yelling and cheering. Our commanding officer, Capt. John Kribokapich, told the men to keep it down. What the captain didn't know was that some of the men had gotten hold of some sake and were all lit up. They wanted to go out and attack the Japs that night. It took a while for Capt. Kribokapich to get them to settle down. He threatened them with court-martial if they didn't.

*Paul E. Cooper holding a can of pork and beans. The photograph was taken on the island of Maui shortly before the war ended. By this time he had survived four island invasions, including Iwo Jima. "We had just gotten our new 155mm howitzers and were training for the invasion of Japan that [coming] November."*

On June 29 we were moved forward into a wooded area. K Battery lost six men that night. We were close to the ocean and a few men from each section were going down to the ocean to clean up. The army had an armed guard on the beach and we had a Marine guard down there. Bill Dunlap, George Goble, Lovern Wiltzen, and I decided to go down and clean up. When we got to the edge of the wooded area we met Cpl. Horace Cobb, Pfc. Smart, Pfc. Stewart, and Pfc. Ruzo. They went ahead of us, and weren't gone more than two or three minutes when we heard some shooting. Pfc. Ruzo came running back and said that Japs had killed the other three. We didn't have our weapons with us, so we ran back to our positions to get them. Capt. Kribokapich stopped us and said he would get a tank to go into this area. I don't remember what happened after that because I didn't go in with the tank.

On July 2 at about 0300h Pfc. Chester Eller and I were on guard duty. Over on our right side, near a tree line, we had a trip wire. It was a fine wire that stretched about four inches above the ground with C Ration cans tied to it with little rocks in them. If the wire was hit it would make a noise that would alert us. This is what happened around 0300h that morning. This trip wire set off a signal that something was happening out in front of our position. Then these dark figures appeared. The guard on the left yelled "Halt!" three times, but they kept moving towards us. He opened up on them, and Chester and I did too. I had an automatic weapon so I fired more rounds than the others. The next morning we went out when it was light enough to see. There were some dead Japanese soldiers and some small children — all dead. Sgt. Alonzo B. Rawlinson started dressing me down; he said I was a murderer. I told him I wasn't the only one shooting. He said that didn't matter; I was expending more ammunition than the others. So because of that I was responsible. About that time Lt. Joe Fegan from Mike Battery got hold of Sgt. Rawlinson, turned him around, and gave him hell. He said, "What if those Jap soldiers had gotten through and into one of our foxholes. What would you have done then, Sergeant?" That was the first and only time that I heard an officer get onto a non-com in front of us lower ranks. Rawlinson was a good sergeant, but he was so upset about what happened to those children. I was upset too, but there wasn't much I could do about it. I was just protecting our position.

On July 9, 1944, Saipan was declared "secure." That day we moved back to the south end of the island to get ready to go on to Tinian. We set up our guns on the 17th to fire on Tinian prior to the landings. The invasion itself was delayed for a few days to see how the landings on Guam would go. There were ninety-six 105mm and twenty-four 155mm howitzers lined up hub-to-hub, firing on Tinian — right at the beach head where the landings were to take place.

On July 27 at midnight we stopped firing and went aboard a LCT with all of our equipment and men for the short trip to Tinian. We were told the ride would be a short one — maybe two or three hours. We didn't have any place to sleep — no bathrooms and no food. We stayed on this LCT that night, the next day, the next night, and the next day until about 1500h when a lot of our men came down with high fevers and dysentery. They then took us aboard the USS *Cambrian*. I remember I was right behind Capt. Kribokapich when we went aboard. We all looked like a bunch of drowned rats. None of us had any rank showing so you couldn't tell a captain from a private. We were met by this Marine lieutenant in pressed, clean khakis and he started dressing Capt. Kribokapich down about what a sorry bunch of Marines we were. Capt. Kribokapich let him go for about thirty seconds before he got his attention. The captain said, "Get us fed, showered, and clean clothes!" We got good service after that. We never were told why we had been left on the LCT for such a long time.

From left to right: *Harold Nowak, Paul Cooper, his son Ben, and Augie Fischer. All three of the former Marines shown above started out together with the formation of the Fourth Marine Division early in the war, fought through the Marshalls, Marianas, and Iwo Jima together, and were all separated from the service at the same time in November 1945.*

We left that ship on August 1st and went back aboard the LCT and landed on Tinian that evening. We stayed on Tinian until the 10th. During this short period of time we did mostly guard duty. When we weren't doing that we played softball.

During our operations on Saipan and Tinian our battery fired 8,420 rounds of ammo. Each round from our 105s weighed a little over 49 pounds. We left Tinian aboard the USS *Typhoon*. Operation Forager was over for us.

## Sixth Provisional Marine M.P. Battalion

### James A. Moore

*James A. Moore was born in 1919 in Los Angeles, California. From 1939 to 1944 he worked for the Douglas Aircraft Company as an engineer-designer. He received exemptions from military service because of a number of secret programs he was working on for the military during war time. His deferment status was ended in 1944, at which time he found himself drafted into the U.S. Navy. After his discharge from the military in 1946 he was given his old job back at Douglas Aircraft and retired from there in 1976.*

With all the exemptions I got I never figured I would be called into the service, but in June 1944, by order of President Roosevelt, all exemptions for men age twenty-five were canceled no matter what they were doing. I was officially drafted into the Navy. However, during swearing in time, and on advice from a friend, I volunteered for the U.S. Marine Corps. I was informed that the Marine air wings needed technically trained men.

I received basic training at San Diego, California, and advanced infantry training at Camp Pendleton where I entered into the anti-tank school. During my

*Pfc. James A. Moore in California in 1946 after his discharge from the Marine Corps.*

training the battle for Saipan was in progress and we trainees were under tremendous pressure to prepare for future engagements. Men with technical backgrounds were not needed or even respected by the NCOs [noncommissioned officers]. As a matter of fact, they looked down their noses at all of these aircraft men that were being pulled into the Marine Corps.

The heavy loss of men to the Fourth Marine Division on Saipan was made up for by forming the Twenty-fourth Replacement Draft at Camp Pendleton. All the men completing anti-tank school, approximately 1,000 of us, were placed in this draft. We entered the Pacific area November 16, 1944, and were attached to the Fourth Marine Division rear area base on the island of Maui. We trained as a separate unit from the division's combat veterans. In the later part of November of that year I was assigned to the *APA Newberry* and practiced mock landings on various Hawaiian Islands.

The invasion of Iwo Jima was top secret. I only learned of the invasion by accident. I was visiting a friend of mine, Lt. (j.g.) Harry McGuggin, on Ford Island. It was my last liberty and Harry was with a group of fighter pilots. We had had a few drinks and one of them said, "Do you know where you are going?" I said, "I don't have the foggiest notion." Then one of them said, "Well, you are on your way to the island of Iwo Jima." That still didn't register. However, it did later.

On the way to Iwo Jima with Task Force 58 we were told that our part in the battle would be that of observers, not combatants. Anti-tank men would be needed for Okinawa.

On February 19, 1945, we arrived off of Iwo Jima and watched from our ship as five waves of Marines stormed the beach. Actually the fifth wave was a group of Seabees that got decimated. The Japanese held their fire during the landings of the first four waves, then opened up on the fifth wave, which was all Seabees. Within a few minutes they had no officers and very few NCOs left.

After the initial landings were completed the Twenty-fourth Replacement Draft was broken into small work parties to unload APAs and LSTs. When that was completed we returned to the *Newberry* to await further orders. When we came back to our ship we were told that we weren't going back to the beach, and would we contribute blood. A lot of the men, thinking they wouldn't be going back in, donated blood. However, those orders were changed and we did go in. Some of these men who gave blood were shot and died from trauma.

About the fourth day of the invasion they started sending us back to the beach as replacements. The Fourth Marine Division went up against 18,000 fully entrenched Imperial Japanese marines and soldiers. I was sent in on February 24, the day after the raising of the American flag on Mt. Suribachi. I was assigned at first to sort out loose equipment that had been dropped on the beach. One of the first things that I put my hands on was a gas mask holder that belonged to Gunnery Sergeant John Basilone. Now, John Basilone was a Congressional Medal of Honor winner at Guadalcanal and was credited with killing 200 of the enemy with a machine gun during a banzai attack. He got on the island at Iwo and was killed right there on the beach. This didn't give me much enthusiasm for what lay ahead.

The next day I was sent forward to a dugout where there was a man with a typewriter and a file system. He asked for my name, rank, and serial number. Then, he handed me a "V" mail blank and told me to write home. "Remember, this might be your last letter ever to go out," he said.

My first real duty in the forward combat area was carrying stretchers from what they called the "Meat Grinder" to Hill 382. This I did for two days. I was the only survivor from that group of stretcher carriers. During one of my last times forward I rescued a man who was wounded and laying in a shell crater. This was after the man who was with me was shot and killed. I was able to get the wounded man back, and the captain who was in charge of that unit was so excited that he wanted to give me a medal. But instead of accepting a medal I asked the captain to make sure I was rescued if in a similar situation some day. By an ironic twist of fate that is exactly what happened.

Later, on March 8, 1945, we were engaged with the enemy in rather rough territory. It was all gulches and ledges, and caves— plenty of cover for the enemy but not much for us. At the end of the day my unit dug in. There were two Marines from the Third Division with me in the same foxhole and we were well out in front. That night some Japanese tried to infiltrate past our foxhole. I threw a hand grenade at him and killed him. However, I didn't realize there were two other Japanese with him. They ran back behind some rocks. With star shells lighting up the night they could see our positions pretty well, so they threw their own hand grenade and it came right in our hole. It killed the two men next to me. I saw the grenade and curled up in a fetal position. The grenade must have gone off about three feet from me and I took the blast from it in my back. It blew me out of the foxhole. I was bleeding, paralyzed from the waist down, and partially blinded. It took a few hours before my vision returned. A corpsman came and told me the two men who were with me were dead, and he didn't know what he could do for me. He dragged me to the back of our lines where he put me under a poncho and gave me a shot of morphine. He then told me I was probably going to bleed to death. I told him to get Capt. William Eddy, the one who wanted to give me the medal. He had promised me that if I ever got in such a position he would come and rescue me or at least try to help me in any way he could. The captain came and got me back to a pick-up spot and got on a field phone. He ordered a Jeep to come up because he said he had some wounded that needed attention. Capt. Eddy was told they weren't sending any Jeeps up to the front because it was too dangerous. Capt. Eddy yelled back that if they didn't send a Jeep he was going to call his men off the line. He said he had had 212 men in his company and was now down to 17 effectives left. So they sent a Jeep up and I was taken to an aid station. I waited until dawn to get into surgery, where they pulled four or five large pieces of steel out of my back. So, you could say I traded my life in against the medal he wanted to give me and I've never been sorry for it. Capt. Eddy won the Navy Cross during his service in the Pacific, and his father in World War I had won the Congressional Medal of Honor in France. Capt. Eddy was an impressive person and eventually became an Episcopal priest.

I was evacuated from the island in an amphibious tractor. It took me out to the USS *Solace*, a hospital ship. Eventually, I could stand up but had no feeling from the waist down for quite a while. This continued until just before we reached Guam when I started to get some feeling down towards my feet. I complained about one of my feet hurting, so they took me into the sick bay and discovered that I had two pieces of shrapnel in one of my feet.

In addition to my physical injuries I suffered terrible nightmares for about seven years after I got out of the Marine Corps. Subsequently, I found out that that was not unusual; it was quite common among combat veterans.

I spent a month in the hospital on Guam, then was air-lifted to Pearl Harbor where I spent another month in another hospital. When I was finally let out I was given a B classification. That meant I was no longer fit for combat. All of us with this classification were sent down to the Marine Corps Transit Center where we were told they were forming a unit to go to England. That sounded a lot better than the forward Pacific area. Well, it turned out to be a ruse. A lot of us volunteered, not realizing that this was a police battalion being organized to go to Saipan.

It took quite a while to get from Pearl Harbor out to Saipan, and in the meantime our commanding officer, a Lt. Colonel Chalpant, decided he was going to take some of the islands in the Northern Marianas that had Japanese radio operators on them. He had fought on Guadalcanal but was not well thought of and had at one time been relieved of his command in the field for showing bad judgment. He was eventually court-martialed and removed from our command. General Edson of Edson's Raider fame was the presiding judge.

In the effort to take Pagan Island we suffered one casualty. I don't remember his name but I do remember he had been badly wounded in a previous island battle and was one of those Marines who was given a B classification after he got out of the hospital in Pearl Harbor. He was shot in the arm during the Pagan operation and died of trauma. I don't think he was more than eighteen or nineteen years old.

The rest of us landed on Saipan and wound up on the middle of the island. It was on what was called the Cross Island Highway.* We arrived in the evening and didn't realize that the area had been abandoned by U.S. forces for a while. In the meantime, some Japanese stragglers had moved in. They were using the tents, the toilet facilities, and showers. There was quite a bit of confusion that night as to who should be staying in whose tent. Anyway, by the next morning the Japanese had cleared out and we had the area to ourselves. There were no injuries or deaths as a result, just a lot of shouting and yelling back and forth.

In Headquarters Company we had sixty men, and almost all of us had Purple Hearts. Maj. Claude Cross, our executive officer, looked up my service record when he discovered that I couldn't walk or stand more than half an hour at a time because of the wounds I received on Iwo. He had me detached from all further field duty. My new job was to make maps and to screen incoming communications from the Fleet Marine Force Pacific, which was a pretty nice job. I was in the battalion's headquarters office, so I was in a position to observe a lot of what was going on.

There were a lot of things of real interest on Saipan. We were involved in the surrender of Japanese stragglers. We helped in the training of the Chamorro police force, and the assigning of Japanese POWs to different work details. I watched all of this and was amazed at the winning over of the Japanese through the care they received. We always let them take showers, gave them good food, movies, cigarettes, and clean clothes. And I don't think anybody realizes the effect that our Hollywood movies had on the POWs and also the Chamorro natives. They would see these movies and interpret their meaning differently than we would. What they really liked were cowboy movies, and it was common for a POW or a Chamorro to ask a Marine, "Are you a Texan?" I asked one native what he found so unusual about American movies. He said something to the effect that ... "Well, when you live in a hut with a dirt floor and a grass roof and you see these people in the movies who are supposedly poor and down on their luck, living in an apartment with hot and cold running water, driving a car and dressed well, you assume that everybody in America is rich, and everybody over here is poor."

My overall impression of the Chamorro people was that they were highly intelligent people. When we were training the native police force they caught on to all the things going on around them but kept to their native ways. I think they felt that once we left the islands they would have to fall back on their traditional skills and ways of doing things.

The Chamorros we had in camp who were training for police duty were interested in everything American. They had been under the domination of the Japanese for thirty years and they were ready for something new. We were teaching them how to use weapons, principally the carbine, a lightweight .30-caliber weapon. The weapon of choice for the natives seemed to be the jungle knives we had. When we finally graduated a group of them they wanted to go out and look for Japanese stragglers, but they didn't want to go out looking for them with guns. They wanted to go after them with knives. We more or less discouraged that.

One of the things I found interesting was that both the Chamorros and Japanese POWs started manufacturing souvenirs. It was a phenomenal industry. We had a very talented Japanese POW who was painting silk handkerchiefs. You supplied the handkerchief and he did the painting. It would take him about fifteen or twenty minutes, and he was charging $20 a handkerchief. I don't know how much money he went back to Japan with but it must have been a lot.

We had a real opportunity with our POWs to introduce them to democracy, and we almost completely eliminated their caste system while they were on island. Regardless of rank, we took the most talented POWs and made them supervisors. As an example, in some cases we had Japanese privates ordering around Japanese officers.

We had two very talented POWs directly in our camp. We called them Toki and Mogi. They were assigned to our wood shop, making furniture and shipping boxes. Toki had been captured on Iwo Jima and we were interested in why he gave up because there were so few prisoners taken at Iwo. Toki told us that we had sunk his destroyer off Iwo and he swam ashore. The Japanese Army wanted him to fight as a machine gunner. Well, he didn't want to do that so the minute the Marines landed he gave up. We asked him about "loss of face," and he said he came from one of the poorest farming areas in all of Japan and losing face was nothing after everything he had gone through.

Toki was an intelligent man. He wasn't very tall—maybe 5'3"—thin. He had been around the world a few times with the Japanese Navy, and had driven taxis in Tokyo. As a taxi driver he had managed to pick up

**Now called Capitol Hill.*

enough English to converse with people. He was a very fast learner and became bilingual simply by being around English speaking people all day as a POW.

I once asked Toki about the charges of atrocities committed by Japanese troops in China, the Philippines, and other parts of Asia and the Pacific during the war. I asked him if these charges were true. His response astonished me. He said most of the atrocities were committed by Koreans. I said, "Why Koreans?" He said, "Because they were trying to show the Japanese soldiers how tough they were."

Toki's sidekick, Mogi, couldn't speak a word of English but the reason he was of value to us was because he was very cooperative and trustworthy. When you consider that these two were working in the wood shop with knives, saws, and even stacked weapons; we couldn't take chances with most POWs because they could have decided to turn on us. But with Toki and Mogi we learned to trust them to the point that they became an integral part of that group working in the wood shop.

We had a lot of fun with Toki. We had a young American recruit who came over after the war was already over and was bragging about his ambition to get in a fight with a Japanese soldier, so we stagged a fight between Toki and this Marine. Twice, Toki beat the Marine to a pulp and the Marine finally admitted he was wrong, put his arm around Toki and said, "Lets go get a beer."

One day some Seabees came into the office and complained about being shot at by Japanese stragglers while trying to put a road through the jungle not far from our camp. They wanted our colonel to do something about it. But our colonel, not being the bravest man in the world, told the Seabees not to worry; it wouldn't last. Well, it only got worse and after more complaints, and our colonel not doing anything about it, the Seabees went out on their own with automatic weapons. When they were done they brought back three dump trucks filled with the bodies of Japanese soldiers and dumped them outside of company headquarters. Our colonel didn't know who dumped these bodies in front of his office, and nobody would tell him. He had a problem because he had to report it to the Swiss Red Cross. We all got a big laugh out of this because nobody liked this colonel.

One day at the Battalion Headquarters Office I looked out the window of the Quonset hut and there stood a Japanese officer with about a platoon of men, fully armed and neatly dressed. They were all standing in parade formation. They wanted to surrender to a high ranking American officer. Our colonel, who was not the bravest man in the world, didn't want to go out and accept their surrender. We finally did get an officer to go out. It was really amazing to see these fully armed Japanese out there going through a formal surrender.*

In time thc natives started returning to their usual life style. In the morning the doors to their huts would fly open, the shutters over the windows would open, and all the kids would be chased out. They even had their animals inside. It was funny to watch the goats, chickens, and different animals come out of these huts. Then the mother would go over to the window and let her hair hang out so that the oldest daughter could go outside and comb it.

I also thought it interesting how the native men would take their children down to the beach. One of the ways a Chamorro father would teach his son to swim was to take them out to the end of these rock groynes and toss him in the water and just walk away.

Their fishing technique was interesting. They made long spears out of metal rods, then started a fire and hammered a barb on the end of these rods. They would walk along the shoreline and throw one of these spears maybe 20 feet out and hit a fish. Now if you take in to consideration the refraction of light in the water, that took a lot of skill. Also, they would go out on the reef. With one hand they would pat the water and scare the fish out, then spear them. I was always amazed at how resourceful they were.

The native village, when I was there, was off limits. We had Chamorro guards with semiautomatic weapons and a barbed wire fence around the compound. This Japanese straggler tried to sneak in to see his Chamorro girlfriend one night. He was detected by the Chamorro guards, and by the time they stopped shooting him there wasn't much left of him. The problem was that every death had to be reported to the Swiss Red Cross, and it was hard to explain why this man was shot up so bad.

Before the war ended it was interesting to go over to Kagman Point and watch these B-29s coming back from bombing Japan. Many were crippled — one or even two engines out, and to land they would have to lift up over a cliff coming in on their approach. Many of them just couldn't make it so the planes were put on automatic pilot and the crews would bail out.

Towards the end of the war we had a large contingent of black sailors and soldiers. Many of them were

**This was Captain Oba and his organized band of Japanese stragglers who held out on Saipan until December, 1945. The book,* The Last Samurai, *by Don Jones tells the full story.*

involved in loading and unloading the ships down at the harbor. They felt they were being discriminated against — that their quarters, their food, and their life style didn't measure up to what the white military personnel were getting. So for several days they went on strike. They refused to load and unload ships.

We had black Marines on Saipan also, but they were never in any kind of trouble — never had any problems. The officer in command of these black Marines was a gentleman from Richmond, Virginia. He was very much a Southern gentleman. Early on he stood those black Marines out in front of him and said, "When you are a Marine I don't know what color you are. As long as you conduct yourselves as gentlemen and Marines you will be treated just like any other Marine." That's the way the Marines treated their men, but the Army and the Navy had problems that finally led President Truman to integrate the armed services.*

Once the war was over we had quite a time adjusting to camp life. At the very end of my tour of duty in 1946 I was at an open air theater when the first civilian woman came in with her three children in hand. There was always a lot of noise and chatter before a movie, but when that woman and her children walked in everything became suddenly quiet. I heard men starting to cry. They realized the war was really over and that it was this woman and these children they had been fighting for. It was very emotional.

There was also a morale problem once the war was over and we were still on Saipan. We were getting letters from home and reading articles that were enclosed in these letters about how inhumane the bombing of Japan was. My mother attended a Unitarian Church in Santa Monica, California. The minister would get up on the pulpit and tell the congregation what a crime it was for using nuclear weapons on a defenseless nation. Well, we had been in foxholes fighting hand-to-hand with the Japanese Imperial Army and we thought it was a great idea to end the war with the bomb, get the war over with, and stop the killing. None of us wanted to think of all the mangled bodies on Iwo Jima and the idea of seeing more of the same if we had to invade Japan. We wanted that sort of thing to end and we wanted it to end in a hurry, which it did thanks to the two atomic bombs dropped on Japan.

**Maug Island**

ROBERT OWENSBY

*Robert Owensby was born in Springfield, Illinois, in 1926. He graduated from high school in January 1944, and enlisted in the U.S. Marine Corps that May. As a member of the Fourth Marine Division he fought on Iwo Jima, where he was wounded. After his discharge from the hospital in Hawaii he was made part of a Marine MP outfit and spent the rest of the war in the Mariana Islands. Mr. Owensby is an architect and lives in Naperville, Illinois.*

I landed on Iwo Jima as a rifleman in C Company, 24th Regiment on February 19, 1945. I spent the first few days taking supplies to the beach and off-loading them, then taking wounded Marines back to ships for treatment. I don't remember the exact day I went ashore to enter the fighting, but I remember as the ramp to the LCVM was lowered several rounds of rifle fire whistled past. Fortunately none of us were hit.

As we headed towards the front we were led past what must have been about 200 dead Marines. The graves detail was going through, looking at the dog tags, and writing down information prior to their burial. I certainly didn't think it was a good way to be initiated into combat.

On the morning of the second day we were ashore we were taken up to just behind the front lines. I was with Jim Parker, Phil Baldwin, and a couple of other guys from the replacement draft that made up part of C company. We must have been maybe 200 or 300 yards behind the lines. I think we were in an area they called the "Punch Bowl," because there were cliffs behind us and I could see lots of dead Japs up there. It looked like they were killed by naval gun fire — not from being hit, but from the concussion. Their eyes were bulging out, but it didn't look like they had any other wounds.

The next day the whole First Battalion, Twenty-fourth Regiment, went forward to the front lines. We started taking mortar and artillery fire about noon. My friend Jim Parker was an assistant machine gunner. He was carrying ammunition up to the front and jumped

**Newspaper and magazine reports from that period indicate that black Marines overall were not treated much better than blacks in other branches of the military.*

*Robert Owensby, on the right, with another Marine. Photograph taken on Iwo Jima.*

into my foxhole just as a mortar barrage started landing in our area. Jim said, "I've got to join my machine gun group." Then he jumped out of my foxhole and ran maybe 15 or 20 yards over to another hole where his machine gun was. It was just a couple of minutes after that a mortar round fell in that hole, killing Jim and the rest of that crew.

The day after that C Company was up around a Japanese strong point called "Turkey Knob." It was a Japanese communications center — a big concrete block house. This was the first time I had actually seen live Japanese soldiers. We were trying to move around their flank where they were dug in in front of the block house. We got around on their right where we could sight down their trench. I could see three or four Japs running down the trench, trying to get into a cave. I got off a few rounds at them, then my M-1 jammed. By the time I got it unjammed they were all underground. Shortly after that our platoon leader directed us to fall back about fifty yards because we started coming under heavy mortar fire.

Sometime after that the company was pulled out of the line for of couple days of rest. We moved back to what was called Hill 382, which had been taken several days earlier. However, being in reserve on Iwo was not what you would call R&R, rest and recuperation, because we frequently came under Japanese mortar fire. We were dug in right near the end of airstrip #2. We were sitting there one day watching the Seabees clearing it off and getting it ready for our use when a B-29 landed on it. It came in from the south, landed, and came to a stop not far from where we were dug in. The pilot hurried up and turned that plane around and gunned it back down towards the south end of the runway because he was starting to take mortar fire. Later on, I was told that that was the first B-29 to land on Iwo Jima. It was quite an occasion since having an emergency airfield for the B-29s was one of the reasons for our being there in the first place.

The Japanese on Iwo absolutely refused to move. Most of them were underground and most of the time you couldn't see them until they fired on you. This was my first taste of battle as a young Marine and I was scared shitless. After the first few days I really didn't think I was going to make it. I had seen so many of my friends killed and wounded. Some of the deaths were just terrible, the way they were blown apart — arms and legs blown off. These were friends I had been with for months. I was closer to these men than the friends I had back home. I often think of them and what they might have done with their lives had they survived.

I was hit by fragments from a mortar shell while we were still on Hill 382, and patched up by a corpsman. Then on the 8 March I was hit by a hand grenade thrown by a Japanese soldier who was on a rocky cliff above us. The grenade rolled down the cliff, hit my backpack, and exploded. Cans of rations and a package of letters from my girlfriend absorbed most of the impact, but I took fragments in my neck, back, and extremities. I was able to walk back to an aid station with the help of a corpsman and was taken to a hospital ship, the USS *Samaritan*. It was determined that I had over 100 grenade fragments in me. Most of them are still there.

The hospital ship took us to Guam and after a couple of days those of us who could walk were put aboard the USS *Bland* and sent to Pearl Harbor. After a couple of weeks in the hospital at Pearl I was sent to the Marine Corps Transit Center. The Transit Center was where they sent Marines being discharged from the hospital, and those coming from the mainland for a second tour of duty. Eventually I was assigned to the Sixth Provisional Marine MP Battalion, which was being activated. Most of the enlisted Marines were veterans of previous combat in the Pacific theater. Most all of the officers with the exception of the battalion commander, Lt. Col. Chalfant III, and the executive officer, Maj. Cross, had no previous combat experience.

In June 1945 we boarded ship and were sent to Saipan. After being on Saipan for only a couple of days we were told that certain companies would be sent on an operation to the islands north of Saipan to mop up Japanese troops that might be holding out up there. The islands that my company was assigned to were Agrihan, Asuncion, and Maug. I was made a BAR man, and we left from Saipan on LCIs. [landing craft, infantry].

When the LCIs pulled up on the beach at Agrihan the ramps dropped and we came off on the run and pushed inland to form a perimeter in case of any strong Japanese opposition. As we came down the ramps all of the natives were standing there watching us. We had some Chamorro guides with us from Saipan, and after we set up our perimeter they were able to determine that the Japanese troops who had been on the island had departed for one of the other islands further north. I remember two of the Chamorro guides had the name "Antonio." One was a little heavier than the other so we called them Big Antonio and Little Antonio. Before leaving Agrihan we left some rice and other foodstuffs for the natives.

The next day we landed on Asuncion, and again there were no enemy soldiers. We had our lunch there on the beach, and while we were there one of the guys—his name was Adams—developed a case of appendicitis, determined by a corpsman who was with us. The LCI then radioed back to Saipan and a Martin amphibious bomber was sent up to get him.

On the following day we arrived off Maug Island. Maug was quite a bit different from Agrihan and Asuncion in that there were no beaches to land on. We

*Maug Island, photographed by Robert Owensby from the deck of an LCI prior to the landing of Marines from the Sixth Marine M.P. Battalion.*

*The Sixth Marine M.P. Battalion barracks on Saipan, 1944–1945.*

managed to get ashore only by rubber boats and being very careful. During our landing one of the boats was overturned by the waves. There must have been half a dozen Marines in it, and they all lost their weapons. We did eventually get most of our people ashore and formed up a skirmish line. We were told that there were Japanese soldiers but we didn't come across any that first day. However, we did find some evidence that they were there. They had some gardens and there was a radio tower on the summit which the Navy had periodically shelled.

That night we made camp in a cave close to the water. Over the next few days we organized patrols made up of NCOs and a half dozen Marines to go around the island and see if we couldn't find these Japanese troops. I was fortunate enough not to run into any, but one of the patrols did find a bunch of them in a cave. They wouldn't surrender so the Marines flipped a few grenades in and killed about six of them.

It was too hot in the cave where we had set up camp so we moved the camp closer to the summit near where the Japanese had their radio tower. One night one of our troops was standing guard duty around our perimeter when he heard movement just outside our camp. Robert Hopper, who was standing guard, saw a Japanese man coming toward his position. Hopper had a Japanese-English dictionary with him and used it to try and talk to this Japanese by flashlight while at the same time trying to keep an eye on this guy. By then a couple of other Marines had come up to see what was going on. I was up in that radio tower while all this was going on and all I could see was a few heads moving around, and this flashlight. The Japanese man surrendered and over the next couple of days more of them came in to surrender. I guess they saw the good treatment that the first one had received. A few days later we were shooting craps with these Japanese soldiers. Here were these Marines who had been through combat and all the killing that went with it, sitting on this island shooting craps with the enemy.

A few more days of patrols turned up Japanese soldiers who had committed suicide. With us was a Nisei from Hawaii who served as our interpreter. In talking to the captives he determined that there was only one more Japanese soldier left on Maug, and since we were unable to find him we assumed that he too had committed suicide someplace where we couldn't locate his body. After raising the American flag over the island we departed Maug and headed back to Saipan.

Much of what we did on Saipan was uneventful after our adventures in the northern islands. We pulled a lot of guard duty. Some did road patrols in Jeeps. Some guarded the Red Cross compound, others the nurses' compound. One of my duties was guarding Japanese POWs who were sent out on work crews. Each of us was assigned ten prisoners and we would take them out on a work detail. The work was monotonous; the days were ten and twelve hours long. Usually we got the same group of prisoners every day so I got to know some of them pretty well. Most of them I enjoyed being with; I can't remember any of them giving me any problems. One of them was a sergeant in the Japanese Army, and his name was Saito. He could speak a little English so I let him pass out the work orders to the rest of the crew. The Japanese prisoners I worked with were amazed at all of the trucks and heavy equipment they saw driving by every day.

Most of the time I took my prisoners to work at a

lumberyard run by black army troops. The officers were all white and they would drive down to the lumberyard every once in a while to see how things were going. They didn't seem to spend much time with the black enlisted men. On occasion one of them would have an Army nurse in the Jeep with him. One time a Japanese prisoner sidled up to me. He looked over at the officer and the nurse sitting beside him and said, "In the Japanese Army everybody had women, not just the officers."

On the last day of the war I was down at the lumberyard with my prisoners. We had received word that the war was over and all the ships in the harbor started running up signal flags and blowing their whistles. Of course this got the attention of the POWs I was guarding. They stared out at all the activity. After a minute or so one of them came up to me and asked what was going on. I said, "War is over. Japan and United States no longer fighting." He looked at me for a few seconds then smiled and said, "Oh, Tojo and FDR now buddy-buddy."

In looking back and remembering the dropping of the atomic bomb — the only comment I remember was, "Well, this will end the war sooner." So a few Japs got killed; well, we were killing them anyway. We all believed it was the right thing to do, and if it was going to get us out of there and back home without us having to go back into combat we were all for it. I have no respect for those people who were not involved with what was going on in those days— those second guessers who never heard a shot fired in anger and never had to crawl through the mud and blood.

## Marines Don't Cry in Public

### Robert Roland

*Mr. Robert Roland was born and raised in Alexandria, Virginia. He graduated from high school in February 1943. His two older brothers, Dick and Lacey, enlisted in the Marine Corps shortly after Pearl Harbor. Mr. Roland followed their example and headed for Marine Corps boot camp in January 1944, and served with the Fifth Marine MP Battalion on Saipan. Mr. Roland is a retired United Airlines pilot.*

Although dates, times, and names have slipped from my memory over the years, there are certain events I will never forget. When I arrived by bus at Parris Island, South Carolina, for Marine Corps boot camp we were greeted by a sergeant, a Pfc., and a corporal. The sergeant, we found out quickly, was the chief drill instructor of our platoon. His name was Tuxberry. He was a small, skinny runt of a guy and had already done a tour of duty in the Pacific, which he quickly let us know. He was the most foul-mouthed man I have ever met. There were about thirty of us "shitheads," as Tuxberry labeled us, and I will never forget his words to us as we stood there that first day. He said, and I quote, "All you sons-of-bitches may have given your souls to Jesus Christ before arriving here, but there is one thing you better God damn well get through your thick skulls, and that is as long as you are on this fucking island your asses belong to me."

Sergeant Tuxberry wasn't kidding. Boot camp was a hell hole as any Marine who went through Parris Island knows. Before it was over I just knew that if ever I got into combat and Tuxberry was there I was going to shoot him in the back. But in retrospect, I came to see that Tuxberry was just doing his job. He hardened us up and got us ready to go off and kill people we didn't know.

It was early July 1944, after more advanced training at Camp Lejeune and Camp Pendleton, that we left aboard ship from California. Throughout the month-long voyage no one would tell us where we were going. It was easy to see by the wake of the ship that we were zig-zagging our way across the Pacific.

The shipboard routine was the same, day in and day out — sleep, eat, play poker on deck, exercise twice a day, senseless guard duty, and salt water showers with a soap that never lathered. Only as the island of Saipan came into view were we officially informed of our destination.

I don't know what happened to everybody who was on that ship, but a hell of a lot of us got off on Saipan. I was with Al Rohr and Dick Lowe, two men I had become good friends with while at Camp Pendleton in California. We became known as the "Three Musketeers," but it was always in the back of our minds that somewhere along the line the Marine Corps was going to split us up, because the Marine Corps can't stand the idea of three guys being happy together. That was our thinking, that somebody would split us up.

After disembarking on Saipan we were taken by truck from Tanapag Harbor over to the east side of the island to a place called Kagman Point. All around us, all we could see were tents. Among the more interesting aspects of those first weeks and months for Al, Dick, and me was talking to those Marine vets who had not only fought on Saipan, but had been involved in other operations. Of course, all of us replacements were as green as could be and had never looked another man in the eye with the intent of shooting him. However, we fully expected to be involved in future combat-related operations and wanted to know what it was like. Our questions often went like this: "Were you scared the first time you saw combat? How scared? What did it feel like when you saw a buddy killed?" Then, there was the question we asked most often — "What was it like to kill your first Jap?"

On one occasion we took a work detail out to the northern part of the island — Marpi Point. By that time we all knew about the mass suicides that took place there, where Japanese jumped to their deaths. Lt. Killick, who was also on his first tour of duty in the Pacific, was in charge of the detail. He decided we should all go and take a look over the cliffs. Some of the men who were with us on that detail were men who had fought with the Second Marine Division all the way up the island. They told us how loudspeakers had been set up to try and stop the Japanese civilians from jumping. We walked over to the edge where we could look to the rocks below. It was quite far down and I was sure I could see body parts lying among the rocks. It left me with a sickening feeling because we were told that not only had Japanese soldiers committed suicide there, but civilians had also committed suicide, including women holding babies in their arms. That gave me a deep feeling of sadness as I stood there.

I can only describe those first few months on Saipan as endless hours of boredom. I spent much of my time on guard duty around the perimeter — guard duty around the island, and guarding different compounds, especially supply compounds, because we were having trouble with Japanese stragglers breaking in and stealing supplies.

I also spent quite a bit of time guarding Jap prisoners. Most of them were easy to get along with, even likable. But there was this one POW I came to call the "Okinawan Kid." He was an arrogant S.O.B. He said he was a pilot and that he had shot down Americans, and he had been shot down himself there near the harbor on Saipan. He boasted about all the American planes he had shot down, and used his hands to show how he did it. He would say "Americans," then spin his hand down to show a plane crashing. This started to get to me. There was a part of me that admired him because he had the guts to express himself where the others didn't. But one day I had him and some other prisoners cleaning out a drainage ditch, and he had a shovel. Again, he started making remarks to the other prisoners, and I sensed that he was saying something about me. I went over to him and he gave me one of his shit-eating grins, so I started baiting him. I told him what I was going to do to his mother and sisters, if he had any. I went on and on, and I said, "If you're married, you know your wife is banging every Japanese soldier she can find." I did everything I could to get him to react.

Finally, I could see I was getting to him. He started to lift his shovel and I took my carbine and smashed him on the side of the head. He wasn't so boastful after that.

Finally, word came down that we had been attached to the Second Battalion, Eighth Marines, Second Marine Division. Now, we felt like we belonged to something, where before we had felt like transients.

Again the "Three Musketeers" survived. We were still together and managed to get our own tent. A fourth guy tried to work his way in with us, but we managed to keep him out. Off to one side of our tent I put a desk. We started fixing it up like it was home. However, we still felt like we were in a replacement battalion. Then, we finally got what we wanted. We were told that an MP Battalion was being formed — a military police battalion — and we were going to be a part of it. All three of us were put in C Company of the Fifth Marine MP Battalion.

The Fifth Marine MP Battalion — what an outfit! Among our duties was patrolling the island, investigating thefts, and hunting down Japanese stragglers still hiding out in the jungle. Most of the stragglers seemed to have moved up toward the northern end of the island. Some of the thickest jungle was up there, and there were lots of caves. In looking for them we would usually go out early in the morning, coming back the next afternoon — spending one night in the jungle. Most of the time these searches were uneventful.

There was one foray when Al and I were together, but Dick was back at the camp. I never thought we were going to see a Jap out there. I had by that time been on five or six forays and hadn't seen anything or anybody. This trip was to be different. It was just before dark and time to bed down. We were sitting around eating our cold C rations, and preparing to sit it out for the night. The whole platoon was pretty well dispersed, but Al and I were sitting on an embankment that led down to a creek. On the far side of that stream were some coral cliffs. Al and I were just sitting there talking in low voices. Al was a smoker and had just about gotten me hooked on cigarettes. He pulled out a cigarette and handed it to me, and as trained, we cupped them in our hands so the light wouldn't show too far away. This was just about as the sun was going down. Suddenly, there was a burst of gun fire. From the other side of the creek came a stream of tracer bullets. Fortunately, they were a little high — just above our heads. A Marine knows that every fourth or fifth round is a tracer, and as we saw them coming toward us it was as if they were in slow motion. They didn't seem to be moving at the speed of a bullet. Then we heard the plop of rounds hitting the embankment above our heads— maybe three feet above our heads. Without a word, Al and I dove head first down the embankment. There was a fallen tree — an old rotten tree we were trying to hide behind. I could feel Al's head pushing up against my feet as if to make me move up a little bit so he could get the rest of his body behind that log. There was no more shooting after that first burst of gun fire. We laid there for a few hours. Then about midnight we heard a single shot. I slept fitfully behind that log for the rest of the night. I really wasn't frightened; I don't know why.

When I awoke around day break, Al was gone. Then I heard voices coming from above, so I got my gear together and crawled back up the embankment. Most of my platoon was gathered around something on the ground. I shoved my way in to see what everybody was looking at, and there was a dead Japanese soldier. He was lying flat on his back with both arms spread-eagled and his head rolled over to the left side. The entire right side of his skull had been removed as if a surgeon had done it with a saw. It was like looking at an oyster shell holding the grey matter. And in his brains was a smoldering cigarette butt. When I saw that my first thought was, "I hope Al didn't do that." I would have guessed that the dead Japanese was only about fourteen years old and there he lay dead. My thoughts turned to some mother back in Japan who would receive word that her son had been killed in battle. Then one of the Marines, who I found out later had been through other campaigns, reached over and roughly grabbed the Japanese soldier by the belt and ripped his shirt off. Somebody said, "What are you looking for?" And he said, "I'm looking for a money belt. Japs always carry money belts." Well, this Jap didn't. Another Marine veteran of combat saw that the dead soldier had some gold teeth, so he took the butt of his rifle and banged him on the jaw, hoping to extract the gold teeth. Whether he did or not I don't know, because at that point I turned around and walked away. I went over to where I thought no one would see me and sat down. Although my eyes were dry, inside my heart was wrenching, not at seeing the dead soldier but at seeing the way some of my comrades had treated that dead body. That bothered me a great deal.

Pretty soon Al came over and sat down beside me and put his arm around my shoulder. He knew what I was feeling. When I turned to look at Al he had tears running down his face.

On another patrol, in the middle of the day, while coming across a clearing we saw what looked like a woman waving a white flag. Nobody got excited because it was obvious that it was a woman, but we were careful — you never knew. She made it obvious that there was something she wanted to tell us but she couldn't speak English, so the lieutenant assigned three or four guys to take her back to camp. An interpreter was brought in and as the story goes this woman said she was with a group of about twenty Japanese who wanted to surrender, but before surrendering they wanted to have one last party. She wanted the Marines to provide the beer and sake or whatever, along with some other things. The Marines were to leave all this at an appointed place in the jungle, then on the day after their party they would meet at this jungle clearing and surrender. Well, somebody higher up must have approved of this because on the next day all these supplies were taken into the jungle and dropped off. Then the next day, at the appointed place, they surrendered.

It was about this time that some of us were asked if we would like to go on an operation to some of the islands north of Saipan. Dick Lowe and I volunteered. Al had some other duties and couldn't go. This operation, I found out later, was arranged by a Lt. Colonel Chalfant III. We were an entire company of men, probably 100 to 130 men under the command of a captain. We landed on Anatahan without opposition. The whole operation was looked upon as a joke. Some of the men were asking, "Why do we want to come here? Why take a chance? These islands were bypassed. If there are any Japs, they aren't going anywhere." Well, nobody had any answers. We wasted an entire day there and we saw neither hide nor hair of them, so we headed back to Saipan.

A couple of days later I heard that Lt. Col. Chalfant had conducted an unauthorized operation. Not only had he put men at risk, but there was not one medical officer attached to that group and I think that is what got him in trouble more than anything else. All of a sudden Lt. Col Chalfant wasn't around any more. Nearly fifty-four years passed before I learned that Chalfant had been court-martialed and separated from the Marine Corps.

Many years later, in a book store, I came across a book called *The Lost Men of Anatahan*. I came home and read the book in one sitting. It turns out the book was written by a Japanese man who was on Anatahan the day we landed. In the book he makes fun of this contingent of Marines that had invaded their island. It was not until 1951 that those few Japanese inhabitants of Anatahan were taken off the island by the U.S. Navy. In 1999 I was put in touch with the Navy commander who "rescued" them.

It was right after the Fifth MP Battalion was formed that I met a guy from Islay Field (now Aslito Airport) who told me that a certain bomber wing, whose number I can't remember, was over on Tinian. I had gone to high school and played basketball with a young boy named Eugene Barry. We were pretty close and we had double dated a lot. Gene had gone into the Air Force pilot training program, but for whatever reason he didn't make it and had ended up in gunnery school. This chance meeting with this Air Force guy taught me that Gene's outfit, B-29s, was over on Tinian. It took me about a month or so, but I managed to hitch a ride over to Tinian. I located his outfit, but Gene was out on a bombing raid, so I had to come back to Saipan without seeing him. We finally got together on Tinian at a later date and it was quite a reunion. We spent the entire day together. About a month had passed and I received one more letter from Gene. I wrote back and told him I was going to come back at the first opportunity. When I went back I discovered that Gene had disappeared while on a raid over Tokyo. His B-29 was shot up pretty bad. According to other air crews who saw his plane go down it had a couple of engines gone. They saw his plane ditch in the ocean and that is the last that anybody ever heard of Gene Barry. It took me a week before I was emotionally able to write a letter to his folks back home.

Many years later, when I was a pilot for United Airlines, I was on a layover flight to Hawaii. My wife was with me on this trip and we drove to Punch Bowl Cemetery where I had been several times before. On previous visits I spent my time walking among the headstones, reading the inscriptions. This time, however, I walked over to a bronze-granite wall that I hadn't paid much attention to on my previous visits. After only a few minutes I saw the name Sgt. Eugene Barry. At that moment a thousand thoughts coursed through my mind as I remembered our times together, both in peace time and war. Sensing what I was feeling, my wife walked up behind me and put her arms around my waist as I tried to sneak the tears away from my cheeks.

When I first arrived on Saipan in August of 1944 I was not aware that my two older brothers were on their second tours of duty in the Pacific. As I came to find out later, Lacey had been on Tinian with the Fourth Marine Division, and Dick, the oldest, had been with the Third Marine Division on Guam. After Tinian, Lacey went home and that would be the end of the war for him. However, Dick later became part of the newly formed Sixth Marine Division. He was wounded on Okinawa and received a medical discharge.

One day Al and I were sent out on patrol and Dick [Lowe] had the day off. We encountered some Japanese stragglers and there was some gun fire, but the only casualty was a sergeant who was shot through the hand. When we got back we didn't see Dick around. We went to the mess hall to eat that evening and still couldn't find him. He didn't come back to the tent that night, so we went to headquarters around midnight and reported it to the Officer of the Day. The O.D. said there wasn't much they could do about it that late at night, but if he didn't show up by morning they would start a search for him. The next day Dick still wasn't there. His bed hadn't been slept in. Somebody said they had seen Dick thumbing a ride on the Cross Island Road that ran near our camp, so the search began in that area. They had quite a few men out and found nothing that first day. It was the following day that they were working the cliff area just north of Kagman when one of the search parties found Dick's body. He had been walking along a narrow stretch of beach. It looked like he had climbed down the rocks to get there. He must have been shot by a Jap straggler. He had been hit once in the head and once in the shoulder.

We had all been together since we first arrived at Camp Pendleton. I remember when Lacey once wrote to me and said, "Bobby, never get too close to anybody. That way it won't hurt so bad if they get killed." Now, I knew more than ever what he meant, because Al and I wept in our own separate ways— not in front of anybody because Marines don't cry in public. They only cry in private.

My brother Dick came home from the war a different person. He came back with what we today call

Post Traumatic Stress Syndrome. In those days we called it "Gone Asiatic." He was a different person altogether — short of temper; totally unlike the person he was before the war. I used to watch him come into his house and if there was a piece of lint on the floor he would go through the roof. Sometimes he would walk into the house, and in the old Marine Corps tradition, run his hand above the door sill, and if he found dust he yelled at his wife. And his wife, Rose, was a wonderful woman. I had some encounters with him and they weren't very nice. Sometimes I would say to him, "This is not the God damn Marine Corps. These people aren't your butt privates and boot recruits. These people are your wife and children and you better start getting your act together!" He never did get his act together, and in 1960 on a lonely hilltop not far from his house he sat in the front seat of his car and put a 20-gauge shotgun to his chest and ended it all. The war was finally over for him.

My other brother, Lacey, wrote to me once during the war that while he was on Guadalcanal, he and another Marine had thrown a Jap prisoner out of a Jeep and killed him. They then went to the officer in charge and told him that the prisoner had tried to escape and they had to kill him. That bothered me when I read this. That was my brother telling me this.

Many years later, while I was still flying for United, I would try to visit Lacey about twice a year. The war seldom came up in our conversations but it did on this one visit. For whatever reason, I reminded him of that letter he wrote to me about throwing the Jap out of the Jeep and killing him. I didn't get any real response from him, but as I continued to talk about it tears started to flow down his face. I sat quiet for a minute or so. Then he looked at me and said, "You know, Bobby, that has bothered me all of my life. Since I left the Corps, that man has crossed my mind a thousand times, and I don't feel good about what I did to him." I never brought the subject up again. Lacey died three years later.

# Mr. Leary

Carl Matthews

*Carl Matthews was born in Texas in 1924. He wears a Purple Heart for wounds he received during the battle for Saipan. After World War II he went to Howard Payne University in Brownwood, Texas. Over the years he has held a number of positions, from Baptist missionary to mental health planner. He now lives in Roswell, Georgia, and is involved in his church and other community activities.*

My son was in his thirties when he came to me one day and said, "Dad, you named me after your friend Leary but you never told me much about him." Mark was right. I had named him Mark Leary Matthews, but I had not talked in depth to anyone about the time I had spent with his namesake in the United States Marine Corps during World War II.

Morning roll call had sounded at Camp Pendleton, California, that fall morning in 1943 and the men from Company G, 23rd Regiment, Fourth Marine Division, emerged from the large green barracks that we called home. Hard training had been the order of the day for too many long days, but the time would come when we would be thankful for every hour spent learning how to stay alive. The second platoon had been without a leader for several weeks, but we had been informed that a new platoon commander was to be presented at roll call. The Company Commander, Captain Frank W. Snepp, came forward to introduce several new officers who would be serving in various capacities in the company. It was obvious that they had all recently completed Officers Candidate School — all second lieutenants — all in new uniforms — all closely cropped hair — all ramrod straight. The captain introduced James Stanley Leary, Jr. It was announced that Second Lieutenant Leary was to be assigned to the second platoon as a permanent platoon leader. We were glad to have someone on board on a permanent basis, but our minds were filled with apprehension as we observed this new officer. Did he really know anything, coming to us without any experience? The answer would come in the weeks to follow. We began to live by the book. Mr. Leary was determined to impose on the second platoon every rule and regulation that Officers Candidate School in Quantico, Virginia, had ever mentioned.

Mr. Leary was not quite twenty-three years old but he tried to give the impression that he was much older and wiser. He gave commands in the deepest voice he

*Second Lieutenant James Stanley Leary. Photograph taken at Camp Maui, Hawaii. Mr. Leary's body was never recovered. Two other Marine Corps officers lost their lives in attempts to recover Mr. Leary's remains. The company eventually bypassed the area and there are no official records indicating cause of death or disposition of remains.*

could produce — words clipped and crisp. He was determined to do everything absolutely right, so much so that what he tried to do, at times, was amusing. However, we didn't laugh. We recognized that he was frightened by his new command and we were going to give him the benefit of the doubt.

Initially, he kept his distance from members of the platoon. After all, officers were not supposed to fraternize with enlisted men, or so they taught at Quantico. So he did his thing and we did ours until we began overnight field maneuvers. Then we had Mr. Leary all to ourselves, away from the Company Commander, away from the other officers. That was when his generous and gregarious nature, bottled up for days, exploded. He was our platoon leader and after a few days we were all his.

I had served as a runner when Lt. Baker was with the company and Mr. Leary retained me in that position. I was always close at hand should the platoon leader need me. We began to live in the field for what seemed like weeks, but after a few days we knew that we had been given one of the better platoon leaders. We learned that he did know many things about his work and what he didn't know he soon learned to ask our platoon sergeant, Jack Campbell. Sometimes he would even ask me. Soon he was just one of the guys in the platoon but he would quickly regain his military bearing when it was required.

We had the happiest platoon in the regiment. Life was hard but Mr. Leary made us see the funny side of even the most difficult moments. He made sure his men were not unfairly treated. He solved our problems and listened to our complaints. Again and again he went to bat on our behalf. And we gave him a little more than we would have given the average platoon leader.

On January 13, 1944, we boarded the USS *Sheridan* and sailed from San Diego for the Marshall Islands with a brief stopover in Hawaii. We were to assault Roi-Namur, two atolls that together covered less than one square mile. Captain Snepp, our company commander, said our company would be in the second wave and would land on the atoll called "Roi." Roi was five or six feet above sea level, completely flat and with large airplane hangars on the east side of the island. Landing strips crisscrossed the island, using up almost every square foot.

We secured Roi in eight hours, but days passed before all the Japanese snipers were purged from the concrete drainage system under the runways. G Company had sustained one death and a few wounded. The young man who was killed was John Howly from Pennsylvania. The fighting on Namur continued for another day or two, then we returned to the USS *Sheridan* and headed to the island of Maui. Maui would be our home for the next several months.

Training was intensified, and more time was spent in the field than in camp while on Maui. More and more Mr. Leary had me attend staff meetings with him, and I experienced a new sense of importance and self-worth by being present with this group composed mostly of officers. It was exciting and I was impressed. My admiration and appreciation for Mr. Leary grew with every day. He was truly a leader of men. He was quick to pick up on the total plan for an operation and grasped quickly his role in its execution. He became a role model for the men in the Second Platoon and for many others who knew him. He never smoked, never told dirty stories, and he never expected more from his men than he was willing to give himself. His spirit in the middle of adversity became contagious, and he built a platoon that could always come through difficult times.

On May 25, 1944, we left Hawaii aboard LSTs and troop ships like the USS *Sheridan*. The horizon was covered with more ships than I knew ever existed in the world. We had no idea where we were going, but we knew it was going to be a big operation. The next day we learned our objective would be the Mariana Islands and our specific objective was an island named Saipan. Our platoon was included in the first wave, attacking the center of the town called Chalan Kanoa. Our objective was to secure the town as quickly as possible and move to the foothills beyond, and eventually to the Japanese airfield.

The town of Chalan Kanoa was a cluster of concrete-walled buildings with metal roofs. There was a sugar cane field behind the town. The sugar cane had been harvested and was completely clear except for stubble. It extended for about five or six hundred yards to where the foothills began. It was five-thirty in the morning on June 15, 1944, when we entered the huge cavern in the bow of our LST and took our places in the amphibious tractors assigned to us. Mr. Leary checked each man, making sure he had all of his required gear. One by one each of the tractors lumbered towards the doors of the LST, down the ramp, and into the water.

It was almost daylight as we left the LST and began to make our way to the rendezvous point directly offshore from where our platoon was to land. The big Navy guns were now firing directly over our heads—round after round they fired, and we could see the explosions on the hillsides where they landed. Navy planes were bombing and strafing the beaches. This was D-Day and H-Hour was closing in fast.

We began our approach to the beach well out of range of the Japanese guns, but as we moved closer to the beach shells began to hit and explode in the water. I stood by Mr. Leary looking out at the operation and we had identified several landmarks that Intelligence had talked about. There was a tall smokestack to our left, just where it was supposed to be. Garapan was to the left of that, and Chalan Kanoa was straight ahead. We were on target.

I was watching as one of the amtracs on our left received a direct hit and disintegrated. Other shells were coming much too close to our own tractor. It was at that moment that I decided to do less looking and do some serious praying. I glanced behind me and there were several men — mean and ugly Marines— already on their knees, some with rosary beads in their hands and all with their heads bowed. I joined them without any embarrassment. My hand touched the New Testament in my breast pocket, wrapped securely in heavy plastic to guard against the water smashing over the side of the tractor. The fact that it was there gave me comfort.

Seven hundred tractors reached the beach in twenty minutes. By noon 8,000 Marines clung to a narrow beachhead, four miles long — one Marine for every 2'8". Our tractor soon reached shallow water, and moments later we were stopped on the beach just a few feet from the palm trees. We climbed over the sides of the tractors quickly for tractors were prime targets for the Japanese artillery. The beach was a madhouse with individual Marines trying to find cover. Artillery shells were landing and snipers were picking off Marines before they could leave the amphibious tractors. One little Marine, Tony Marriro, from New York didn't move quickly enough from where he lay in the sand and one of the tractors ran over his legs.

There was ample evidence that the Navy had bombed and shelled the area heavily, but there was evidence as well that there were quite a few Japanese still in defensive positions.

Our platoon quickly assembled and we began to make our way through the jungle-like area between the beach and the village of Chalan Kanoa. Frank Wittie, from Texas, with a wife and child, fell dead from a sniper bullet. We pushed on, pausing only for a moment of private grief. We had been trained not to assist those who had fallen. Snipers expected comrades to rush to the fallen — then they became targets as well. But we were alert for snipers. As quickly as they were discovered they were dispatched to their ancestors. We directed round after round into the tops of palm trees just in case snipers were there. Sometimes the rounds found their mark and we could see the sniper fall or dangle from a rope that held him in the tree.

We were clearing out the snipers as we moved through the village but the Japanese artillery located in the hills was pounding us without mercy. We were attempting to push our way through the heaviest of the artillery fire when we heard the sound of tanks. We had jumped across a ditch earlier and since we had no defense against tanks Mr. Leary ordered us back to that ditch. We had just reached the safety of the ditch and had barely caught our breath when the tanks came into view. They were our tanks. What a beautiful sight.

Encouraged by the arrival of our tanks we began to

make our way back to the point where we began our retreat. We passed Wittie, still lying where he had been hit. Three other men from our company — McDonald, Baxter, and Anderson — were all together and had received a direct hit from an artillery shell. One of the men had been an avid gambler and had won several hundred dollars while he was on the LST, but it wasn't going to be worth much to him, now. Navy corpsmen followed us and attended to the wounded as best they could.

By nightfall we were only 200 or 300 yards from the beach. We had gone through the village of Chalan Kanoa and were on the edge of the sugar cane field. The Japanese had constructed a large underground concrete bunker, and we set up our platoon command post there. A Marine artillery battalion landed and moved into position just to the rear of our right flank. I had mixed feelings about them being there. I knew we needed their help, but I also knew that when they began firing they would draw Japanese artillery fire in return. Fortunately, as the artillery dueled throughout the night no shells fell in our vicinity.

We could hear the action on our right flank where the Third Platoon had dug in for the night. The Japanese were attacking that area with cries of "Banzai, banzai!" followed by hand-to-hand combat. Several Marines died during the attack.

The Japanese artillery quieted during the early morning and we received word from battalion headquarters to move forward across the sugar cane field. The field was flat and there was absolutely no protection. Every Marine moving across that field would be exposed. However, when Mr. Leary gave the order to move out, we moved. Our objective was Aslito Airfield on the south end of the island. It was a miracle of God that we reached the cover of the foothills without any casualties. We had moved up the hillside to the first rise when we were advised that we had penetrated the line beyond the point where we were supposed to be and that we were to hold our position until further notice. We dug in and experienced light casualties from sniper and mortar fire. The wounded were evacuated by the Navy corpsmen. One corpsman by the name of Paige risked his life many times to attend the wounded. He was later killed on Tinian.

The Japanese tried to rush our position several times during the day, but we were well dug in and turned them back with each attempt. When night came we were concerned that a large Japanese force might attempt a banzai attack as had been the case with the Third Platoon the previous night. Most of us had not slept for forty-eight hours and we needed some rest. We took turns watching and listening so that we could get some sleep. One of the Japanese wounded was not far in front of our lines and he moaned and screamed throughout the night. One man in our platoon yelled, "Will someone please shoot that son-of-a-bitch so I can get some sleep?" The moaning and screaming stopped before dawn and we assumed the poor soul had died.

We were ordered to move out early the following morning and learned that our objective had been changed. We were told other units had caught up with us and that we were to secure the middle of the island, cutting the Japanese off from the airfield.

We began a push over the hills in the center of the island. One of our first objectives was to take some heavy gun emplacements that Intelligence had detected from aerial photographs taken prior to the invasion. We expected heavy resistance as we made our way in that direction but much to our surprise Japanese resistance weakened. We moved cautiously until we came to the first gun emplacement. It was no gun at all. It was an elaborate wooden imitation of a sixteen inch gun, complete with grey paint and camouflage nets. That was fine with us because it gave us a few hours without casualties.

Orders came to regroup and form a line across the middle of the island and begin a concentrated push towards the northernmost tip of the island. G Company was positioned almost in the center and it appeared that the rugged terrain in front of us would not be simple to take from the Japanese. We dug in and rested for a day while other units were getting into position.

Once the other troops were in place we began the push north, a move that would force the Japanese towards the high cliffs located there. The native Chamorros began to appear in ones, twos, threes, and even whole families with small children. I thought they would run back but they were hungry and thirsty and when we motioned for them to come to us, they did. We moved them out of the line of fire and into a depression where we shared our rations with them.

One Marine company discovered some Chamorros in a cave and counted more than 100 individuals as they

Opposite, top: *Taken from Agingan Point, this photograph shows the part of the western reef and the lagoon where members of the Fourth Marine Division came ashore on 15 June 1944, a week after the landings in Normandy.* Opposite, bottom: *A Fourth Marine Division tank — one of several that didn't make it ashore on 15 June 1944. It still stands abandoned off the coast of Saipan.*

came out. All Chamorros were taken behind our lines and interrogated. We were told that Japanese soldiers were often found in these groups and that the natives were usually quick to expose them.

Casualties were frequent and the push through the rugged terrain of the mountains became more difficult. The valleys in the mountains were dotted with little farms and farm houses and we often came across animals that had been left behind. One by one men in our platoon were killed or wounded, but some deaths affected us worse than others. Bob Howard, a young boy from New York, was hit. The sniper who shot him was quickly discovered and killed. Then we ran to where Howard lay on the ground beside a little farm house. He was conscious, but everyone including Howard was aware of the severity of his wound. Mr. Leary told Howard that he was going to be all right, but Howard looked up and told Mr. Leary that his wound was bad and said, "Mr. Leary, I don't want to die. I'm too young to die." He was dead two or three minutes later. I had never seen Mr. Leary so shaken. He walked behind the farm house for a few moments, and I was crying too.

It was the next morning and we still hadn't received orders to move out when Mr. Leary said, "Carl, why don't you read us something from that New Testament you carry." I didn't know much about scripture or where to look for special words of comfort and encouragement, but the New Testament included the Book of Psalms and I had memorized the Twenty-third Psalm during vacation Bible school in Dawson, Texas, many years earlier. I knew where to find that and I began to read. The fellows nearby stopped talking and it was as if we were having a service. When I had finished nobody prayed an audible prayer but the Lord was listening that morning from some hard Marines engaging in silent petition.

The mountains were filled with small caves, crevasses, ravines, and all sorts of places to hide. We began using flame throwers in places where we knew the Japanese might be. I always felt bad when the Japanese would run out of the holes, almost naked but with

*The north end of Saipan — Banzai Cliff— where many Japanese men, women, and children were pushed or jumped to their deaths rather than risk capture by American forces.*

fuel and fire from the flame throwers covering their bodies, screaming and dying. But if we had given them half a chance we would have been the ones dying.

We had used mortars very effectively and at times were assisted by our artillery located far behind us. Then they brought up a new weapon, rockets mounted on the rear of a vehicle. We were experiencing some resistance one day when one of these rocket units pulled up. Once they were in position twenty or thirty rockets shot out into the air. Another group captured a Japanese officer who spoke a little bit of English. He said he would have killed himself rather than be captured except for the fact that he wanted to see that automatic artillery.

Almost fifteen days had passed since we had landed on the beach at Chalan Kanoa. We changed socks regularly, washing them whenever possible and dried them on the run, but we had no chance to change our dungarees. Most of us had begun to lose weight and we were all bone tired. Then one day we received some good news. The U.S. Army was coming to relieve us. We held our positions and here they came. Their uniforms were clean. They had blankets and an extra pair of shoes. Most Marines just had a poncho and some extra socks.

Once relieved by the Army we marched down to the beach where we washed our dirty dungarees in the surf. After resting on the beach for a while we put on our wet uniforms and retraced our steps back to the foothills to bed down for the night. Led by Mr. Leary, we all helped ourselves to some "Ten-in-one Rations" stockpiled for the Army troops. We were in a guarded perimeter and could sleep all night without interruption, and not in foxholes. We were told that we could remain there for three days of rest. We were preparing breakfast the next morning when we were told to prepare to move out. Why? Because the Japanese had broken through the positions we had left with the Army, and we were needed to plug the gap.

We pushed hard to reach the positions we had left but when we got there everything was relatively quiet. The Army, however, had hardly taken any new ground. They were right where we had left them and they were firing their weapons like crazy. I stood there for several minutes just watching. I wondered what their target might be. I couldn't see anything in the direction they were firing. I asked one of the Army men what they were firing at and he said, "I don't know." Then I said, "Then why are you firing if you don't know what you are firing at?" He replied that an officer had told him to set up position and start firing. Marines never would have wasted ammo like that.

The Army packed up their shoes, blankets, ponchos, extra dungarees, and all the other gear they carried up there and left. We never saw them again, but we never left the line again either.

The men of Mr. Leary's platoon learned to rely on each other completely. Once, several men from our platoon being led by Mr. Leary were moving along a dry creek bed. The banks were sometimes eight to ten feet high. We made our way along cautiously, ever on the lookout for the enemy. Mr. Leary and I were in the lead. The balance of the patrol was following. All had been quiet since we had left our position. Suddenly, that ended with the sound of an automatic weapon firing at the end of our group. We had unknowingly passed a small cave in the side of the creek bed. It harbored several Japanese and when we passed them they came out and prepared to open fire on us. Fortunately for us, a young man from Harrison, Missouri, named Lawrence D. Vanzant had lagged behind. He saw the Japanese as they emerged from the cave and opened fire with his BAR. He fired one clip into the Japanese who had emerged from the cave and a second clip into the cave itself. Vansant saved the lives of several or perhaps all of the men in that patrol by his quick action. Mr. Leary praised him and told me he was going to recommend Vansant for a commendation. But Mr. Leary never lived to write up that commendation and Vansant was killed on Iwo Jima.

Enemy resistance increased as we progressed up the backbone of the island. By this time the airfield at the south end of Saipan was in operation and air support became available from that point on. We had large pieces of brightly colored oilcloth that were spread in front of our lines when air strikes were scheduled. The pilots could easily see the bright hues of the oilcloth from the air and would strafe or bomb the enemy, sometimes just a few yards in front of the oilcloth panels. Artillery battalions constantly shelled all suspected enemy positions. In addition, G Company had a very efficient mortar squad that could place live rounds in areas close to our positions. The artillery would at times fire anti-personnel shells that were set to explode over enemy positions, raining sharp pieces of shrapnel on whoever was below.

One day we called for artillery support and that meant we were to hold our positions. That was always a good time to rest or grab a bite to eat. I was sitting with my back against a tree when the first rounds of anti-personnel rounds began to explode. All of a sudden I heard a whoosh and a thump, and there at my side was a large piece of shell about six inches in length. I

*Taken from Mt. Tapochau, this view shows the landing beaches of the Fourth Marine Division with Lake Susupe in the foreground and Tinian in the distance.*

reached over to pick it up and quickly dropped it. It was still hot.

We continued to move through the rugged terrain of the mountains and were now near the ridge that ran north of Mt. Tapochau. Our platoon was on the right flank of the Twenty-third Regiment, and the Twenty-fifth Regiment was supposed to maintain contact with us to prevent enemy infiltration of our lines. One day, in extremely difficult terrain, the two points widened until we were perhaps 200 to 300 yards apart. Word came to close that existing gap but we didn't have sufficient manpower. Our company's strength was probably half of what it was when we first hit the beach. Mr. Leary told me to send a message up to the Twenty-fifth. I had my semaphore flags and Mr. Leary suggested that I use them. I responded that signal flags would probably draw fire. He responded that we didn't have any alternative. I stood up and started to wig-wag. I got out probably one wig and one wag before the Japanese started to fire. I was on my way to the ground before the bullets had a chance to arrive, pausing long enough to throw those flags as far as I could.

Mr. Leary then decided that I would have to go personally and convey the message to the Twenty-fifth and inform them of our position and lack of strength. I chose a ravine that offered some degree of protection and headed in the direction of the Twenty-fifth. I was really frightened. The ravine ended much too soon and I was faced with having to cover several yards of open area that offered no protection at all. Two men that Mr. Leary sent along with me ran first without drawing any fire. Then it was my turn. The first two men must have alerted Japanese in the area because they started firing at me as soon as I reached the exposed area. Bullets were kicking up dirt all around my feet, but my feet were moving too fast to be hit.

When we reached the colonel in command of the Twenty-fifth my adrenaline was squirting by the gallon. I was breathless and shaking like a leaf. I will never forget the gentleness of that colonel. He said, "Son, just sit down here for a minute before you tell me why you're here." He handed me his canteen and after I took a sip of water I gave him the message. Then I led a reserve company back to our position by another route.

*One of the few remaining large caliber Japanese guns (believed to be a 155mm) still in place on Saipan. It was guns like this that caused more than 2,000 American casualties on the first day of fighting on Saipan. Of the more than 700 LVTs used for landing troops and equipment on Saipan, more than 200 were lost — many as the result of the accurate fire laid down by these big Japanese field pieces.*

Near noon a few days later we had pushed across relatively easy terrain and taken up position in a rather large gully which looked across a large expanse of farmland. On the far side of the field there was a large grove of tall palm trees with heavy vegetation underneath. Our move into that position had been very quiet and few shots had been heard. We were there for some time waiting for other units to get into position. The distance from the gully to the palm trees was perhaps 150 to 200 yards.

We received orders to move out and began making our way across the open field. We were probably two-thirds of the way across the field when we began to receive heavy fire. Men fell right and left. Those of us who could raced for the shelter and safety of the gully where we had been. Wendal Nightengale, my buddy, a BAR man and tent mate, was one of those hit. He was trying to get up and make it to the gully. Before I could think of what to do Richard Freeby dropped his rifle and went racing across the field against the hail of bullets. He began pulling Nightengale towards the gully when additional shots hit Nightengale. Nightengale was killed and we watched as Freeby ran back to the gully. He was not hit but his backpack was riddled with bullets, and he cried. That was the greatest act of bravery I had ever seen or ever hoped to see. He later received the Silver Star for valor.

Death had come to every platoon in G company that day. Mortar squads lobbed one shell after another into that palm grove. Tears were mixed with sweat as they dropped the rounds into the mortar tubes. Artillery was summoned and soon they had shells screaming overhead and landing in the palm trees. When the shelling stopped we were given the signal to again attack the palm grove. The remaining men of G Company raced over the bodies of their comrades who laid in the open field, swearing vengeance with every step. Every bush that moved became the recipient of hundreds of rounds of small arms fire. One Japanese emerging from a hole in the ground was forced back in by the bullets hitting his body. It was all over in a few minutes but we had all aged a lifetime.

We continued to push the Japanese further and further towards the northeast end of the island. The further we pushed them the more resistance they put up. It was almost dark when we took up position on the backside of a long ridge. We had experienced a series of bad days. More men had been killed and wounded. We received replacements but they couldn't produce the way the men who had trained together could. We had been a part of a team that had formed strong personal ties.

We had been on the island for almost three weeks and were becoming drained physically and emotionally. Small willow trees grew along the top of the ridge near where we had dug in and the Japanese kept raking the trees with machine gun fire throughout the night. When morning came the leaves from those trees covered the ground like snow.

Throughout the night we could also hear the Japanese talking on the opposite side of the ridge. We were well aware that there was a concentration of Japanese only a few yards in front of us. Later, when we were alone, I told Mr. Leary I didn't know if we would come through the next few hours alive. I also told him that I had come to appreciate him more than any man I had ever known. He expressed some words of appreciation and we shook hands.

It seemed like it took an eternity for daylight to come. There was something about the sun coming up that provided hope. One of our artillery units had sent a spotter up to us. He crawled up to the ridge just before an artillery barrage was to start. The spotter was on my right, on his stomach, talking on a field telephone. Mr. Leary was on my left. The spotter crawled a few feet to where he could peek over the ridge and spot the initial rounds. The first shots fired by our artillery were always fired well in front of our lines with subsequent rounds brought closer as the spotter directed. We heard the first round whoosh over head and explode. The spotter brought the next round back a few yards but still not close enough to hit the concentration of Japanese in front of us. The spotter called for another round and brought it back still closer. We didn't hear the whoosh of that one, but we felt the explosion just a few yards away. The round had almost made it over the top of the ridge but had, instead, landed in the middle of our position. My ears rang and I was dazed. The spotter was still on his stomach and his dungaree jacket was in shreds. The flesh on his back looked as if someone had run it through a meat grinder but he never ceased to give instructions. He redirected the fire and the Japanese forces felt the full impact of the barrage. They were either killed or routed.

The events that followed, for me, remain hazy. Later that day, or perhaps it was the following day, we were on a high plateau where there was a stone wall separating a large open field. The edge of the field dropped off sharply, perhaps by sixty or seventy degrees down to a relatively flat area that reached all the way down to the ocean. We rested for a time behind the stone wall, then moved across the open field without resistance. We began moving down the steep cliff, and still no resistance. We could see to the north for several hundred yards, and I had spotted a number of Japanese near a grove of trees. I watched them through my binoculars and pointed them out to Mr. Leary. They were officers in full uniform and swords, standing completely in the open. We hadn't received any fire for about thirty or forty minutes. Mr. Leary and I were talking when a burst of machine gun fire erupted. I instinctively fell to the ground. Somehow I knew Mr. Leary had been hit bad. J.P. North was just above us and I heard him call for a corpsman. I remember telling North it was too late for a corpsman, that Mr. Leary was dead.

My lights went out and did not come on again for eight days when I found myself on board a hospital ship, the USS *Samaritan*. My days on the hospital ship remain fuzzy. Some sailors were lifting weights above the wardroom. One of them dropped a heavy weight on the steel deck above and the explosive noise frightened me. I trembled and began to vomit.

Ten years would pass before I would learn some of what happened during those seven or eight days from July 8 to July 16 or 18. Frank Routh began to fill in the gaps for me during a reunion in 1955. After Mr. Leary's death he said that resistance on that slope became such that the company was forced to withdraw all the way back to the stone wall. Several attempts were made to reach Mr. Leary's body and remove it — not only his but several others. More men were killed in the attempt to recover the bodies. Routh said I had been collecting hand grenades at one point after the company had retreated to the stone wall and somebody noted that I was walking in the open field in the direction of the cliff. Several men called to me to come back, but to no avail. Routh said he ran after me, catching up with me in the middle of the field. He said he asked me what I was doing. I assured him that I knew where the machine gun was and that I thought I would go down and knock it out. Routh said I was fighting like a tiger as he struggled to restrain me. He said he eventually dragged me back to the company area, and after removing the hand grenades, turned me over to a Navy corpsman.

Physicians aboard ship and at the hospital in New Caledonia found that my left ear drum was ruptured, infected, and draining. They also thought I might have had some internal bleeding and a concussion. They informed me that my problems began back at the time of the blast from the artillery shell, but that I had been able to perform despite my injuries. The doctors indicated that I had bordered on emotional and physical collapse for several days, that the final fade-out was delayed by the fact that I had placed my total confidence in Mr. Leary. As long as he was leading I could function. When he was gone my mind moved into neutral. When my leader died, I gave up.

Mr. Leary was constantly on my mind. I wanted to convey my condolences to his family in North Carolina but could not bring myself to write what I wanted to say. Then, one day when I was home on hospital leave, I composed a brief letter to Mr. and Mrs. James Stanley Leary, Sr., in Ahoskie, North Carolina. I had completed my final effort on behalf of my deceased platoon leader. A few days passed and I received a letter from Mr. Leary's mother. She wanted to know more details. I just did not have the emotional strength to respond to her.

My new assignment was the Marine air base in Quantico, Virginia, and I reported there January 1, 1945. Meanwhile, Mrs. Leary waited for my response, which did not happen, and was not going to happen. She then addressed another letter to my mother, Mrs. Carl Matthews, Sr., in Hubbard, Texas. My mother responded and told Mrs. Leary that I had been assigned to the airbase in Quantico. A few days later I received a special delivery letter from Mrs. Leary. I then requested and received a long weekend pass. I took a bus to Ahoskie, North Carolina, arriving at ten in the evening. It was two in the morning before bedtime came. I was emotionally drained by then, but buoyed by the way Mrs. Leary sat straight in her chair, posing one soft question after another, always with a smile that seemed to say, "No matter what has happened I have peace within."

There were times when Mr. Leary would leave the room, always to return. The children, ages from seven to their early twenties, sat in silence. That night was the beginning of a wonderful relationship that was to last with Mr. and Mrs. Leary for almost forty years, and with the family to this very day.

# 7 The Army

## Military Intelligence Service Attached to the Twenty-Seventh Army Division

BENJAMIN HAZARD

*Professor Benjamin Hazard was born in South Lancaster, Massachusetts, in 1919. He was attending the University of California at Los Angeles when the United States entered World War II. He was two weeks short of graduating with a degree in chemistry when he entered the United States Army. He was in the Military Intelligence Service and was attached to the Twenty-seventh Infantry Division (Army) during the battle for Saipan. He is a retired East Asian history professor, and lives in San Jose, California.*

In junior high school, high school, and at UCLA some of my closest friends were Nisei. I became interested in learning the Japanese language, and while attending UCLA took adult education language classes at night for two years in order to learn Japanese. The classes were for three hours one night a week. Then in 1940 they saw the war coming at UCLA, and introduced the study of the Japanese language. I think that was the first time it was taught there, and I took the class. Our teacher was a young lady, a Kibei.* After Pearl Harbor, in January of 1942, she was relocated to an internment camp and a Korean man came to teach the class. All of my Nisei friends from California were evacuated to internment camps, also.

I was two weeks away from graduation when I went into the Army. That was December of 1942. I had a 2-S deferment, being that I was a chemistry major. That was considered a critical occupation back then. Two majors from the War Department were traveling through the United States, visiting all the institutions of higher learning where Japanese was taught, looking for Americans of non–Japanese ancestry who had some knowledge of Japanese. By that time I had four years of Japanese language training. So, they invited me to volunteer. I only had two more weeks before graduation, but the thing was, the war was going on and they needed people. My uncles had fought in World War I, my two grandfathers had fought in the American Civil War, and both sides of my family had fought in the American Revolution. I felt like Oliver Hazard Perry, "my country, right or wrong." Pearl Harbor made it awful easy for me.

I was recruited right into the Military Intelligence Service, and in January 1943 I was sent to Ann Arbor, Michigan, for an intensive course, which was supposed to be for a year. There were about 250 of us in my company. We were divided up into sections, eight men to a section, and we studied Japanese eight hours a day. We had a three-hour exam each Saturday. That was supposed to be for a year, but they needed bodies in a hurry, so after six months they took the top thirty-five people from the company. Most of them were sons of missionaries who had lived in Japan. I was one of the

**An American of Japanese ancestry who was born in the United States, went to school in Japan, then returned to the United States.*

*Second lieutenant Benjamin Hazard standing at the side of a captured Japanese truck. He is holding a captured Japanese sword and flag. The photograph was taken the day after the Gyokusai.*

few who wasn't. So, from Ann Arbor we were sent to Camp Savage in Minnesota. We were there for six months to learn military Japanese terminology and organization, and upon completion I received my commission.

I had high school and college ROTC, but after I enlisted in the Army I never received Basic Training. I could have used it on Saipan.

After I was commissioned I was sent to JICPOA (Joint Intelligence Center Pacific Ocean Area) in Hawaii. There I was interviewed, and since I was the best shot in the group, and because the Twenty-seventh Infantry Division was getting ready to go into action, I was told I would go with them because I could defend myself. That was the only reason. This was in April or May of 1944. I would meet the language detachment just once before we sailed for Saipan, and that was for a dry run of the division's assault landing we did on Maui. At that time I met the entire language team.* I could sense that team leader, Tim Ohta, particularly resented me coming there. I could understand that; here I was just out of school and he already had two operations under his belt, and I didn't know my way around.

We were broken up after that, and there would be two men to each regiment. Some of these men had been in combat before. They were all Nisei except me. They had been in two other operations, they knew their way around, and they were well received by the division. The tone was set by General Ralph Smith and Lieutenant Colonel Van Antwerp. The general said, "These are American citizens, and they are American soldiers. We will treat them as such." Plus, they had already earned the respect of the men in earlier operations, especially at Makin in the Gilbert Islands (now Kiribati).

The Nisei from Hawaii and the Nisei from the mainland were like two different ethnic groups. The Nisei from Hawaii did not speak English with the same fluency as the Nisei from the mainland states, and the Nisei from the mainland had their families in

*Tim Ohta, Hoichi Kubo, Nobuo Kishiue, William Nuno, Richard Mortisugu, Frank Mory, Joe Fujino, Larry Saito, Roy Higashi.*

internment camps, while the ones from Hawaii did not. I became very close to many of these men after the war, but not on Saipan because it was an officer–enlisted man sort of relationship then. I did sleep in the same tent with them after Saipan was secured to protect them from some of the American soldiers who might resent them. But, I was ordered out and told that it was not fitting for officers to be sleeping in the same tent with enlisted men.

When I first got to Saipan I didn't even know how to use a field telephone. When I first used a field telephone I could hear Major Herzog talking to me, but he couldn't hear me because I wasn't pressing the "butterfly lever." I didn't know this until I got back to division headquarters. That's no way to learn, plus I was under small arms fire at the time. I had not gone through basic training. This was O.J.T., on the job training.

I landed on Saipan on the 17th of June, 1944. We landed on the northern sector of the Fourth Marine Division. Our landing craft couldn't go right up to the beach, so we had to wade ashore and we were under mortar fire. I had never been under fire before. We got to the beach and dug in. I dug a foxhole that I thought was adequate, but that evening we were strafed by a Zero fighter, and I felt like I was on a pedestal. After the plane left I dug my foxhole down deeper until I couldn't look over the edge.

Division headquarters spent several days on the reverse slope of the bluff behind Agingan Beach while the

*Members of G-2 Section, Twenty-seventh Infantry Division (Army): Lt. Col. William M. Van Antwerp, G-2, is third from right, bottom row. Maj. Jacob H. Herzog, Assistant G-2, is second from right, bottom row. The Nisei linguists of Language Detachment attached to the G-2 Section were not present for this photograph. They were still with their assigned combat units, and at POW camps, interrogating prisoners. The photograph was taken at Magicienne Bay, Saipan, in July 1944.*

*A view of Death Valley, Saipan, where the Twenty-seventh Infantry Division (Army) took such heavy losses — as it looks today.*

165th Battalion was clearing Aslito Field. We pitched blackout tents for working at night. While there we came under artillery fire. The Japanese were walking it up toward us 50 meters with each jump. They walked it right up to division headquarters, and I thought the next barrage would be right on top of us. That is when it stopped. We were still there the next day when Major Herzog said to me, "We've taken Aslito Airfield, and I want you to take a squad from the recon platoon up there." We were going through the sugar cane fields, and there was a narrow gauge railroad there. I'm leading and think it is easier to walk along the railroad which was above the cane. This sergeant says, "Lieutenant, don't you think we should get off the skyline?" I allowed that he was right, so we went back into the cane. Again, this was something I should have learned in basic training, but I didn't have basic training.

On the way to Aslito we came across a Japanese man who had killed his baby son because he was told that the Americans would kill the child. I found out later that this man hung himself in remorse when he discovered that we weren't the demons the Japanese military made us out to be.

We got to Aslito Field and this Japanese fighter plane came in for a landing on it. Everybody opened up on it, including me, and the plane crashed towards the end of the runway. Believe it or not, the pilot survived. He had been told in Guam that the Japanese still held Aslito. He climbed out of the plane and became our prisoner.

Meanwhile, my mission was to look for documents. The Signal Corps had already strung wire from division headquarters to the Japanese command building at Aslito Field. The wire was wrapped around a concrete pillar. I was on the phone on the west side of the pillar and the concrete above my head was being chipped away by Japanese fire coming from the other side of the airfield. In that building I was able to get documents and airplane engine logs. I didn't know until after the war that the Army made a training film called "A Scrap of Paper," which was based on the fact that the examination of these engine logs in Hawaii showed that the engines on Japanese planes were breaking down because the ball bearings didn't have enough tungsten to harden the steel. This, in turn, led to the bombing of tungsten mines, and ball bearing factories as primary targets for B-29s. This was all based on those documents that I found.

I came back to division headquarters that evening, and was later sent to a road junction that lead to Kagman. By this time I was no longer with division headquarters. We were taking Japanese prisoners from two different regiments of the Twenty-seventh Division. I was just behind our advance units where I would do secondary interrogations of prisoners. The Nisei were doing the primary interrogations. Third interrogations were done at a POW camp in the rear. I had to be two miles away from division headquarters so that any escaped prisoners could not tell the Japanese where our division headquarters was. This was scary because here I was two miles away with only fourteen or fifteen MPs. Some of them were used to escort prisoners, so we were never at full strength. These MPs would make a sweep every morning of our area as soon as we got out of our foxholes, and almost inevitably they would kill some Japanese infiltrators. At night it was really hairy. One night a herd of oxen came through our area. We were wondering if the Japanese were driving them through.

While we were at this road junction several hundred Japanese cut off at Naftan Point made a breakout. Just behind us was a field hospital. Behind them was a Marine tank company. The tank company had been taken out of the front lines for rest. Anyway, there was a ding-dong of a firefight going on. The Marines were fighting from their foxholes. Fortunately, they had light machine guns on their tanks. I think that is what saved the men. Some of the fighting got down to entrenching tools when the Japanese got into their positions. Fortunately for the hospital, the Marines were between the Japanese and the hospital. That is what kept them from overrunning the hospital and us. The fourteen or fifteen of us—we wouldn't have been able to stop them.

The Japanese used to shell that road junction like clockwork, at ten in the morning and three in the afternoon. Right below us was a Marine Corps salvage dump. They had a master sergeant there who had won the Congressional Medal of Honor in World War I. The Marines had put him with the salvage dump in the rear to keep him from getting killed. He was one of their living treasures, so to speak. The Japanese houses had these concrete cisterns where they collected rain water. This Marine was using one of those to get away from the artillery fire. A shell hit the lip of this cistern and he was killed. Even in a rear area you could get killed.

From the road junction I followed the division through "Death Valley," just behind them and just forward of division headquarters. There was no way to wash; we didn't shave. I wore the same set of fatigues until the island was secured. I found I was breaking out with all sorts of skin diseases—dermatitis, fungus. At one point we hit a Japanese supply dump and went through it. I took out a Japanese tropical jacket and what they called "comfort bags" which were sent to Japanese troops. Each bag had one tenugui (hand towel), one fundoshi (loincloth), as well as a bar of non-sudsing soap, postcards and a stub of a pencil to write home with. I took out about twenty tenugui from these "comfort bags," and put them in my pack. I used one to wipe myself down every day, then I threw it away. At night I took a branch and hung my fatigue jacket out. Like I said, we had no water for washing. All we had was water distilled by the engineers from ocean water. We would get enough to drink, not enough to wash ourselves. So I would wear this Japanese tropical jacket to sleep in at night while my fatigue jacket aired out.

The first day I was on Saipan there was the smell of fresh blood. The only time before this when I smelled massive amounts of fresh blood was when I was going to college and I went to slaughterhouses to get the placentas from dead pigs in order to extract the hormones. That smell is unique. And like I said, when I landed that first day there were all those dead Japanese, and dead Americans. All that blood—you could smell it. But, I never smelled it again after that first day because there was always the odor of dead bodies in the air, and I became an expert on how long a Japanese body had been dead—not by the smell, but by the color.

After "Death Valley" we crossed over to the west coast near Tanapag Harbor. Before we crossed over I was near a road, and there was a house there. I was there for a number of days with the MPs—just the MPs and myself. I remember there was a dead woman—a Japanese woman, who had been dead for some time. By this time I wasn't bothered by the sight of dead people, but one of the enlisted men just couldn't stand the sight of this dead woman there, so he took his entrenching tool and put several spades-full of soil over her face. He didn't want to see her face.

After we crossed over to Tanapag we settled into the Japanese naval warehouse at Tanapag Harbor. North of that was the Japanese flying boat base. There was a creek between the warehouse and the base. We had our

*Japanese pilgrims, many of them from Okinawa, return to Saipan and other Pacific islands where they once lived to remember those who didn't survive. The author came across many sites such as this, where loved ones left prayer sticks, letters, flowers, and other memorabilia for those lost to them so many years ago.*

telephone set up inside. At night we always went into foxholes, and I always had the habit of improving my foxhole if I stayed more than a day or two. I would dig little niches in the side of the hole and put my hand grenades in them with the tape off the release. This was a ritual I went through every night. Another thing I would do is take out a fundoshi. I had about twenty of those, too. This way I was able to have a change of underwear. So with those towels and Japanese undergarments I was able to have a little more comfort than the average G.I.

Fortunately, I never had diarrhea. Most of the others did. I never used my spoon when eating. The Nisei and I would take branches, peel the bark off, and use them as chop sticks. We would eat our "C" rations with those, then throw them away. That way I never got diarrhea until I went back to division headquarters and ate in the Officers' Mess.

We were getting prisoners in and interrogating them the whole time, and we were able to relay the information directly to division headquarters by telephone; something I wasn't able to do coming up through "Death Valley." Now, I had daily contact with Lt. Colonel Van Antwerp and Maj. Herzog. It was the fourth of July that we took in a Japanese civilian who painted the hulls of flying boats. That was the first time we had any indication there would be a Gyokusai. He had surrendered freely, and he said there was going to be a Gyokusai July 7th. The Japanese on Saipan knew the end was near, and they still had radio contact with Tokyo. Now, the Gyokusai can only be ordered by Imperial General Headquarters in Tokyo. This is not the same as a banzai attack. This is an attack until annihilation. The battle cry was, "Seven lives to repay the nation." In other words, "Take seven of the enemy with you." The attack actually resulted in the reverse of that. The intent was to take as many of the enemy as possible, and none of the attackers were to survive. Literally,

*The remains of a Japanese tank, possibly a Model 97 (1937) 57mm tank gun.*

it means, "Smash the jewel!" The jewel being the Japanese military.

The next prisoner we got in was from the equivalent of our Marines, the Fifty-fifth keibitai. He came in on the 7th of July. That is the day of the Tanabata Festival. According to Chinese, and later Japanese mythology, that is a time when the spirits of the dead are supposed to return to earth, which is also a good time to die, because you can join your ancestors. I was aware of the significance of Tanabata because I had been exposed to Japanese history and religion in my Japanese language courses. I tried to explain this to Lt. Colonel Van Antwerp, but he said it was nonsense. He couldn't understand this concept of Tanabata being a good day to die. Other cultures had that, too—the American Indians had it. This prisoner was taken by one of the Nisei, Hoichi Kubo. It was this prisoner that gave us the tip off that the time of the attack would be midnight of the 6th. Hoichi Kubo called battalion and regimental S-2 (intelligence) about this prisoner. He then took the prisoner back to regimental headquarters. The prisoner was then interrogated by the S-2, the executive officer, and the commanding officer of the 105th Regiment. This information was sent back to us, then the prisoner was brought back to us about dusk. Now, Dick Kishiue was there with me at Tanapag Harbor. With this prisoner we knew what was up. We knew the roof was about to fall in. I remember calling Van Antwerp with this information. I was still talking with him after midnight on the 7th of July. He told me since it was past midnight, and the Japanese had not attacked, they probably wouldn't. I now know that our interdictory fire from artillery delayed the Japanese attack.

That was a night I will never forget. That word Gyokusai had not entered the American vocabulary. This was not a banzai attack; this was something completely different. This was not a bunch of yelling and screaming, then coming in. The Japanese knew they were going to die. They came in singing. You could hear them in the distance. There were between 4,000 and 6,000 of them. Like I said the attack was delayed until the morning of the 7th, and the full impact was

*The remains of a Tori Gate — part of a Japanese Shinto shrine as the author found it, buried in the jungles of Saipan.*

not felt until dawn. The high point for Dick Kishiue and our little group was when we moved out to our foxholes along the south side of the creek bank. Thank God there was a Marine Corps heavy machine gun covering the bridge over the creek. It was first light and here came one Japanese officer and about twenty enlisted men. This was the deepest Japanese penetration. They started to come down to the creek when the Marines opened fire on them. Then I started firing on them, and one by one Dick Kishiue and the MPs opened up, and we mowed them down. The machine gun did most of it. We waited to see if there was any movement, and if there was we fired on them again. Then, I signaled to the Marines that I was going over. I checked the bodies for identification, and I took the officer's sword. I still have that sword.

The next day I went with a regiment of the Second Marine Division and passed through what was left of the 105th Regiment of the Twenty-seventh Infantry Division. I went out just in back of their skirmish line. I could tell how long a Japanese had been dead by the color of his skin. They were dark brown when they were alive. When dead they turned green, then black. The ground was covered with bodies. In this trench close to where the Second Battalion of the 105th Regiment had been I noticed that there were a couple of Japanese bodies that looked awful alive to me because of their color. With me were a couple of MPs. We were immediately behind the skirmish line of the Sixth Marines, and I said in Japanese, "Come on out." They had covered themselves with dead bodies, and struggled out from under them. There was one officer and one enlisted man. I told them to surrender and they refused. The officer shouted, "Tenno heika, banzai!" Long live the Emperor! I knew the officer was not going to surrender. He sat down with his sword and was going to commit suicide. I could tell that the enlisted man was waiting for him to do that so he could surrender, but he couldn't surrender while the officer was still alive. Meanwhile, this MP sergeant who was with me had a

Thompson submachine gun. There was also a Marine Corps photographer who took a picture of me talking to these two Japanese. A few weeks later this photograph appeared in U.S. papers with the caption, "Japs Do Surrender!" But they weren't surrendering, and right after the photograph was taken this MP sergeant shot them both with his submachine gun. I started to chew him out when he said, "Well sir, I wasn't going to give them the pleasure of committing suicide."

There were a number of Japanese at the time of the Gyokusai who played dead. The day after the Gyokusai, while I was searching for documents, one tried to attack me with a grenade. I fired on him with my carbine. About four rounds hit him in the chest, and I thought he would never go down. He did go down, but it seemed like it took forever, even though it was probably only a couple of seconds. I made a point then to go to ordnance and get myself a .45, because I knew if I hit someone with a .45 they would fall.

Near the beach there was a 37mm gun of the Second Battalion, 105th Regiment. They had been firing canister shot at the Japanese during the Gyokusai. About a hundred yards, muzzle high out from the gun was a stack of Japanese bodies. Around the breech of the gun were eleven dead Americans. As they were killed they were rolled aside by the others who continued to man the piece.

Some time after the Gyokusai I went with the 165th Regiment to the Marpi area in a mop up operation. I don't remember as vividly all that happened in the mop up, because my life wasn't in jeopardy at any time. But I do remember I was on the high level ground above the cliffs on the east side south of Marpi Point and a man from a tank platoon attached to the 165th came in and said, "Lieutenant, somebody is down in this coral fissure, and they're moaning down there." It was about a 10 foot drop, so I jumped down with a .45 in each hand. There were three Japanese enlisted men and one civilian. Then there was a boy about 12 years old, and he was the only one alive. The rest had killed themselves with hand grenades. I was looking at him and he seemed all right, but he was moaning. Then I raised his sweater and his abdomen looked like hamburger. He told me his father had placed a grenade against him. I called for a medic. He jumped in and gave the boy a shot of morphine. The boy spoke Japanese, and told me his mother was Chamorro and his father was Japanese. There were some houses near by, so we got a piece of corrugated iron roofing. Four of us lifted the boy on to it and lifted him straight up. The medic then asked the medical officer for some plasma. The medical officer said, "We don't give plasma to Japs."

Before this I had been helping the doctors at a M.A.S.H. hospital near Chalan Kanoa, so I asked the medics from the 165th to take him there. I knew this boy was now an orphan, so I picked up some yen and went to the M.A.S.H. unit the next day. I talked to one of the surgeons about the boy, and he said, "Yes, I remember him. He died on the operating table." Now, I have seen a lot of deaths; I've seen friends killed, but a child ... I cracked up. The division headquarters surgeon, Major Smith, was a fine man. He is the one who pulled me through over the next three days. I think just everything built up, and the death of this boy triggered what happened.

While I was still on mop up duty in the Marpi area I met a young Okinawan girl, about eighteen years of age, who had strangled her young brother because the Japanese military had told her that if the Americans captured them they would kill the children and rape the women. When she found out that none of this was true she was so angry that she asked for a rifle so that she could go out and kill Japanese.

When the division left for Espirito Santo, the language detachment and I were placed on detached service with G-2 Section, Headquarters, Garrison Force, Saipan. Later, a Japanese warrant officer who had been Admiral Nagumo's secretary was flown back from Pearl Harbor. He had been with Nagumo all the way through to his suicide, and knew where his various headquarters caves had been. We arranged with Garrison Force, Saipan, to go back to one of these headquarter caves that overlooked Garapan. We had a platoon of Marines and about 15 Okinawans with picks and shovels. When we got up there we found fresh footprints around the mouth of the cave. We sent the Okinawans to the rear. The Marines put rounds in the chambers of their guns and took the safeties off. The Japanese warrant officer went up to the mouth of the cave and called for whoever was in there to come out. Finally, we heard this voice inside, "Me friendo." They were two Seabees who had been out souvenir hunting. They knew there were Japanese guerrillas in the area, and they heard us speaking to the Warrant Officer in Japanese, so they thought we were Japanese. They couldn't stand up for fear. I've seen men afraid, but nothing like that.

One of my duties was that of "materiels censor" for all military units on Saipan. I went to all of the military units once a week to clear souvenirs for shipment. During a "shake-down" of the Twenty-seventh Division one of the officers found a Japanese situation map that showed all the Japanese forces in the Central Pacific, including Guam, and Pelileu. This had been taken by an enlisted man and wasn't found until the division was being sent down to Espirito Santo,[3] after Saipan had been declared "secure." If we had that before our attacks on Guam and Pelileu it would have made it a lot easier for us. It would have saved lives.

I left Saipan on New Year's Eve of 1944, and was sent to Leyte in the Philippines. I returned to Saipan in 1994 where I participated in the dedication of the monument to the dead of the Twenty-seventh Infantry Division.

*Benjamin Hazard on his eightieth birthday in October 1999. On the wall in back of him are his medals and other memories.*

*Espirito Santo is an island in the New Hebrides.*

## A Nisei's Story

### Nobuo Richard Kishiue

*Nobuo Richard Kishiue was born to Japanese immigrant parents. He was drafted into the U.S. Army before Pearl Harbor. In February 1942, his parents, along with other Nisei, were removed from their homes and sent to internment camps. During the Saipan operation Mr. Kishiue was a member of the Language Detachment, G-2 Section, of the Twenty-seventh Infantry Division, then commanded by General Ralph Smith. After the Saipan operation, when the Twenty-seventh was sent to Espirito Santo for rest and recuperation, the language detachment remained behind on Saipan on detached service with the G-2 Section, Garrison Force. They were then charged with searching caves for stragglers, and assisting with the administration of Camp Susupe, as well as conducting surveys of the Japanese civilian population for intelligence information. After his discharge from the military Mr. Kishiue went back to farming in California. He retired from farming in 1990.*

My father's name was Nobataro Kishiue and my birth mother's name was Yoshiko. They came from Wakayama Ken, Japan. I don't know the year but it had to have been before 1920. They didn't talk much about life in Japan except to say that life was pretty harsh in those days and they wanted to seek a better life by going overseas to the U.S. However, even in the United States they found life was all hard work and perseverance. My mother died when I was four years old. After she died my father went back to Japan and remarried. The name of his new wife, my stepmother, was Otami. We lived in Kings County, California, near the town of Armona. My dad made a living by farming. At that time Japanese immigrants could not own land. the land that he farmed was leased to him. After the Alien Land Law* was passed my father could no longer lease land, and had to find employment as a farm laborer on a ranch. He did that until Executive Order 9066† came into effect in February 1942.

**This was enacted by the California Legislature in the mid–1920s to prevent aliens, especially Orientals, from owning land. It remained in effect until the late 1940s when it was repealed.*

*†Executive Order 9066 was issued by President Roosevelt and enforced by the U.S. Army. Americans of Japanese ancestry were removed from the western coastal areas to internment camps in the interior of the United States.*

My life before the war wasn't much except going to school, working in the fields, and harvesting crops in the summer. We never went anyplace because of the Depression, and I had to work and help the family make a living. I didn't have much time for play, not even when I was in high school. We didn't have segregated schools when I was growing up and I didn't experience any discrimination in grammar school, but I did experience some when I went to high school. For example, I was not allowed to join any of the extracurricular clubs, although I was accepted into the California Honor Society.

I went to Japanese school every Saturday, where I studied Japanese language and culture. After finishing high school I had to work full time as a farm laborer to augment the family earnings.

Some of the Nisei I knew in the Hanford area served in the 100th and the 442nd Regimental Combat Teams* during World War II. Fortunately, none of them were killed in action in Europe but some were wounded.

I was drafted into the U.S. Army in November 1941, and did my basic training in California at Camp Roberts. I was on leave on December 7, 1941, when the Japanese bombed Pearl Harbor. I didn't know what to think. All of us who were on leave were ordered to report back to camp as soon as possible. I wasn't treated any differently than my Army buddies during basic training, but after Pearl Harbor all of us Nisei were taken off of K.P. and guard duty. The Caucasian draftees were envious of us because those were the two worst duties.

When I was doing my basic training there were four Nisei in our company. There was myself, Tim Nizokami, Tim Tokuno, and Art Takahashi. I was friendly with all of them, but because of Executive Order 9066 we were all transferred to Camp Robinson, Arkansas. (Art Takahashi and Tim Mizakami were killed in action in Europe. Tim Tokuno, I met again after the war. He was a member of a V.F.W. Post in Oroville, California, and I met him at a state convention.) While at Camp Roberts we learned that our families would be interned. When I transferred to Camp Robinson, the base commander said that any Nisei who felt he needed to go back to California to help their families relocate would be given emergency leave. I took the leave and came back to California to see how my folks were doing. They were at the Fresno assembly center at that time. I was not allowed to go into the camp even though I had my uniform on. I had to talk to my father at the fence. There was nothing I could do except give him a little encouragement. My parents' feeling about the situation was that it was just something that couldn't be helped.

*Nabuo "Dick" Kishiue, Military Intelligence Service, attached to the Twenty-seventh Infantry Division (Army) during the Saipan operation.*

I had a younger brother and two half sisters. My younger brother did not go into the service, and was interned with the rest of my family. His draft status was 4-C, which was "enemy alien," even though he was an American citizen.

When we went back to Camp Robinson all they would let us Nisei do was police the camp and do janitorial work. I did that kind of work for about nine months. While I was there a group of Caucasian officers came and interviewed us. They asked me to translate some Japanese into English. One of them was a major who had interviewed me before while I was at Camp

*Combat units made up of Nisei from Hawaii and California. They served in the European Theater during World War II.*

Roberts in California. After this second interview at Camp Robinson, this major — his name was Dicky — asked me if I would volunteer for the language school at Camp Savage, Minnesota. I said, "Since I'm in the service and if I'm ordered to go there, then I'll go." So the first part of December 1942, I was shipped out to Camp Savage, Minnesota.

From December 1942 to June of 1943 I was in school learning the Japanese language — reading, and writing Japanese military terminology, and anything else they could think of. Upon graduating from the school I was sent to Fort Smelling, where I was assigned to a language team that consisted of ten men. They were Tim Ohta, Hoichi Kubo, Tom T. Mori, Richard Moritsugu, Larry Saito, Joe Fujino, Jack (Shigeo) Tanimoto, William Nuno, Roy Higashi, and myself. Tim Ohta was the team leader, and he was a staff sergeant. Most of the rest of us had the rank of T/4 and T/5.

From Fort Smelling we left for our overseas assignment in Hawaii. While there we did some translation work. We did translations of Japanese documents and soldiers' diaries that had been captured in the Pacific. Then we were assigned to the Twenty-seventh Infantry Division (Army). That was in September 1943. We were introduced to all of the officers, including General Ralph Smith. General Smith welcomed us with open arms. He told all of the others that we were on their side and an important cog in the operation in the Pacific. The G-2 Section was headed by Lt. Col. Van Antwerp. His executive officer was Major Herzog, and the enlisted men were Master Sergeant Daley and Technical Sergeant MacIntire. They all helped us get used to our new surroundings and provided us with everything we needed to do our assignment. We didn't have any problems with the Caucasian military men because we were taken around to the different units and they were told to familiarize themselves with us — that we were Americans and on their side. In fact, the Army was the first branch of service to accept Nisei as military intelligence personnel. The Marines at first were skeptical but later on, through the work we were doing for the Army, found we could help them in many ways.

Later, while in combat, we were given bodyguards, sometimes a whole squad. Even around camp we had a couple of Caucasian soldiers to protect us. The bodyguards were to protect us from both Americans and Japanese. In combat they were there to protect us from other Americans and keep us from being captured by the Japanese.

Our first mission was in the Gilbert Islands [now Kiribati] — that was Makin Atoll. I was on a troop ship with the 165th Regiment, Second Battalion. I was a Coast Guard ship called the USS *Leonard*. On that ship one of the sailors was a movie actor by the name of Cesar Romero. When everybody found out he was on the ship they would gather around him when he was trying to work and ask him questions. Finally, orders came down to leave Cesar Romero alone so he could work.

The morning we were supposed to go into battle we were topside getting ready to go down into the landing craft. We could see the battleships bombarding the island of Makin. I could see coconut trees on the skyline, but when the bombardment was over there was nothing but bare land. I was in the third wave. That's when the Japanese threw everything they had at us. After the battle, Jack Tanomoto and I stayed for another two months cleaning up the paper work, mostly translating some Japanese documents left behind on the island. Completing that, we were sent back to Hawaii to rejoin the rest of the division.

In April of 1944 we set out for Saipan, first stopping at Kwajalein Atoll. In the early part of June we were off the coast of Saipan. That night we heard over the radio that the Marines had secured the air base on Saipan — Aslito Airfield. We thought since they had secured the airfield we could wait 'til morning to land and help the Marines out. Then about two o'clock in the morning they woke us up and said, "You guys are going in to help the Marines out because they're battling right on the beach." I landed on the beach about two hours later — on Yellow Beach, at Chalan Kanoa with the 165th Regimental Combat Team. The Twenty-seventh moved in towards Aslito Field. However, before the airfield was taken I was sent out to see about helping some of the civilians who had been rounded up. There were women and children who had had no food or water for a couple of days. They were to be given food and water first, but there were some rowdy Korean men who broke ranks. We had to slap a few heads to control these men.

When the 165th took the airfield I was sent out to see what I could find in the way of documents at the airfield headquarters. With my bodyguards standing by, I started sorting out documents that I deemed important for division headquarters. I was about to go back into headquarters when I heard the chatter of machine guns coming from the sky. I saw two Japanese Zeros and two Navy Hellcats in a dogfight. One Zero was shot down, but one Hellcat made the mistake of going after the other Zero. The Zero made a quick circle inside the Hellcat and shot him down. The Zero that shot down our Hellcat started to land on the airfield. You can imagine the confusion when this took place. Men on both sides of the airfield opened fire on the Zero as he landed. I took cover and was I surprised when the pilot was taken prisoner and brought to where I was. I asked him where he came from and why he landed. He answered that he had left Guam to help his comrades on Saipan and did not know that the airfield had been taken by U.S. forces. After getting more information from him I sent him back to Division Headquarters for further questioning.

After this I was pulled back to Division Headquarters, and from there sent to various regiments that needed me for documentation work. That was about the time that we saw a change in the command of the Twenty-seventh Division. I was really sorry to see Gen. Ralph C. Smith go, because he was a soldier's general. He really thought about his subordinates before putting them to unnecessary risk in battle. I don't remember exactly when he was relieved of his command, but after he left we had interim division commanders.

About three days after General Smith left, however, I was sorting out captured documents when somebody I had never seen around headquarters came up and started to ask me questions. He picked up a magazine and asked me about it. I told him it wasn't important. Then he picked up something else and asked me about it. Not knowing he was our next commanding general, I told him to get the hell out because I was in a hurry to sort out the documents and get the important ones to corps headquarters. The next morning I got word from a captain who said he was General Griner's aide and that the general would like to see me. As I approached the general I recognized him as the person I had kicked out the day before. He introduced himself as General Griner and apologized for interrupting my work. After that I got along pretty good with him, and he always called on me to do translations, even if there were personnel more proficient than me.

After General Ralph Smith was dismissed it took us about three days to take "Death Valley" and surrounding areas. After that firefight, Major Herzog, our G-2 executive officer, and I went out to see the results and to get troop identification of the enemy. Upon coming to an area where the previous night the Japanese had attempted to infiltrate our front, we came upon a body that was in a naval uniform. I checked the body for identification and discovered that he was a vice admiral from the Japanese Inspector General's office. He had come up from Truk and had become marooned on Saipan.

The next day I went out with some of the G-2 personnel to make more troop identification. We came across what we thought was the remains of a dead Japanese soldier hanging in the fork of a tree that was about ten feet tall. I told the others that if we left him up there he would stink up the island. As I climbed up towards the body I heard a click. I yelled to the others, "Grenade!" Then there was a loud explosion in front of me. The body fell to the ground as the limb broke. I asked the guys on the ground if they were okay, and they asked the same of me. The Japanese hadn't been dead, and thought I was coming after him. He committed suicide by holding the grenade to his belly.

In July, after Tanapag Harbor was taken, I was assigned to a POW collecting site. On July 6–7 I learned from Japanese prisoners that a Gyokusai* was to be made in the early hours of the morning. We notified Division and Corps headquarters. However, our information must have been taken lightly because no reinforcements were sent up to beef up our lines. On the morning of July 7 what remained of Japanese forces on Saipan hit the American lines. There was a terrific firefight. The charge was stopped just short of our location except for a few stragglers. We escaped the full onslaught. When things calmed down later that morning, Maj. Herzog came by and asked me to accompany him to the site of the Gyokusai. Coming upon the scene I saw a carnage of slain men on the field. The smell of blood in the air stayed with me for a couple of days.

The island was declared secure on July 9, and I went back to Division Headquarters to be sent out on mop up details until the division was sent for rest and recreation at Magicienne Bay. By that time we were getting pretty tired of Army rations, so Kubo, Tanomoto, and I went spear fishing in the lagoon for octopus and

**Refer to the previous oral history,* Military Intelligence Service Attached to the Twenty-seventh Infantry Division, *Benjamin Hazard.*

Opposite, top: *The "Bone Hunters." The Japanese started returning to Saipan and other Pacific islands in the late 1960s in an effort to recover skeletal remains of their war dead. The last big expedition to take place on Saipan was in November 1995. This photograph shows the remains of an estimated 500 or more individuals being cremated at an old Japanese air strip on Marpi Point.* Bottom: *Of the 28,000 to 30,000 Japanese combatants on Saipan during the war, fewer than 1,000 survived. This photograph was taken at a memorial ceremony at the Japanese Memorial on Marpi Point, just below "Suicide Cliff." Seated in the photograph are surviving Japanese veterans and civilians of the World War II generation, along with younger men and women who lost fathers and other family members on Saipan and Tinian during the war.*

used grenades to get fresh fish. We got some rice from the company mess sergeant and cooked our own meals.

One day we got word that there were some chickens in the next valley over. We got permission for a Jeep from Col. Van Antwerp and went chicken hunting. Before going in we let the troops know that there would be some shooting. After that we ate chicken for the next couple of days. We later heard from some Japanese POWs who were in that same valley that they were about to surrender to us when they saw that we were only looking for chickens.

Among other things, I worked at the hospital that was run by the Navy. I was there as an interpreter. The patients were all civilians who were wounded during the fighting. I vividly remember a young girl who was brought in with a large wound in her hip. As the doctor probed the wound maggots came out, and the doctor commented that the only thing that saved her from getting gangrene was the maggots keeping the wound clean.

The only civilians I remember were Japanese and Korean nurses I met at the civilian dispensary which was run by the U.S. Navy. The ones I got to know were Yoshiko Takaesu, Kimiko Okazaki, and Kazuko Koji. There was also a fourteen-year-old Korean girl by the name of Fukuko Takada. I will never forget her because she was handicapped by being blind in one eye but did her work with zeal and was always cheerful. The Navy doctor in charge of the dispensary told me that he was going to have her fitted for a glass eye.

Fukuko would take my dirty uniforms home at night and have her mother wash and iron them. I would reciprocate by giving them soap and rations.

I did not go into any of the caves to get soldiers or civilians to come out, but did go out with loudspeakers calling for people to come out and surrender. Some of the civilians told me about their experiences of being under fire, and hiding in one place then another. Some were held against their will by Japanese soldiers.

One time I was out on patrol with a Garrison Force Team in the Mt. Tapochau area because of a report of stragglers there. We started for the foothills of Mt. Tapochau. About a half hour into the patrol one of the soldiers stepped on a dead branch. It made a popping sound like a Japanese grenade made when it was going to detonate. Someone yelled, "Grenade!" I hit the dirt and there was quite a bit of confusion after that. There men — I think they were from the Twenty-fifth Infantry Division — were a pretty jittery bunch. After that I told my commanding officer that I would not go out with the Garrison Force ever again.

I also registered and interrogated the Japanese civilians at Camp Susupe. There was no surrender of Japanese troops en masse as was the case with German and Italian troops in the European theater, and some were shot by their own people if they did try to surrender.

On Thanksgiving Day, 1944, thirteen Japanese Zeros came over. I later heard that they came over from the island of Rota. They flew in under our radar and raised havoc at the B-29 airfield — Aslito Field. One flew over Camp Susupe, and when I saw the fighter with the rising sun emblem I thought he was going to bomb us. I yelled, "Hit the dirt!" But he went by so fast we just stared at him in awe.

We were flown back to rejoin the Twenty-seventh Division by way of Tinian, Enewetak, Rabaul, and Guadalcanal. In the New Hebrides we were sent around to all of the units in the division to teach basic Japanese, and also to have all the replacement troops familiarize themselves with us, so they would know that we were part of the outfit. Shortly after that we left for the invasion of Okinawa, and were on Okinawa when the war ended.

We Nisei, as second generation Americans, had to prove ourselves loyal to the United States. I am glad that the 100th and the 442nd Regimental Combat Teams, made up of Nisei from Hawaii and California, got publicity during the war while they were in the European Theater, because those of us in the M.I.S. in the Pacific Theater were a secret outfit — the eyes and ears of the U.S. Armed Forces in the fight against Japan. We weren't even allowed to talk about what we did during the war until twenty-five years after it was over.

When I came home from the war I never experienced any resentment from members of my home town. However, only about one-third of the Nisei from the Hanford area returned to the area after the war. They made their homes in other parts of the country where they scattered after being released from the camps.

# The Thirty-Third Coast Artillery Battery

ROLAND FRONHEISER

*Roland Fronheiser was a non-commissioned officer in the U.S. Army and spent fifteen months on Saipan in 1944–1945. After the island had been declared secure his battery started training for the planned invasion of the Japanese home islands. Because of the dropping of the two atomic bombs and the surrender of Japan that followed, his training was never put to the test. He returned to his hometown in Pennsylvania, and like most veterans, married, took a job, and raised a family. In the spring of 1996, Roland returned to Saipan for a short visit. Roland died suddenly on 1 December 1997 at his home in Boyertown, Pennsylvania.*

I celebrated my twenty-first and twenty-second birthdays on Saipan. I have always considered myself fortunate for having served with the guys I served with. They were all great guys—guys that did their job and that was it.

I am of the opinion that artillery accounted for a lot more enemy dead than they will ever get credit for. Heavy artillery never seems to get any credit. You will never hear of a heavy artillery commander who was thought of as a hero, and I don't know of any heavy artillery outfit that ever had a movie made about it. Yet I'm sure they accounted for a lot of enemy casualties. As far as I know there wasn't a guy over there looking for any credit. We were just trying to get a job done, then go home.

Only old artillery men like myself know what artillery could do. Our 155mm "Long Toms" shot 25,395 yards, which was about fifteen miles.

Before we landed on Saipan we were sent to jungle training in Hawaii. There they were shoot-from-the-hip-happy. For one week we didn't do anything in jungle training except try to hit something shooting from the hip. On Saipan our mess hall was right on the edge of a ravine. One day we were standing in the chow line at supper time and we always had guards at the edge of that ravine. On this one particular night I remember a guy by the name of Colper was standing guard with a BAR [Browning Automatic Rifle]. All of a sudden one guy yelled, "Hey Colper, over there—there goes a Jap." He was crawling up the other side of the ravine, and Culper swung his BAR around and shot from the hip. He was shooting up into the trees; hell, he never came close to hitting him. That shooting from the hip training that we got never worked. We missed more Japs than we ever hit. Anyway, at that point Sergeant Percel jumped behind a .50 caliber water-cooled machine gun and sprayed that area thoroughly with .50 caliber bullets. He emptied a whole belt-full in there, and when he got done he asked the captain to go over and see if he had hit anything. He hadn't.

We hardly ever left that camp, and when we had the chance we took it, even if it was only to get supplies. We had only one phonograph record in that entire camp. It was "Sentimental Journey," and that song was played day and night for fifteen months in our mess hall.

There was one week when the Army sent a bunch of soldiers up to do our guard duty because we were all down with dengue fever. It was hell, and most all of us came down with it. I laid on a pile of Jap lumber for a whole week, hoping I would die.

When we set up our camp there were dead Japs all around, but at first we made no attempt to bury them. It was considered too dangerous. They swelled all up and the fat oozed out around their leg wrappings. The smell and the flies were terrible. There was a terrible fly problem on Saipan. There were flies all over. We used to eat with one hand and chase flies with the other. I have lived for a long time around cattle and things where there were a lot of flies, but I have never seen flies like there were on Saipan.

We were there at the time of the banzai charge* but did not fire our guns in support of the Twenty-seventh Army Division being overrun by the Japs. Those Japs got good and drunk before the charge. They were miles away from our camp but we could hear 'em whooping it up all night long.

Like I said, we didn't fire our own guns during the charge. We were known as an eight-ball outfit and not good enough for the job. In those days practically nobody wore shirts so you couldn't tell who was Marine and who was Army, but I can tell you that some men driving seven and a half ton Army prime mover trucks fetched our guns, and used them to beat back the Jap attack. There was a sense of urgency in the outfit that day like I have never seen before. It was mass confusion. Nobody knew what the hell was going on.

When they brought the guns back one of the truck

**The Japanese referred to it as the Gyokusai, or breaking of the jewels.*

*First Sgt. Roland Fronheiser. Saipan, 1944–1945.*

drivers told me that at one point the Japanese had pushed the Marines back under the guns, and that they had to cut the fuses beyond the safety point to stop the banzai charge. The artillery men had intensive infantry training and at that point they took up small arms and helped fight off the banzai charge.

They brought the shells up in dump trucks and dumped them in the mud. The artillery men were firing so fast that they were shoving those shells in the guns, mud and all. We were thoroughly trained to wipe those shells completely clean before they were rammed home, but of course during a banzai charge you don't have time to wipe them off. When we got the guns back we didn't know that at the time, but when we started firing at Tinian one of the guns was firing four hundred yards short. That one gun was so bad it had to be replaced. We asked for a new barrel. They didn't bring us a new barrel — they brought us a whole new gun. But I will never stop wondering about my buddy, Ernie Bittenbender, who was in the Second Marine Division and was killed by shrapnel in the head during the battle for Tinian. If one of our guns was firing four hundred yards short — imagine — it could have been our gun that killed him. Shortly after the banzai charge some of the Marines came back and actually hugged our guns. I saw one of the Marines even kiss one of our guns.

After the banzai charge we were given the dirty job of burying fifty dead Japs. We put them in a pile and tried to burn them. That didn't work and few of us ate dinner that night. A colonel came by and saw what we were doing and gave us proper hell. He then had a bulldozer come, dig a trench, and push the smoking, stinking mess into the trench. That was somewhere north of where our guns were. I think they built a road over where they were buried.

The Marines had a habit of burying Japanese and letting their feet stick out. There was one buried right there where our guns were mounted for a long time with its legs sticking out, just from the knees up. One day our captain walked by and saw those feet sticking out and said we should be ashamed of ourselves. Of course, that dead Jap was there when we got there. The Marines had buried him like that, and we just left it as a memorial to the Marines. But, we eventually had to cover 'em up.

You know I was scared the entire fifteen months I was on Saipan. Those Japs were always trying to sneak into our camp. I think they were after food more than anything else. Going to the latrine at night was one of the scariest things I ever had to do. That ravine was full of snail shells and whenever one of those Japs stepped on one it made a crunching sound and the whole camp would open up on that ravine. There were nights when no one would get any sleep, especially when this one fellow — I can't remember his name — was on guard duty. So one night the captain asked me to go with this guy and stand guard with him. He wanted to see if my presence would allow the rest of the men to get a little sleep. Well, I went up there and he was just plain scared. He kept saying, "Japs! Japs everywhere!" and would fire off a clip into the bushes. It was so dark that night you couldn't even see your hand in front of your face. But you know something, after about two hours out there with this fellow I was seeing Japs everywhere too, and I was firing off as much ammo as he was.

Sometimes they fired back. One night they started shooting just behind my shelter half. Sgt. Crocksford kept calling out my name, "Dutch, you all right? Dutch!" he kept calling. But you know, my heart was beating so fast it went right up into my throat and I couldn't talk. That happened to a lot of fellows. They got so scared they couldn't get a word out, and we had men in my outfit that were a lot braver than me.

Some of those men were always looking for excitement. They would volunteer to go out on patrol. I never volunteered. I went if told to, but I didn't volunteer. One time three men from my outfit, against orders, went to an area that was off limits. They were looking for souvenirs. They were walking along the other side of that ravine with their arms full of Jap rifles and other things they had picked up when they ran right into a group of Japs. We figured the Japs must have thought our guys were other Japs because of the type of guns they were carrying. I think each side must have realized that the other side was the enemy about the same time. One of our guys jumped over the edge of the ravine and rolled all the way down. The Japs threw hand grenades after him. He came into camp all cut up and so frightened he couldn't talk. When he finally did get a word out all he could say was, "Japs!" The other two men were found by one of our patrols on the beach.

One night when I was sergeant of the guard, one of the other guards kept calling "Sergeant of the guard. Sergeant of the guard. Japs in the plotting room. Japs in the plotting room." As soon as I heard that I headed for the plotting room with my M-1 Garand. A Lt. Sheeting followed along with his M-1 carbine. This was at night and as soon as we get close to the plotting room this lieutenant turns on a flashlight. Can you believe that? As soon as he did that I slapped it out of his hand. I think he realized that he had just done something stupid, because he apologized to me. Japanese were even reported to be in our mess hall one night. When we ran up to the guard who reported it I asked him why he didn't open up with his .50 caliber. He said, "Oh no! I'm not going to put holes in our nice new mess hall!" It is funny the things you remember fifty years later.

*First Sgt. Roland Fronheiser of the Thirty-third Coast Artillery Battery, photographed on Saipan in 1944–1945. The gun is a 155mm "Long Tom."*

It seems the bravest things I did in the service was to do things that the officers were scared to do. Whenever they were afraid to do something they got me to do it. I believe there were about 45,000 Americans on Saipan when the first shipload of beer came in. The captain came to me and said, "I want you to take 40 of the best men we have and go down to the docks and put a guard on each truck that takes a load of beer to the distribution point." We were down there for a couple of days while they were unloading this beer from the ship. Eventually, the stevedores came up out of the hold and said the ship was empty. When my men all came back I started marching them off the dock when the Officer of the Day stopped me. He asked me where I was going, and I said, "Back to my outfit. The boat is empty." He said, "No it's not. Go look." Me not being too smart, I handed my M-1 to the corporal and went back to the ship. I went down into the hold of the ship. Sure

*Roland Fronheiser in 1996 on the island of Saipan for his first and only visit since 1945. He died about a year and a half later.*

enough, there were six big stevedores, all with big knives in their belts. One of them said, "Little man, what do you want?" I said, "What are you gonna do with that beer back in the corner?" "We is all gonna put it in our truck tonight," he said. I went back up and told that lieutenant, and he said, "They can't do that. Here's my .45. Go down and make them move it." Boy, what a spot. I looked over at the corporal and he just shrugged his shoulders. I told that lieutenant, "Look, I'm damn scared. There are six big guys down there." I said, "You better stick up here by the hold, and if I start shooting you better finish the job." To make a long story short, about the bravest thing I did during the war was down in the hold of that ship. I forced them six guys to unload the rest of that beer at gunpoint. Aside from going to the latrine at three o'clock in the morning with Japs running through the area, that was the scariest thing I ever did during the war.

After fifteen months most of us were rock happy and would have done anything to get out of there, even if it meant invading Japan. We didn't have to do that, of course, because of the bomb. I don't care what anybody says, if we had had to go into Japan it would have been a terrible thing and I'm not so sure we could have pulled it off. After the war ended in Europe they started rotating men home and replacing them with younger, less experienced men. The efficiency of our outfit suffered as a result. Those younger troops didn't share the desire of us more seasoned troops to get the job done, nor did they share our hatred of the Japs.

We spent the remainder of the war training for the planned invasion of Japan. We were stockpiling chemical shells to use against the Japanese. In one of the many lectures they gave us in preparation we were even told we would have to shoot children as young as six years old because they might be concealing hand grenades.

You know I am glad we didn't have to go into Japan. If that war had gone on too much longer, and the casualties had gotten worse, I think the American people would have lost the will to win. But not everybody was as happy as me about not having to invade Japan. I remember Sgt. Crocksford — he was really looking forward to going into Japan. He always let everybody know how disappointed he was that we didn't.

## Field Artillery Officer

### EDMUND JOSEPH LYGA

*Edmund Joseph Lyga was born in 1917. In June 1941, he was drafted into the U.S. Army. Lt. Lyga was the executive officer for "B" Battery of the 531st Field Artillery, which was made up of 155mm "Long Tom" guns. Their guns were mounted near Agingan Point on Saipan, and fired on Tinian in support of the Marine landings on that island in July of 1944. Mr. Lyga is a retired high school teacher and principal.*

I would guess that we were about 6,000 yards out from Saipan when the Twenty-seventh Infantry Division (Army) landed on the beach. I was watching the landing with field binoculars from the ship, and I saw all of the mortar and artillery fire that the Japanese were placing on that beach. I remember thinking to myself,

*Edmund Joseph Lyga as a young officer in the 531st Field Artillery. This photograph was taken in Hawaii.*

"My God, I'm going to have to go into that beach pretty soon!" That was about 0530h when they went in, and I would guess that it was sometime that evening when my unit went in. We took off to find our position where we were going to place our guns. I remember walking maybe a mile, and it was getting dark. There was still a lot of firing going on — machine guns and rifles. And in the evening there were many flares going up. They kept the night constantly lit up. I don't think the front lines were more than 100 or 150 yards in front of us. We were told, as officers, to be awful careful because the Japanese liked to pick off the officers more than anybody else. So here I am walking along with just my pistol and I see this enlisted man coming along with a pretty good load. I asked the enlisted man if I could help him, believing that if maybe some Japanese did spot us he would say, "It doesn't pay to shoot him. He is just a Pfc."

It must have been well after dark when we came to a hole in the ground. We were made to understand that this was a Japanese ammunition dump, or gasoline dump that exploded. We stayed there overnight. The next morning when we got up our skin was red in spots, and itching. I suppose that was from the chemicals that were in that dirt.

We started out the next morning, and I remember going just a short way when I saw my first dead Marine, a big blond haired guy, maybe six-feet-two. His rifle was laying there and I figured why leave that gun there? So I picked it up and walked a little further. We crossed a narrow gauge railroad and found where our gun positions would be. We set up our guns facing the island of Tinian. Our guns were 150mm guns—"Long Toms." A gun is different than a howitzer. A howitzer is short-barreled compared to a 155mm gun. The projectile that is shot from both a gun and a howitzer is approximately the same. However, the howitzer when fired — its trajectory was higher. In other words it sort of lobbed them in. The 155mm gun was long-barreled, and the projectile went out at a tremendous velocity. Also, its trajectory was rather flat as compared to the howitzer.

After the guns were dug in I went out and found an O.P. [observation post] that looked from Saipan to Tinian.* That was Agingan Point. I looked at Tinian through some powerful glasses that the Japanese had left, and spotted three Japanese guns on Tinian. They were pointed straight up in the air, and no Japanese around that we could see. I picked the first Japanese gun on the right and sent orders back to my gun battery, giving them the range and the direction. When they announced that they were ready to fire, I told them go ahead and fire one round. It landed a little over the target and to the right, if I remember right. I sent back instructions to the guns to try to hit the target or land short. We always figured that if we got within fifty yards of a target we were close enough. Once on target I told all four guns to "Set out your stakes on your aiming point." Then we were all set to fire. We didn't have to wait too long; I believe it was the first night that the first round came our way from one of the Japanese guns on Tinian. One of those rounds landed right under our number one gun position — under the barrel. It didn't do much damage. I think it must have been from a small caliber gun, or it was a dud. We let out with a few rounds from our guns and that was the end of it.

The first real excitement we had was when all hell broke loose at number one gun. I was connected to all four guns by telephone. I called number one gun and said, "What's going on!" I didn't get much of an answer. Nobody was talking. Finally, when it all settled down, I went to number one gun, talked to the corporal in charge, and said, "What in the hell is going on here?"

**Tinian lays about three miles south of Saipan. Saipan and Tinian are two peaks on the same mountain, most of which is under water.*

*This Japanese bunker with the remains of a Japanese tank resting on top of it is on the west side of Saipan, and defended one of the beaches where U.S. Marines took more than 2,000 casualties on the first day.*

Well, nobody knew. This was late at night and everybody found themselves up and fighting. I told the highest ranking enlisted man — I don't remember his name — to count his men. He counted his men, and it turned out one of the men was missing. On checking, we found some blood, and about a hundred yards from that gun position we found one of the guys. He had been stabbed, and he was dead. We knew there were no Japs in there — the gun pit. The only conclusion I could come to was that one of the guys had a nightmare. He dreamed that there was a Japanese in there, and he came up swinging and fighting with his knife. Then everybody else jumped on him, and I had to assume that is how the guy got stabbed. To this day I don't know if he stabbed himself by accident, or if somebody else stabbed him.

We did very little firing on Tinian for quite some time. There was very little to fire at. However, there was a time when General "Howlin Mad" Smith* was at our O.P. While he was there a plane — a U.S. plane — came and strafed a cave in a cliff on Tinian. I saw a lot of tracer bullets going out. Another U.S. plane followed him and the tracers from that second plane were glancing off of that cliff and going towards the first plane. "Howlin Mad" got all excited when he saw that. He wanted to know what in the heck was going on. He said, "Where is your other O.P.?" "It's down the line about a half a mile on Obyan Point," I said. "Call him!" says General Smith. So, I called. I said, "Lt. Doty, General Smith wants to talk to you." Lt. Doty wouldn't believe me. He thought I was trying to pull a big trick on him. He absolutely refused to believe that General Smith was there. After telling him a few times, "No, no, he is here and he wants to talk to you," old Smith took the telephone away and talked to Doty, and Doty talked to him. Lt. Doty was reprimanded for that, but never lost rank, and later became a battery commander. He didn't get much from it, but it was on his record. Gen. Smith went away after that and it was the last I ever heard from him.

**Lt. Gen. Holland M. Smith was commander of the V Amphibious Corps during the invasion of Saipan.*

Opposite, top and bottom: *A well camouflaged Japanese bunker built into a limestone cliff on the north end of Saipan.*

*A recent photograph of Edmund Joseph Lyga and his wife, Bernice.*

We never actually fired on any targets on Saipan because our guns were only 200 or 300 yards from the beach and our orders were to position ourselves facing Tinian in case we received enemy fire from there. Those were our orders right from the first day.

After things on Saipan settled down, I remember looking around a little bit — looking here and looking there. Once I went to Floyd Doty's O.P. From his place I could see a big cliff off to the left, towards Naftan Point. There were two caves in that cliff. Since things seemed pretty settled I decided to take a walk over there. I went on top of that cliff and looked down to the ocean. It must have been about fifty feet down. We were told that was where lots of civilians, especially women and children, jumped off and committed suicide. I went back to my O.P. and while I was there some unit, and I don't know who they were, brought a 37mm gun up there and fired into those two caves. After firing for a while, they picked up and left. Where they went, and where they came from, we didn't know, and nobody else seemed to know.

That night after that small gun pulled out, the men at Lt. Doty's O.P. heard some mumbling. Our men challenged them, and just like that everything turned quiet — not a sound. There was no firing, but whoever it was took off in one direction and Doty and his group took off in another. They took off for our battery. One of the enlisted men said to me later, "I was crawling on my hands and knees. I looked to my right, and there was a Japanese crawling right next to me. So I came to some sugar cane that was in wind rows. I crawled in there and stayed until morning."

I remember about three days after the banzai attack (Gyokusai), I was in my foxhole at my guns. I think this was early in the morning, and a terrific smell hit me. I looked out of my foxhole and American trucks were coming into our area with bodies with rigor mortis set in — arms and legs sticking out. The trucks were taking these guys to the Twenty-seventh Division Cemetery, which was just a short way from us. We used to fire our guns over the Twenty-seventh Division Cemetery, and over my O.P. to hit Tinian.

We didn't do a hell of a lot of firing on Tinian until it became time to go into Tinian. Three days before the invasion we started pounding the beaches. When the Marines went into Tinian they found very little opposition. Originally, our main objective was to fire counter battery in case any artillery on Tinian fired on our forces on Saipan.

There was another artillery unit next to us on Saipan. It was maybe 150 yards from our position and some of their men went out on a little sightseeing — picking up souvenirs. They went on top of a cliff, and down the cliff on a rope. When they got down there and started investigating they found a cave. Somebody inside the cave opened up on them. When that happened, they left. Of course, they had to crawl back up the cliff using that rope. One fellow didn't make it. When the others got back to their unit they formed a party and went back to the cliff and back down to the cave. When they got there they found that the Japanese had killed the American and cannibalized the body.

After Saipan, we went to the Philippines, then Okinawa. We were on board ship heading back to the Philippines when we found out the war was over. I don't remember anybody crying because we couldn't go into Japan.

Opposite, top: *This Japanese pillbox can be seen today on a point of land near the town of Garapan, Saipan — now part of American Memorial Park, dedicated to the more than 3,000 Americans who died taking the island.* Bottom: *Japanese defensive station on Saipan.*

# The Navy

*(8)*

## Navy Civil Affairs Unit

### Harris Martin

*Professor Harris Martin was born in Japan the year of the "Great Earthquake," as it was known in Japan—1923. He returned to the United States in 1940 to go to college. In 1942 he enlisted in the U.S. Navy. He worked in the intelligence section of Civil Administration at Camp Susupe on Saipan from June 1944 until May 1945. After the war Professor Martin attended Stanford University where he attained his master's degree in history. He was recalled to active duty during the Korean Conflict, but returned to his studies two years later, eventually earning his Ph.D. He retired from San Jose State University as a full professor in 1988. He now lives in Aptos, California.*

My father was old enough to be my grandfather. He was born in 1875 and ended up in Japan by chance, by way of China. He was a fairly devout Christian youth—he was a Methodist, but he was not a minister. He left China during the Boxer Rebellion and was on his way back to the United States by ship when it pulled into Nagasaki. A launch came out to the ship and he heard an American voice calling up from the launch, "Is there anyone who can stay here for a year and teach English?" That was his introduction to Japan, and he stayed two years. That was from 1900 to 1902. He decided in 1913 or 1914 that he wanted to go back out to Japan and teach. He married my mother and went out in 1914. My brother and two sisters were born in Japan. My father was a professor of English at Aoyama Gakuin (Aoyama University). It was a Methodist college.

He was dropped from the university staff at the time of the Great Depression and we moved to Kobe. He stayed in Japan, which was the smartest thing he ever did. He was in his fifties and he couldn't have found a job in the States at his age during the Depression. He had a family of four children and I was the youngest. And like I said, it was the depth of the Depression so we stayed and he taught English in Japanese schools. I did not go to a Japanese school, but to a Canadian school in Japan. I learned Japanese, but not well. What I learned was children's Japanese.

In 1940 I came back to the United States and went to college: first to Sacramento Junior College because we had relatives in Sacramento. Then my folks came back to the States. They were evacuated on the advice of the United States government before the war started. By that time my father had been reinstated in the mission and had been assigned to work at a Japanese church in Tacoma, Washington. In Tacoma I went to the College of Puget Sound, now the University of Puget Sound. I was in Tacoma for about 15 months before I enlisted in the U.S. Navy.

When the war broke out between the United States and Japan the Army and the Navy began to pick up people who were born in Japan—young men and women too—to see if they would be useful to the war effort. The Navy got to me first. Or I should say I enlisted. I didn't know enough Japanese to help them but they knew I had a background and they sent me to the Navy Language School which was then at Boulder Colorado. After I was already in the Pacific they moved it to Stillwater, Oklahoma. There were several hundred people in the school at the time I was there. These were people who had some background in Japanese, or had lived in Japan. Those of us who had lived in Japan were called the "B.I.J.s"—Born in Japan people. And there were other people who had shown an aptitude for languages. We had a concentration of brilliant people there. B.I.J.s were not necessarily brilliant, but the others were. Many of them became leading scholars in Japanese studies after the war. There were no Nisei in the Navy program at that time. The Army, however, did take Nisei. Most of them at first did not become officers, but some were commissioned through the ranks so that by the end of the war there were a handful of Nisei officers. I really don't know why the Army took Nisei and the Navy didn't. Perhaps it was distrust, or snobbery—I don't know.

Like I said, I didn't know Japanese very well when I went to the language school, but I had an ear for it, which helped me a lot. Of the four Japanese-speaking men in my Military Government Unit in Saipan, I was the most facile of the four, simply because I had this background that they didn't have. They managed to get along, but they couldn't converse in Japanese as easily as I could.

I was at the language school for fourteen months, from 1 December 1942 until March 1944. I first went overseas in April 1944. I was sent out to Pearl Harbor to the Joint Intelligence Center Pacific Ocean Area (JICPOA), which was under CINCPAC, and was translating documents with a whole bunch of other language experts. Then as the Marianas operation developed four of us were picked out and put with a Military Government Unit. There were others from the language school who received their commissions with the Marine Corps, and they were assigned to Marine Corps field units.

It was probably the middle of May 1944 that I learned I would be going to Saipan. At that time I was assigned to what was called a Navy Civil Affairs Unit. The Navy used the term "Navy Civil Affairs Unit." On Saipan, after the battle when the Fifth Amphibious Corps left the island, we came under Army administration and they used the term "Military Government Unit."

Before we left Hawaii, however, we were taught a little bit about civil affairs, but not much. I was given the task of teaching the enlisted men in the unit some words in Japanese in preparation for this. The landing on Saipan was on June 15, 1944. We were on the USS *Sheridan*, an APA. We didn't go ashore until D-plus five, but we watched the landings. Some of the assault troops were from our ship. We could see some of our

*Professor Harris Martin as he looks today. He was born and raised in Japan, returning to the United States in 1940. During World War II, because of his Japanese language skills, he served Naval Intelligence.*

landing craft being hit by Japanese artillery and we watched Japanese tanks as they counterattacked from the low hills below Mount Tapochau. Towards dusk we could see much more of the battle because of the tracer bullets. One of the things that caught my attention was the flame throwers. We couldn't see it clearly, but we could tell what was happening, and we had field glasses. And too, we had doctors on our ship and many of the wounded were brought to our ship.

I knew the Japanese had been charged with fortifying the islands before the war, but I think the only one they had fortified was Truk. Saipan they hadn't. The biggest guns they had, the naval guns, weren't even mounted yet when we landed. They were still at Tanapag Harbor. The only real fortifications they had were pillboxes, and air raid shelters. The plain fact of the matter was, their defenses, even though they gave us a hell of time, were not very good. And they really didn't have first class troops there. They did have a unit from the Kwantung Army,* which sounded very impressive, but it had been slapped together before being brought to Saipan. What I'm trying to say is that the nucleus of the Kwantung Army had been dissipated from all the years of fighting in China, so it really wasn't what it had once been. Certainly there was no shortage of brave Japanese soldiers, but Saipan was not the fortress that Iwo Jima was, for example.

We went ashore on landing craft, but by D-plus five they had already put floating piers out so we got off on those. We moved into a little school in Chalan Kanoa that still had a roof and windows. We were there for a few days before we went out to Susupe and pitched tents. The Marines had big howitzers right beside us and they scared the hell out of me each time they fired, because they lifted me right out of my bunk. I really didn't have much to do the first few days I was on Saipan. We had several civil engineers who were Navy officers, and they started the process of laying out the plans for Camp Susupe. They were pretty flimsy buildings they put up. They had corrugated tin roofs and were open at the sides. The floors were maybe two feet off the ground so they wouldn't get wet inside. The most important things were drainage and privies. The camps were divided up into different cooking centers so that people belonged to this cooking center, or that cooking center.

I dealt primarily with the Japanese, not the Chamorros, although I saw them all the time. The Marines were bringing in prisoners even before we got there — before the camps were set up. Everybody was kept under guard no matter if they were Japanese, Korean, or Chamorros and it took us a while to get the idea of separating them. It was during this early stage of separating people and organizing the camps that some Nisei troops from the Army came to where we were holding the prisoners. I could see these Japanese civilians just staring at these Japanese in American uniforms, almost with open mouths. Most of the Nisei were bigger and huskier than the native Japanese. Later, it was the Nisei from the Army who came to the camps to ferret out Japanese soldiers who were trying to pass themselves off as civilians. So even though I was in the intelligence section of Civil Affairs I was not charged with that particular responsibility. I didn't deal with prisoners as an interrogator at the time they were captured.

There were some very able interrogators, most of whom were B.I.J.s like me, but who spoke really good Japanese. Some of them were of American and Japanese parentage. There were a couple of full-blooded Caucasians who had gone through the Japanese school system, right through Tokyo University. These people were the ones who interrogated the prisoners who were especially knowledgeable. They were so good that I think it took the Japanese by surprise to find Americans that could speak Japanese at that level, both in the forward areas and at Pearl.

I remember hearing about one interrogator — not that he used brutality, but he was very forceful in his language. He used rough language, and he threatened prisoners. I don't think he ever physically abused anybody. However, I do know about situations where prisoners were killed. I know about commanding officers who told their men not to take prisoners. We've all read about that, and that happened. I know of worse things that happened, where actual mutilation occurred, like taking of teeth and other parts of the body. These things did happen, and yet some people take a certain amount of comfort in the idea, or claim that Americans weren't quite as bad as the Japanese because this was not a policy. However, for example, if a commanding officer says, "Don't take prisoners," for that unit, that is a policy. When Japanese ships were sunk and American planes strafed the survivors in the water, and there wasn't a court-martial because of it, then that can be accepted as having been a policy, or at least something that was overlooked. My whole point is, when people claim that the Japanese were particularly cruel I can think of occasions when Americans were particularly cruel, too. I think it is also true, however, that we never, during the war, organized a unit like 731— the Ishii Unit.†

At first we fed the civilian prisoners on Japanese rations, then we began to import rice and stuff like that. We had big stores of rice on the island that we had captured and we were able to use a lot of that. However, a lot of the stores we should have been able to use we weren't able to because our own troops were so destructive. They stuck their bayonets in cans just to see what was in them.

We were told to keep our eyes and ears open for anybody who had an official position with the Japanese, and the Army and Marines were bringing in Japanese daily in trucks. I would be there trying to case them. I saw this one woman who had been in a cave and when

**Also spelled "Guandong" according to the new "pinyin" romanization of Chinese.*

*†A Japanese biological warfare unit in Manchuria that experimented on live human beings.*

she came to the camp she was trying to nurse her dead baby. These people had been through hell and many of them were hysterical. However, I was mainly concerned with the men. When they came in I would ask them, "What did you do before the invasion?" This one man told me that he had been a policeman. When I found this out I took him to our administration people. His name was Akira Hirasawa. We became very good friends, and he later told me after he had been appointed police chief of the Japanese camp that he was convinced that I was taking him to be shot. The fact that he had been a policeman, and that I had showed so much interest in him, convinced him of that.

Another Japanese, an older man by the name of Kotari, was appointed as Hirasawa's clerk. He had worked for the NKK before the invasion. I spent a lot of time talking to these two. That is the way I kept aware of what was going on in the camp. For example, whenever there was any question about something that happened in the camp that we didn't know completely about I went directly to Hirasawa. I suspect there were things he didn't tell me. For example, Captain Oba* infiltrated some of his men into the civilian camp, but we didn't know about it at the time. One night some of his men were caught trying to sneak into the camp farm we had for the Japanese civilians and there was a big shoot-out. I was down at the beach watching a movie. I saw the tracer bullets and heard the racket. The next morning I went to the farm. When I got there I came across a pile of .50 caliber shell casing that we must have fired from a machine gun we had set up there, so I figured they must have fired across the field in a certain direction. When I went around in that direction I found a body. He was wearing a Japanese naval uniform. It was a sad sight; he was a very handsome young man. I had seen lots of dead Japanese after the battle, but most of them had been dead for several days, and they were bloated. This guy was freshly dead. His leg was broken. It must have been a .50 caliber bullet that broke it. I didn't frisk him or anything — I didn't touch him. I just reported it to administration.

There was another incident that happened on this farm, but it wasn't associated with the shoot-out. It was a poem written in Japanese that was found at the farm. It was very touching, and the thing that impressed me so much about it was the allusion to nature and to insects. It was not the sort of poem you would expect most soldiers to write. It was a sensitive poem, full of longing and feelings of connection with nature. It touched me at the time. I am sorry I didn't keep a copy of it.

I remember one morning after a Japanese air attack, Hirasawa told me that breakfast tasted extra good that morning. Of course, we shot down all of the Japanese planes, but he was happy that they had at least attacked. You know the Japanese for months after the American landings were looking for the Japanese Imperial Forces to return, which of course never happened. Hirasawa remained an ardent Japanese when it came to the Japanese military, but he also became very friendly and trustworthy in all matters except possibly were it touched on the interest of the Japanese military. I don't think he was likely to volunteer information about that, but as far as management of the civilian population in the camp I think he was completely open and honest.

One day after the B-29s started their bombing raids against the Japanese home islands I took Hirasawa and Kotari out to Isley Field. Of course, from the camp they could see planes coming and going, but there was this feeling on my part that they should understand that this was final, that there was not going to be any comeback by the Japanese. They were really astonished by what they saw, and this was early on, before the large, almost daily raids against Japan got going.

In time we started sending Japanese civilians out on work details, and this gave them some income. We had like a little PX where they could buy things, and they had craftsmen who made things to sell to U.S. military people on the island. Plus, they were allowed to do some farming.

I first heard about Amelia Earhart on Saipan when somebody from Fifth Corps headquarters came down. They came to the Chamorro camp to interrogate some Chamorros. The information all came from the Chamorros, not the Japanese. And it was the Chamorros who said there was an American woman flier who was brought by the Japanese to Saipan, and who was executed by them. Who the first American was who heard it from a Chamorro I don't know, but the person who was investigating this had orders from higher up. I sat in on one of these interrogations and became interested in it after that.

Some time after Fifth Corps left Saipan a Chamorro said that the woman flier had been buried at Talofofo. I went up to Talofofo in a Jeep with her and one other person. We went up there and looked and looked, but we couldn't find anything.

A fellow by the name of Philip Monahan was in charge of the Korean camp, and I remember the

**Head of an organized band of Japanese holdouts that did not surrender until December 1945.*

antipathy the Koreans had towards the Japanese. I remember the antipathy of many of the Okinawans to the Japanese too. Sometimes when the prisoners were sick they were sent to one of the field hospitals. When they were brought back to camp in ambulances they were brought back all together, Japanese, Korean, and Okinawans. At the Japanese camp I would open the door and say, "All Japanese get out here." If there were any Koreans, they would go on to the Korean camp. But anyway, I was distinguishing between Koreans and Japanese. "Japanese get out here." There was this one old Okinawan still sitting there. So, I said again, "All Japanese get out here," but he didn't move. So one Japanese girl said, "Old man, he says for all Japanese to get off." He said, "I'm not Japanese. I'm from Okinawa." He finally got off. But on the other hand, Hirasawa was living with a Korean girl in the Japanese camp and we never tried to separate them.

The camps did have barbed wire fences around them and some U.S. military people did try to get in, looking for women, and some were apprehended doing so. I was at the court-martial of one, but I wasn't a witness.

Lieutenant Commander Schattle was head of the intelligence unit that I was a part of. He was a cop in civilian life, and an interesting fellow. We called ourselves "Schattle's chattels."

Sometimes when we sent Japanese men out on work detail there were sexual attacks made on these Japanese men by American military men. This was appalling to me, and I suppose to others. I went to Schattle and asked him why there were so many homosexuals in the military. He said they were not homosexuals—these were homosexual acts by heterosexuals. As a policeman he was familiar with this, but I wasn't. The Japanese civilians were annoyed by the fact that American troops were bothering their men, but I don't know if anything was ever done about this. If anything was done about it, it was not handled by Civil Affairs. I might also add that Hirasawa once asked me, "Why don't you have women here for your troops?" He didn't use the word "Comfort" women.

When I got my orders to leave Saipan, boy was I happy. Jeez, I had been there for eleven months, and the war was moving on to other places. Look at what happened between the time I arrived on Saipan and the time I left Saipan. The Palau Campaign, the Philippine Campaign, Iwo Jima, and Okinawa. Saipan was important as a major base, but I felt like I was being left behind. So, when I went back to Pearl Harbor I was happy to be back, but I was also thinking this would be a chance to be sent out to a forward area again. I was tapped, along with some others, to go to Okinawa, but those orders were canceled, and within a few days came the A-bomb and new orders to send us to Japan.

## Gunnery Officer: USS *Twining* (DD 540)

### William VanDusen

*William VanDusen was born in Denver, Colorado, on 27 January 1922. In June 1939, he joined the U.S. Navy as a midshipman fourth class and attended the United States Naval Academy in Annapolis, Maryland. He was supposed to graduate in June 1943, but because of the critical need for naval officers during World War II the curriculum was accelerated and his class was graduated in June 1942. Captain VanDusen spent the rest of his working life either in the regular Navy, the reserves, working as a civil servant for the Navy Department, or as a contract engineer. He is now retired and lives in Orinda, California.*

Upon graduation from the U.S. Naval Academy in 1942 I was assigned to the destroyer USS *Bancroft* (DD 598). I joined the Bancroft in Boston, Massachusetts, and after a number of convoys on the east coast the *Bancroft* transited the Panama Canal. We spent the following year in the Aleutians, culminating with the retaking of Attu* from the Japanese the following summer. On the return of the *Bancroft* to the West Coast I was detached and subsequently ordered to the USS *Twining* (DD 540), which was under construction in San Francisco. The *Twining* was one of sixteen Fletcher Class 2,100-ton destroyers built in the city of San Francisco during World War II. It was commissioned on 1 December 1943. After a shakedown period,† the *Twining* finally set to sea on 11 February 1944, passing under

**One of two islands in the Aleutians taken by the Japanese earlier in the war.*

*†A period of familiarization and training performed on ship immediately after commissioning. At the completion of shakedown, a ship is ready for operation with the fleet.*

*Lt. VanDusen on the starboard wing of the bridge of the* Twining.

the Golden Gate Bridge. It headed west, not to return until the end of the war.

Our captain, Commander Ellis K. Wakefield, was a survivor of the sinking of the cruiser USS *Astoria* off Guadalcanal earlier in the war. He was our commissioning skipper and was in command throughout the Marianas operation.

At Pearl Harbor the *Twining* underwent a series of rigorous training exercises, primarily shore bombardment, in anticipation of what was then an unknown upcoming operation. On 31 May 1944, the next operation was known to be the taking of Saipan, Tinian, and Guam. The *Twining* got underway as part of Fire Support Group One to provide gunnery, anti-aircraft, and anti-submarine protection during the landings on Saipan and Tinian.

On D-Day Minus One, *Twining*, together with the destroyer USS *Stockham* and the light cruiser USS *Montpelier*, arrived at dawn off the east coast of Saipan. Late in the afternoon, *Twining* and the ships in company were taken under fire by a Japanese battery on Naftan Point. It had been a pretty calm day until the talker in the gun director shouted the captain's order to commence firing. At about that same time a large, colored splash appeared off of our bow, followed by another. I saw the gun flashes on Naftan Point and took the battery under rapid, continuous fire with our five five-inch main battery guns. Out of the corner of my eye I saw the *Montpelier* open fire with her 12 or 15 six-inch guns and disappear in a maroon cloud of gun smoke, accented by the flash of gunfire. The Japanese gun battery on Naftan was obliterated.

The captain of the *Twining* was quite concerned that we always steamed with a clear stack — that is, no smoke. You did that for two reasons: number one, it showed that you were operating the boilers most efficiently. And number two, you didn't leave any telltale smoke clouds for enemy aircraft to identify. The engineers weren't quite as diligent as the captain would have liked. As a result he ordered that there be an enlisted engineer on duty on the bridge at all times on a telephone connected to the fire room to report on any smoke that came out of the stack, and to get the men in the boiler rooms to then trim up the blowers to get rid of the smoke. When the Japanese batteries on Naftan Point opened up and the shells began to fall, the captain ordered, "Make smoke!" This would have been typical in order to provide a smokescreen to protect the cruiser we were there to protect, as well as to protect ourselves. The enlisted engineer at the back of the bridge had been so accustomed to the captain yelling at him, "You're making smoke," that he immediately called to the fire room, and said, "You're making smoke." Of course, this resulted in the captain not getting the reaction he wanted. The captain shouted to the fire room again, "Make smoke, God damn it!" And again the enlisted man called down to the fire room, "You're making smoke again, God damn it!" Then out of frustration the captain got on the 1MC, the ship's speaker system, and bellowed, "Make smoke! We've been straddled!" And with that, both stacks belched smoke.

On D-Day, *Twining* continued its support role and that night took up patrol in the channel between Saipan and Tinian. It was rather nightmarish. We were close to the beach and the heavier ships behind us were firing over our heads onto the beach. There were flares being dropped by Japanese planes from Tinian as well as a bomb or two. An officer on the bridge reported seeing a Japanese soldier swimming in the water totally naked except for his sword hanging around his neck. He was headed for Tinian and disappeared rapidly into the darkness as the ship passed him by.

Later, while conducting indirect fire on the beach, *Twining*'s guns hit a large ammunition dump, which exploded which a tremendous cloud of smoke and flame near Aslito Airfield.

On 16 June 1944, *Twining* and its Destroyer Division 106 were detached from the bombardment groups at Saipan and sent out to reinforce the Fast Carrier Task Force* that was shielding the islands from an oncoming Japanese fleet. Because of the fact the *Twining* had additional special radio equipment placed aboard, she was classed as a radar picket.† Together with her division mates, she was stationed about 25 miles due west of the task force to provide early warning of any incoming aircraft or ships. The general mode of operation during daylight hours was to steam west, that is toward the oncoming Japanese forces, and at nighttime to fall back toward Saipan and Tinian. It was my understanding that Adm. Spruance was concerned that the Japanese might perform an end run around us. That was the reason for falling back at night.

June 19, the second anniversary of my graduation from the Naval Academy, grew bright and clear when we went to general quarters. When I got to the gun director and asked the Combat Information Center where the "bogies"§ were, I was informed that they were from 230 to 300 true, ten to unlimited miles.** In other words, the sky was full of them. This was to be the first of a number of attacks that were subsequently going to be known as the "Marianas Turkey Shoot." As the first ships the attacking Japanese aircraft would see were those of DESDIV 106, a number of the Japanese planes peeled off to attack us. This was my first experience with anti-aircraft fire. I noticed the sky was full of contrails and I was quite concerned that with the large number of planes that were airborne, both friendly and enemy, I might inadvertently take a friendly under fire.

A plane seemed to be coming in to strafe us. I dropped down into the gun director to look through my magnified telescope and saw immediately that it was a Japanese Zero. I gave the order to commence fire. The plane was hit when it was so close that I could see the pilot and the white scarf around his neck. The plane was hit squarely, and as it blew apart the Japanese pilot's parachute fluttered out but he did not survive. That was the first of three aircraft we shot down that day. The next two were torpedo planes— Kates— as I recall. They came in low on the deck in a formation of about six. They went around us to head for the main force and we took them under fire. We hit one, which went down, hit the water, and then ricocheted back and hit one of the other planes beside it. So we got two for the price of one. The entire operation lasted twenty-six minutes, although it seemed a lot longer than that to me. By the end of the war the *Twining* was credited with having shot down seven enemy airplanes.

The rest of the day for us was rather uneventful. We did pick up one U.S. Navy pilot who ditched near us. That was another feature of being on picket duty, as we were the first friendly American ship to be seen by returning aircraft. If they were in trouble they generally tried to ditch by us. We then were responsible for pick-

**Task Force 58 under Adm. Marc Mitscher.*

*†These are destroyers that are deployed in advance of the main body of ships, generally some 15 to 20 miles. Their role was to provide early warning to the main body of ships.*

*§Enemy aircraft.*

***Air targets were normally first detected by the ship's air search radar and transmitted orally to the gun director. These targets were identified in terms of their true or relative bearing (in this case, true), and slant range (ten to unlimited) nautical miles. The gun director would then train to the indicated bearing, search at the indicated range, acquire and commence tracking the target.*

*The USS* Twining *being refueled at sea by an aircraft carrier.*

ing them up, and *Twining* recovered some sixteen airmen during the war. We usually received a large container of ice cream from the carrier to which we returned a pilot or air crewman.

As a follow-up to the heavy losses suffered by the Japanese on June 19, Adm. Spruance determined that he would launch an attack against the Japanese carriers and other ships. By that time the distance between the U.S. forces and the Japanese was extreme, but the chance of great success was obviously far greater than any concern for loss of aircraft. So the admiral launched a massive air strike against the Japanese forces. The American planes began to return to their aircraft carriers from their attacks after dark. Many of them were damaged. All of them were quite concerned over the fact that it was pitch dark and they were going to have to land on a darkened aircraft carrier deck. The fleet commander ordered that the picket destroyers, and other ships, turn on their 36-inch searchlights to identify their positions. This we did, which gave us a bit of concern because we were obviously identifying ourselves in a very bold manner to any Japanese submarines that might be nearby. But we kept the searchlights on and pointed them over towards the American carriers that had lighted their flight decks so that the fliers could find their way back and land.

It was a disheartening operation in that so many of our planes went down. The next day we were deployed in a very large, long scouting line. We swept through the area where the American planes had returned in an effort to find and pick up survivors.

On 23 June, the *Twining* was detached from Task Force 58 and ordered back to continue its operations on Saipan and Tinian. *Twining* provided gunfire support many times, but two times really stick in my mind. One of them was a twenty-four-hour period during which we provided gunfire support to the Marines and soldiers on the beach. We pulled in to Magicienne Bay [east side of Saipan] and stayed there providing indirect fire* for that whole time. This indirect fire was the type in which the shore fire control liaison officer would call the ship by radio and give us the coordinates of the target he wished to take under fire. We would fire on it and he would spot it. Then he would give us another target. I was particularly concerned as time wore on, because the shore fire control liaison officer was calling on us to fire closer and closer to our front lines. Because of my concern that rounds might fall short when we got such a situation, I would only fire the guns on the "up-roll," which is a shipboard artillery tactic used ever since there have been guns on ships. That is, if there was going to be any error it was going to be long and not drop short on our own men.

Whether it was to boost our morale or not, I don't know, but our shore fire control liaison officer told us that because of the accuracy of our gunfire the Marines had not only requested that we fire very close to their front lines, but they had requested our ship in particular because of the accuracy and dependability of our fire.

During the night we had a pre-set schedule of random firings into enemy-held territory in order to keep the Japanese on their toes. We also lobbed star shells to continuously illuminate their positions. This was to preclude any maneuvering on the part of the enemy during the night.

On another occasion we were off the west coast of Saipan, near Garapan, when we were contacted by the shore fire control liaison officer who stated that the Marines had been stopped at the southern border of the town. They asked that we deliver a destructive fire on the town. We fired, as I recall, five or ten five-gun salvos set for air busts, which would give the maximum effect against personnel dug in below. After having delivered this fire, the shore fire control liaison officer reported back that we had done an excellent job and that the Marines were now walking into Garapan.

When on patrol off the west coast of Saipan one got an unusual view of the action. If you were at the south and steaming north you would look toward the beach and see trucks and other activity. A little further north you would see clotheslines out with laundry on them. But the further you got to the north, and the closer you got to the front lines, you'd see less and less activity until finally there wasn't any motion whatsoever. Then you knew, of course, those were the front lines.

One event that resulted in a lot of activity aboard ship was when Chamorro women and their children were periodically brought down to one of the beaches to bathe. Naturally, every piece of optical equipment on the ship was brought to bear in order to watch these ladies take their baths.

Oftentimes when we were on patrol off the west coast of Saipan, informal arrangements were made with the Marines on the beach to bring some of them on board. We would send our whaleboat over, pick them up, and bring them aboard. Immediately, some clothing was loaned to them, while theirs was washed by our laundry. They were given dinner. Our gunners' mates cleaned and oiled their weapons. They saw a movie, got a good night's sleep, and were put ashore the following morning. One time, with some of these Marines aboard, there was an air attack. Some of my men reported that the Marines said that they wanted to get the hell off that ship, because if they were on the beach they could dig a hole, and for a bomb to do any damage it would have to land directly on top of them. But on our ship a bomb could land a hundred yards away and down would go the ship with them on board. We all thought that rather amusing.

During the later part of the action on Saipan, the senior Marine Corps/Naval gunfire liaison officer on the beach instituted a series of tours for gunnery officers of the Navy ships that had provided gunfire support. I was given that opportunity one day, and was told to arm myself. I put on my tin hat, which on the beach made me stand out like a sore thumb, in that we painted them grey. And although I was qualified as an expert rifleman, I thought it would be unbecoming for a Navy lieutenant to go carrying a rifle, so I strapped on my .45, which I could just barely hit the broad side of a barn with, and went ashore. As I recall, when we got ashore at Garapan there were a couple of Jeeps there to take our party around. We made a sort of counterclockwise tour of the island. We first drove down to Chalan Kanoa. Then we drove across the island and up the east coast. We went through an area where there had been a tank battle. To me, it was astounding. The whole area was covered with litter. There wasn't a six-inch space that didn't have on it spent ammunition or live ammunition, hand grenades, and playing cards. Everywhere I looked there were playing cards. I don't know if every soldier carried playing cards, or whether some haver-

**Gunfire where the firing ship cannot see the target either optically or by radar.*

*Lt. VanDusen standing beside the main battery gun director of the* Twining. *By war's end the* Twining *was credited with the downing of seven enemy airplanes, gunfire support at Saipan and Tinian, and taking part in the bombardment of the Japanese home islands.*

sack was hit that was full of them, but they were all over the place.

As we stopped something caught my eye, and I went over to it. It was what had been an American field dressing station. There were a few body parts around, and I noticed a soldier's body there. I went over and saw that his body had a tag on it to the effect that he had been injured in the shoulder. He was a sergeant and had been cut in half. Whether that was because of artillery fire or what ... I don't know.

Shortly after finding his body I heard a boom, saw a cloud of dust, and heard some small arms fire. I looked back to where the rest of the party was and saw them scrambling to get under a Jeep. There was no room for me (I'm 6'3" and weighed 230 lbs.). Shortly thereafter a couple of Jeep loads of Marines arrived and they finished off a few straggling Japs in a nearby grove of trees. I surely felt foolish during that episode with my haze grey helmet, useless .45-caliber pistol, and no place to hide.

Further up the coast we went into a reinforced concrete house that had allegedly been the last headquarters of the Admiral Nagumo.* It had been severely damaged by naval gunfire, but at the same time we did notice that there were several sixteen-inch projectiles laying on the ground that did not explode when they hit. This was probably because of the relatively flat trajectory when they came in at fairly close range. In this room was a hand-cranked record player that we

**Adm. Nagumo led the attack against Pearl Harbor. He later committed suicide along with Gen. Saito, the ranking Japanese Army commander on Saipan, in a small cave in Paradise Valley, near the present day village of San Roque.*

cranked up, and there were some RCA records with it that were made in Japan.

We then crossed over to the west side of the island and came down to the beach where Japanese dead had been stacked like cordwood in big piles along the beach. From there we drove back down the coast. At one point we passed a little burial ground which contained two crosses and a Star of David. Around it was a little white picket fence. Someone had taken great care to make this little cemetery for these three men. I thought it would be a shame if they were ever disinterred and brought back and put in a veteran's cemetery, because there was a story to be told there with the Christian and Jewish soldiers or Marines side by side. Obviously, they had been interred by some caring people.

We also visited an enclosure where some women were being kept. A doctor who was there said that many of them were prostitutes, and that they were conducting business with U.S. military personnel through the barbed wire. I thought that presented some pretty tricky problems for the people who undertook that form of recreation.

The Navy established a Fleet Post Office in Garapan after the fighting had passed to the north. One of my gunners' mates had the collateral duty of the ship's mailman, and whenever we were on patrol close enough we would send him over on the whaleboat to pick up our mail. On one trip I got word through the grapevine that he had come back with a bottle of sake that he had purchased from somebody on the beach. I called him to my stateroom and asked him if that was true. He said, "Yes." Then I told him, "Well, you know you can't have alcoholic beverages on board ship. But I tell you what I will do; you gather some of your buddies and we will all go back on the fantail. We'll open the bottle. You can all take a drink, then we will pour the rest over the side." There, the gunner's mate opened the bottle and took a swig. He immediately had a disgusted look on his face. It turned out it wasn't sake at all, but some sort of red fish paste. Naturally, his buddies refused the honor of taking a drink and the fish paste went over the side.

In general, at nighttime we took the picket station to the north of Saipan to give early warning of any enemy aircraft flying down from Iwo Jima. During the day we were assigned various patrol sectors around the island about a mile to two miles off of the beach. What we saw was what we could see through the magnified optics of either the gun director, the range finder,* or binoculars. Also, we didn't hang around in one spot. We were moving all the time so that we wouldn't become a target for artillery or submarines. As a result, we didn't see much detail of what was going on on the beach. Occasionally, I did see people jump off the cliffs, hit the rocks, then skid down into the water. Just north of Saipan was a Sargasso Sea of bodies. It was disheartening, because among the bodies was a woman holding a baby to her breast. One day when we passed through this sea of bodies we spotted the body of a Japanese soldier. Our captain stopped the ship, and we took a grappling hook and hooked the Japanese body to see if he had any valuable intelligence information on him. He didn't.

The Japanese by this time were pushed up into the northern tip of the island and were jumping from the cliffs at Marpi Point. Occasionally, when our day patrol assignment was off of Marpi Point we could see our men in their camouflage uniforms talking to them with loudspeakers, trying to convince them that no harm would come to them, but obviously this was to no avail.

On 7 August 1944, *Twining* departed Saipan after participating in the taking of Tinian. During the entire war, and the approximately twenty months the *Twining* was at sea we lost only one man. He was lost overboard in one of the two typhoons that we went through. Subsequent to the Saipan and Tinian operations the *Twining* operated with the Fast Carrier Task Force and was one of the first destroyers to enter Tokyo Bay at the end of the war. During that period *Twining* took part in the Western Caroline Islands operations— that is, Palau— and the assault on the Philippine Islands, the Leyte operation, Luzon, Formosa, and the battle of Surigao Strait. We had one star for the Iwo Jima operation, one star for the Okinawa Gunto operation, and a battle star for the Third Fleet operations against Japan, including a bombardment of the Japanese home islands. The *Twining* earned eight battle stars during her career in World War II.

We learned that the war was over while on picket duty with the Fast Carrier Task Force we were assigned to. Our aircraft had been attacking the Japanese home

**An optical device in the ship's gun director used to determine the range of a target being tracked.*

Opposite: *Suicide Cliff, over 800 feet high, where Japanese men, women, and children jumped to their deaths. Battle hardened soldiers and Marines watched as women with babies or small children jumped, and stood helpless as fathers shoved their wives and children, then followed them in the long plunge. Pleas made by Japanese-speaking Marines and soldiers over loud-speaker systems persuaded few to surrender. American sailors in small boats pulled some from the water, but the bodies were so thick in places that they fouled the propellors on the boats. Those who missed the ocean and landed on the rocks lingered, sometimes for days, before dying.*

islands at that time. The kamikazes had become such a threat that when we went out on picket duty there were often four of us instead of just one to provide mutual anti-aircraft support. We also had four fighter aircraft assigned to orbit over us to provide additional protection. On 9 August, while operating alone on picket station, we learned of the order to cease fire. We had large numbers of aircraft airborne. The ones with bombs were ordered to jettison their bombs and return to their carriers. The fighters were ordered to stay in the air and shoot any Japanese aircraft that came out. Shortly after this we heard somebody on our radio shout that thirty or so airplanes were taking off from a Japanese field and heading for us. Sure enough, shortly thereafter a Japanese plane starts to make a kamikaze attack on us. We tried to get through on the one radio link that we had back to the main force to tell them we were under attack, but we couldn't get through because Adm. Halsey was on that link congratulating everybody for having won the war, and reminiscing about his days in the Navy. We took the plane under fire and I can remember standing in the gun director and looking up. The plane's target angle was zero—it was coming right at us. We had a good fire control solution, but we weren't hitting the target. I thought this was it and had the strangely reassuring thought that I had just had a shower and was clean! At the last moment the plane pulled out and went out over the horizon where it was subsequently shot down by one of our aircraft. Years later I read a report stating that the commanding officer of the Kamikaze Corps was a Japanese rear admiral* who wanted to commit hara-kiri and gathered around him some three dozen other pilots who wanted to do the same. The Emperor's orders were to stop the killing but they didn't say anything about not committing hara-kiri, so these people jumped in their airplanes. What they were doing was coming out to commit suicide by making suicide runs against us. Had this been a wartime situation I'm convinced that plane would have hit us.

I think the general reaction of the crew on the *Twining* when we learned of the dropping of the atomic bomb was one of relief. Remember, we were a picket destroyer. At Okinawa we were losing roughly a picket destroyer a day in kamikaze attacks. We had on board the operation plan for the invasion of the Japanese home islands. We were to be a picket again and already they had smaller ships assigned to stay with us to pick up survivors if any of us were hit by kamikazes, as they had been doing at Okinawa. That is, they would assign smaller ships like LSIs [landing ship, infantry] to stay with us. They were such small targets, hard to hit, and generally not attacked by the kamikazes. We felt that if we did have to invade Japan we would probably last three days before we were sunk, so naturally the thought of the war being over was greeted with joy.

*The last official photograph of Capt. VanDusen before he retired from the Navy.*

After the war the *Twining* came back to the West Coast and was put into mothballs. It was brought back out during the Korean War, then used as a training ship for the Naval Reserves before being sold in 1971 to the National Chinese on Formosa. It served there for quite a number of years, then was sold as scrap. It is probably now in pots and pans all over the world.

I served on five destroyers both during and after the war, and the *Twining* was the best of all of them in terms of the morale, spirit, and the training of the officers and the crew. I think this is reflected in the fact that the *Twining* has had well attended reunions at least every other year since shortly after the Korean War.

*Probably Admiral Matome Ugaki.

# Patrol Bombing Squadron Twenty-Two

## Bob Willig

*Bob Willig was born in Middletown, Pennsylvania, in 1921. He was working for the U.S. Army Air Force when the United States entered World War II. He joined the U.S. Navy eight months later.*

I joined the U.S. Navy in August 1942. There were too many flags flying and too many bands playing so I left my civilian job. I could have stayed at my civilian job for the entire war but I felt like I had to do something so I joined the Navy. I certainly didn't want to be in one of those trenches or mud holes. That is why I went into the Navy, but I forgot there was a lot of water out there too. After I finished my training I was put on a train and went across the country to San Francisco. I had been assigned to VPB-22. We flew PBM3Ds, a two-engine amphibious aircraft. We had a 13-man crew. The reason we had such a large crew was because we had six gun stations, two flight engineers, a radioman, three pilots, a bombardier, and two ordnance men. The pilots also served as navigators.*

In August 1944, we were put on an escort carrier, the USS *Shipley Bay* and sent to Hawaii. Escort carriers were used mostly to ferry airplanes out of the country and over to the front. That was my first experience on an aircraft carrier.

When we arrived in Hawaii we did some more training before heading out to the Pacific. One thing I remember about flying out of Kaneohe in Hawaii—you took off in the bay and right at the end of the bay there were high mountains. These PBMs were so underpowered, and the pilot had to make a decision to either lift off or try again. Quite a few times we had four or five runs before we could break the water and make the turn away from the mountains.

In September we left Pearl Harbor on the USS *General Patrick*, a troop transport. We arrived at Enewetak in the Marshall Islands on November 4, 1944, and stayed on board ship for three days. From Enewetak we went to Guam where we were supposed to catch a plane for Saipan. I believe it was in Agana, Guam — we walked up this incline. There was a bunch of tents along this path that was just big enough for a Jeep. These other Americans came out with some things in their hands. They were Marines or soldiers who had fought to take the island and I'm sure they went through hell. They said, "They're teeth, man — teeth; they're Japanese teeth! We're selling them. You want to buy some?" I don't know where they got 'em — I can only imagine. And I don't know if they were trying to scare us or impress us.

We left Guam on an Army DC-3 on November 13, 1944, and arrived on Saipan about an hour later at Isley Field. That evening we went to a movie. We were all sitting there watching a movie and all of a sudden general quarters was sounded. We all got up, the movie went off— here there were a couple of Japs setting up a machine gun to spray the guys watching the movie. They had come down from the hills and had infiltrated right there next to where we were watching the movie. I don't know what happened to the Japs, but we didn't go back to the movie.

When we arrived on Saipan we found out that our squadron was back at Enewetak, so the next day we took a plane back to Enewetak. It was about six hours of flying to get back there. We didn't stay very long. We flew our planes back to Saipan and stayed there overnight. Plane #14 sank when it tore its bottom on the coral reef. We lost plane #6 while still on Enewetak, so we lost two planes before we even got to our forward area.

We left Saipan early the next morning and headed for Palau. That was about six and a half hours of flying. At Palau we were stationed off Babeldaop Island in the Kossol Passage which was just to the north of Babeldaop. Kossol was almost open sea and rough. We were told at the time that there were about 40,000 Japs on Palau. We operated off the USS *Casco*, a sea plane tender about eight miles offshore.

After dark there would usually be three or four of us on board the plane, which was tied to a buoy. In fact there was someone on board all the time, but at night especially. One of us would be on top of one of the wings with a rifle or Thompson machine gun. We would be up there in case any of the Japs from the island approached the plane. We didn't have any problems in our squadron but I do know that one of the squadrons did have Japs come out and attempt to

**Pilots: 1st pilot was Lt. Harold Strohoefer. Other pilots were Ensigns Carl Lamb and Lester Stawser. Other Crew Members: Wayne Tadman, Rosario Cannizzaaro, Robert Willig, William Walden, John McMullen, Louis Fusco, Thomas Murray, Lloyd Thompson, and Omer Carrico.*

*Bob Willig in 1944.*

destroy their planes. During the day we had no fear, but of course we had a large part of the fleet always around where we were. That was one of our jobs too—to protect the fleet—keep an eye out for any approaching enemy subs, ships, or any other kind of threat.

We usually took off at dusk and came back the next morning at daybreak. Sometimes we had to come back and land in the dark. When that happened a ship would leave three buoys out among the ships so we would know where to land. Each of these buoys had a light on it and the ships were all blacked out. I remember one time we came in after dark. We had a new pilot; I think he was still training. We saw these three lights and after a while they started drifting in different directions. We didn't know which direction to come in. I was at the waist gun mount, looking out and I could see that we were below the level of the ships' masts. Some of them were only a couple of hundred feet away. It was hard to see the water and it was also hard to judge altitude at night. However, radio contact with the tender helped us identify the drift of the lighted buoys so that we were able to land.

On November 29, 1944, we had been out all night flying and had just finished morning chow when G.Q. [general quarters] was sounded. We were told that the Japs were heading our way with between eight and thirty Bettys [a Japanese Mitsubishi land-based attack plane]. It was a suicide squadron and they were headed for our anchorage. Unfortunately, our plane, *The Whiskey Head,* Crew #11, was on the deck of the seaplane tender *Kenneth Whiting* having its tail rudder repaired. We had torn the rudder off while landing. They dropped *Whiskey Head* over the side and we took off. We were flying around above eight American aircraft carriers and ten destroyers. The Japs did arrive, and they bombed a floating dry dock but only one of the Japanese bombers made it through.

We flew these planes until they just went down. We lost quite a few. As I recall, by the end of our stay out there we had lost ten or eleven planes. One time around the beginning of December 1944, we had just got into the air, then our engine cowling started flying off. We took that plane back and got another one. However, it was fairly dark when we took off, it was raining, there were strong winds, and the water was rough. We seldom wore our Mae Wests. We were fearless—all just a bunch of young kids, even the pilots. But that night we all wore our Mae Wests because we were concerned about the conditions, and we were concerned about getting off the water. We never even wore our parachutes except one time when we lost an engine. But we figured if you had to jump out over that sea you were going to be down there all by yourself anyway, and you were going to drown.

On December 8, 1944, we were flying patrol around Babeldaop. We were flying low, maybe 1,000 or 2,000, feet, and watched Corsairs fighter planes bomb and destroy a Jap radio tower on Babeldaop. There was also a Japanese sub sighted near there. We were flying in and out of the harbors, thinking it would be hiding in there somewhere but we never did find it.

On December 12, 1944, plane #13 crashed on

Opposite: *Bob Willig's plane, the* Whiskey Head, *went down at sea off the island of Yap. This photograph shows flight engineer Rosie Cannizzaro on the bow.*

takeoff. It tried to take off twice and just bounced up and down — the pilot couldn't get off the water. It was damaged beyond repair, and they pulled it on board a tender before it could sink and stripped it. Also, Plane #5, about two weeks before, was badly damaged when it crash-landed at sea after one engine failed. That was while night flying and the crew was picked up.

Flying those PBMs was like landing an ordinary plane in a corn field. You would hit these swells— these swells could be anywhere from eight to fifteen feet high. In these PBMs you would hit one, then another, then another. If you lost too much speed, you lost control of the airplane. Then you just had to hang on and hope that your next hit stopped you.

On December 14, 1944, Plane #14 crashed while coming in for a landing after a patrol. They were actually lost in a typhoon, were three hours overdue, and came in at 8:30 in the evening. When they landed a depth charge came out of the bomb bay and blew the whole tail off the airplane. The plane sank in just a couple of minutes, but it was unbelievable that all hands were saved. Only one crewman was hurt.

On the next day we flew off and into that same typhoon. Those old PBMs were tough. They were like flying tanks. On this same flight we strafed some Jap fighter that was on the ground about ten miles from where we were anchored.

On December 25, 1944, general quarters was sounded while we were eating Christmas dinner. An unidentified plane was approaching, but I don't think any plane got through because I don't remember anything happening. For dinner out there we had some of

*VPB 22, Crew #11.* Front row, left to right: *Louis Fusco, radio; Lloyd Thompson, ordnance; Bob Willig, flight engineer; Rosie Cannizzaro, flight engineer; Tom Murray, radio; Bill Waldon, flight engineer; Omer Carrico, ordnance.* Back row, left to right: *Wayne Tadman, crew chief; Ens. L. Strawser; Lt. H. Strohoefer; Ens. C. Lamb; John McMullen, radio.*

the best food. That is one of the reasons I joined the Navy. I didn't want to fight in the mud, and the Navy had good food no matter where they were because of their storage capacity and freezers. We had turkey for Christmas, and ice cream, cranberry sauce — the works. Even when we went out on a flight we were given a cardboard box. There were twelve or thirteen of us in a crew, and one of the crew would do the cooking. We had a little galley under the flight deck; if I remember correctly it was two little hot plates. Almost always what we got in our cardboard box was steaks or chops, cans of peaches, and a can of corn or two. To do ten or twelve steaks on an airplane was quite an accomplishment. It took two or three hours to get all that done. And there was a pound of butter and a loaf of bread — maybe two loaves of bread.

On the day after Christmas, Plane #8 with crew #2 on board were reported down and lost at sea. Two planes on night patrol were out looking for them after taking their radio bearing. The planes found them and circled over head. They were 180 miles out to sea and a destroyer was trying to tow them in.

It was on December 30, 1944, that one of the planes caught on fire. They were refueling and the gas either from the boat or the plane caught on fire and they were both destroyed. The fellows on the plane — there were three of them — jumped overboard and saved themselves. But one of the crew members from the gas tender was severely burned. He came up the gangplank — I never saw anything like that in my life. He was actually grey all over — no clothing. I don't know how that poor guy walked. He didn't make it. He couldn't have because his whole body was severely burned. That was a sight I hope I will never see again.

In early January 1945, we were out on patrol and we thought we had picked up a Japanese sub on our radar. We went to the area and circled around for almost six hours but couldn't find anything. However, we did try to drop our depth charges where we thought the sub was, but they stuck in the bomb bay. Our ordnance man, Lloyd Thompson, crawled up into the bomb bay. We had to leave the bomb bay doors open because we were afraid that if the depth charges did drop they would drop inside the plane. Thompson was a long spindly guy, and I followed him up. Half of his body was actually out over the open bomb bay and he tried to kick these depth charges out. That didn't work, so we tried to drop them again three or four times. We did get them to drop but only by dropping the extra fuel tanks at the same time.

We would go out at dusk and come back at dawn. It was boring, believe me. There is nothing darker than the middle of the ocean if there are no stars or moon out. And of course you can't have navigation lights on, and the ships have no lights. We would pick up a target on radar and try to find it, but it was very difficult to get a sub once it submerged, especially at night. We did have sonar buoys. We would drop those in the water by parachute. They had an antenna and a transmitter in them. We would drop these in four different areas, forming a square around the area we thought the sub was located. When they hit the water a microphone would drop down and the antenna would stick out above the water. This way if there was a sub in that square we could hear what direction the sub was going, or how close he was to one buoy or another. This we did quite a few times.

On January 12, 1945, we were just returning from a flight when we contacted two small Jap subs. They were suicide subs and they were right amongst our ships in the harbor. One of our planes — Crew #1 — took off to see if they could see them. It was such a small area that we couldn't use more than one airplane. In the end, these subs were sunk by ships' gunfire. Two Japanese bodies were recovered.

On January 21, 1945, we were told that we were going to leave Palau. Believe me, we were all glad to get out of that place. That was rough duty. Many times we would land and it would actually tear the earphones off my head. It was the next thing to a crash a lot of times, we hit that water so hard.

When we left Palau we went to Ulithi, and there we boarded the USS *Cumberland Sound*. It was great duty up there — the water was calm. At times there were so many ships in that harbor you would think it was a city. At night they felt so secure in there that the ships left their lights on. One night we were watching a movie on deck — all outdoors. It was about 8 o'clock at night and this plane came over the top of us — right over the top of our ship. We all looked up because this plane flew so low. We knew it wasn't off a carrier. I thought, "Where in the hell did that plane come from?" I could see that it was a Zero, and about three seconds later there was a loud boom! There was fire and sparks and we knew something was hit right in the middle of the harbor. This Jap got through and hit the USS *Randolph*, a carrier. I don't know how many people were killed. Then about a half a minute later another explosion happened. Two Japs got through. The second one hit a warehouse on the atoll.*

**Originally 24 planes set out on this mission. Most of the planes returned to base with engine problems, or ran out of fuel and crashed at sea.*

On one of our flights we came across the USS *Franklin*. We escorted it for a couple of hours, flying around it. It was being towed back to the States by way of Honolulu. We were at about 1,000 feet when we went around this carrier, and it was full of holes. I don't know how anybody could have survived it. Its color was rust and black.*

On February 26, 1945, we were flying out of Ulithi and we had engine trouble. We were out 300 miles when one of the engines went out on us. We dropped down until we were only a couple of hundred feet off the water. We threw all of the excess gear overboard, everything except water and food. Believe it or not there was an admiral and a commander along with us from one of the carriers. To get their flight time in they would go out on our planes. We did get back to base, and I'm sure the admiral and the commander were just as glad to get back as we were.

Sometime in February we had been out most of the day, and it was late in the afternoon; we were coming down back towards Yap Island. During this period we were bombing Yap. Two or three planes a day would go in and bomb Yap and Ngulu Atoll. Anyway, we were headed for Yap, and we were within sight of it when our starboard engine cut out completely. We turned away from the island and were attempting to get the gas from our starboard engine over to the port engine. We had dropped down quite a bit but were holding our own just above the water with the one engine when it quit too. I will never forget the quiet. Then everybody started running around to see what we could do. Our plane captain, Wayne Tadman, took over the control panel — the engineer's control panel. Others tried to get the auxiliary power going, which they never did. The first place I went to was below the flight deck. There was a hand pump down there, and I felt sure we had an air lock and weren't getting gas to our port engine. I was on my knees and I knew we were going down. I was pumping and every once in a while the port engine would catch. I pumped like that for maybe five minutes. When it sounded like the engine was back and running I would stop pumping until it cut out again. I almost tore my insides out pumping. It's a wonder I didn't break the pump off the wall. Then we hit the first swell. It sounded like somebody dropped all the pots and pans in your kitchen on the floor at one time. That is the sound I remember. We bounced up again and I fell flat on the floor. We hit a second time — more pots and pans. The third time we hit it was like hitting a brick wall. We were stopped, but still floating. I couldn't believe it. I would say from the time the first engine went out until we hit the sea was about twenty minutes. We managed to stay in the air that long.

**On the morning of March 19, 1945, while off the coast of Okinawa, the USS Franklin was hit by two bombs dropped by a Japanese plane. At the time the flight deck was full of planes loaded with bombs and rockets. Most of the damage was the result of the ensuing fire that set off the rockets and bombs.*

*Bob Willig in 1998.*

I'm guessing it was about three o'clock in the afternoon. We were down and we had gotten off a "May Day" distress call over the radio. The radioman was sending in code where we were. He didn't have time to get the whole message coded so he sent the rest of it in plain English. That was a real no-no, because half of his message was in code and half was in plain English. The Japanese could break our code for that week if they had picked it up.

It was getting dark and one of our planes picked up our distress call. They reported our location and went back to Ulithi because they were low on fuel. We were concerned that we would wash up on Yap. The plane was badly damaged and there was a leak in the hull, but we were still floating. I saw the report from the ship that picked us up — they picked us up at ten minutes after twelve that night. Nobody even knew there was a ship there because nobody could turn any lights on. Then I saw this black spot and it was only about a 100 feet away from us. It was a destroyer escort there to pick us up. It was the USS *Alvin C. Cockrell* (DE-366). The seas were rough and to get on board the ship we had to crawl up these nets. Once all of us were aboard ship one of the boat crew fell overboard. It was that rough, but they did save the crewman and we all got away safely. They tried to tow the plane and salvage it, but it was badly damaged and they had to sink it with gun fire.

I want to say that we had the greatest pilots. Lt. Strohoefer was a school teacher in New Jersey before the war. I give him all the credit for bringing us back after that landing in the open sea.

We continued to fly for about another three weeks after we lost our plane off Yap. Then another squadron relieved us and we went back to the States. Our planes were left at Ulithi. I don't know who took them over after we left, but I doubt that those planes were flown much longer. They were actually falling apart when we left. That is how we lost most of our planes; we just flew them until they fell apart.

We left Ulithi on an LST for Hawaii. That thing went along at maybe twelve or thirteen knots and we were on it for quite a few days before we got back to Hawaii.

In the last couple of years I have been getting sentimental, I guess, and I have gotten in touch with quite a few of the fellows I served with.

# 9 The Army Air Force

## B-29 Lead Pilot

RAY BRASHEAR

*Ray Brashear was born in Long Beach, California, in 1919. He joined the first College Pilot Training program at Long Beach Junior College in 1939. In 1940 he left school to join the Army Air Corps. He retired from the Air Force in 1963 and now lives in Sunnyvale, California.*

With the war raging in Europe the United States decided to start building up its military. The Army Air Corps started several "Contract Flying Schools." These were civilian programs paid for by the Army Air Corps. At that time each flying cadet went through primary, basic, and advanced training. Each phase lasted approximately three months. They also started a College Pilot Training Program (CPT). College students could sign up for the program in addition to their normal classes. Flight training was conducted at a local airport. They were in no way connected with the military. However, the first class of College Pilot Training graduates were taken right into the Army Air Corps. I was in that first class in the Fall of 1939, and was fortunate enough to be selected for the advanced CPT program during the Summer of 1940. I never did graduate from college. I had this chance to go into the Air Corps, so I took it. For good or bad I went right to Randolph Field in San Antonio, Texas, without going through the Army primary. Fortunately for me, my advanced CPT instructor was an old Army pilot and he taught me the "Army way." There were four of us CPT students in one room at Randolph Field. The other three washed out, so I was the only one in the room after that and had to do all the housework.

From Randolph I went to the other side of San Antonio, to Kelly Field. After completing that course I graduated on 14 March 1941, as a shiny second lieutenant with a pilot's rating. My first assignment was at Moffett Field, California, when the Air Corps had it. I was sent there as a flight instructor. Sunday, December 1st, 1941, I was transferred to Merced Army Flying Field in California as an instructor.

The following Sunday, December 7th, the war started. I had just bought quite a few civilian clothes in Palo Alto to wear in Merced, but when the war started we could wear nothing but uniforms. In those days we were flying BT-13s, basic trainers. I should have had a clue that the war was coming, but I didn't. Some British pilot had come over and gave a lecture on his combat flying experiences in Spitfires. That got our attention about the war in Europe, but I didn't know we would get involved in it at that time. I was just thinking about flying and my weekends in San Francisco. My student load quickly went from four to eight students after the war started, and I had about all the flying I could handle. I was in Merced for three years. I went from flight instructor, to squadron commander, to director of flying, and finally to director of training for the whole base.

By that time the B-29 program had started and they were looking for experienced pilots. They looked

*Ray Brashear in his "flight line" uniform. Saipan, 1944–1945.*

at the training command and found that most of the flight instructors were well qualified. So, I ended up in the B-29 program. The program was running quite late because of mechanical problems with the new planes. First I went to Sebring, Florida, and checked out on B-17s. That was in 1943. The Fifty-eighth Bomb Wing was still in Salina, Kansas, plus three other bases, trying to get checked-out on B-29s and get the planes combat ready. As a result, they were late in leaving for India. So we sat in Clovis, New Mexico, for about three months before we could go to Salina. When I finally got to Salina we had very little training in B-29s. It was mostly in B-17s, because there were very few B-29s ready and they had all kinds of engine problems. They would overheat, catch fire, and so forth. They were modifying them both at the factory and at the training bases.

Finally, in late October 1944, the Seventy-third Bomb Wing headed for the Pacific. We weren't sure where we were going at first. It was at the last minute that we found out we were going to Saipan. After several weather delays we did get off for John Rogers Field in Honolulu. We spent a couple of days there because of bad weather, then went to Kwajalein Island in the Marshalls. We spent the night there. We finally found out we were in a war zone because all of the magazines and newspapers we had on board were stripped out of the airplane by the ground crews. Newspapers and magazines were hard to get there. We left for Saipan the next day.

The first B-29s of the Fifty-eighth Bomb Wing went to China and India. The first bombings of the Japanese home islands took place from China. That was before the taking of Saipan and Tinian. Planes in India had to fly bombs and fuel over the Himalayas from India to the bases in China. I think it took four or five trips over "The Hump" to get enough fuel to fly one B-29 to Japan and back. General Curtis LeMay was in charge of that.

I think it was the 10th of November 1944 that we arrived on Saipan. There were several B-29s that arrived before us. *Dauntless Dotty* was the first one; they arrived in late October. After a couple of days of briefings we got ready for our first raid on Tokyo. There were several aborted attempts to fly the first missions because of bad weather over Japan. Finally, after about three briefings we got off on the 24th of November. Our first raid was a total disaster. We flew between 27,000 and 30,000 feet and we didn't know what the jet stream was. There were overcast skies and the planes got scattered all over Japan. The planes flew back to Saipan individually except for our group, the 449th Group. They didn't think they could recover all

*Ray Brashear's crew in 1945. From left to right in the back row are Major Ray Brashear, aircraft commander; Dick Hart, co-pilot; Bud Parsons, flight engineer; Ed Bartenstein, navigator; and Don McCabe, bombardier. (All of these were lieutenants.)* Front row: *S/Sgt. Lyle Darling, CFC gunner; Sgt. Bob Wiggans, left gunner; Sgt. Bob Wagner, right gunner; Sgt. Charlie Alder, radar operator; T/Sgt. Ted Douglas, tail gunner; and Ian Stewart, radio operator.*

the planes at Saipan, so we had to go to Guam. But that was a mistake because the runways were not ready, and they didn't have any maintenance. My navigator almost got lost. He made a line of position on his chart. We flew to that, made a left turn, and about ten minutes later Guam showed up. That first raid was a waste — we didn't do any damage. We didn't even know where our bombs dropped. When we got up to our bombing altitude the winds from the jet stream blew us so hard we dropped our bombs by guess.

On that first mission there was very little flak but quite a few Japanese fighter planes met us. I honestly don't know how many B-29s we lost over the target because the B-29s were pretty well scattered, and the Japanese fighters had trouble intercepting them. There were several planes that ditched at sea on that first mission coming back to Saipan. The Japanese still had Iwo Jima at that time, so we couldn't go in there. Some of the crews were picked up by our submarines, and some were never found. There wasn't much of a search and rescue system in the early days of our operations against Japan. We had submarines placed at intervals, but the Japanese pretty much controlled the water at that time.

My co-pilot was Dick Hart. My flight engineer was Bud Parsons. My navigator was Edwin Bartenstein. The radio operator was Ian Stewart. He was the original hippy. It was hot out there, so he would cut the bottoms off his shirts. But in Saipan you could do almost anything — wear almost any uniform. Charley Alder was my radar operator. The CFC (Central Fire Control) gunner was Lyle Darling, the left gunner was Bob Wagner. The right gunner was Bob Wiggens, and the tail gunner was Ted Douglas. My first bombardier was Alfonso J. Piaquadio. He was from Brooklyn. My second bombardier was Don McCabe. He was one of three survivors of an earlier ditching and joined our crew when we later returned from Hawaii.

After that first mission I flew almost every other mission for quite a while. I had a very good flight engineer. He was an M.I.T. graduate, and he nursed those engines along beautifully. I think I had three aborts and twenty-five successful missions before we went to Hawaii for rest.

We had a lot of accidents on landings. Some of the planes had their tires shot out during missions. Some had two engines out. We had a couple of aircraft commanders who said they couldn't take it, so they were pulled off crews and put in staff positions.

Early on, Japanese fighters would attack Isley Field. They only came in on moonlit nights. One night they hit a B-29 that was loading bombs, getting ready for a mission. The bomb loaders were in the bomb bay and the plane was on fire, but they didn't know it. The bomb hoists were making lots of noise. Finally, somebody went into the bomb bay and told them their plane was on fire. They got out of there and it blew up moments later. There was another raid of about seventeen Zeros that came in just about noon. Every day at noon they would blow all of the air raid sirens just to make sure they would work, and that day the Zeros came in at just about that time. When the air raid sirens went off at noon that day everybody stopped and reset their watches. Those Zeros had a field day. They shot up all sorts of planes we had on the ground. I think all but one of the attacking planes were finally shot down. We had pretty good air defense systems by then. I think by April or May of 1945 the Japs gave up and we didn't have too many raids after that.

General LeMay came over from India and took over from General Hansel. General Hansel was an advocate of high altitude bombing, but the weather was so bad over Japan during the winter months that we could seldom see the ground. General LeMay started these low level incendiary raids. I flew four out of the first five raids. That was really scary, flying through those huge smoke columns. When I flew through one I had the bomb bay doors open and you could smell burning flesh.

I led the entire daytime raid on Kobe, Japan, on the 5th of June, 1945. I think there were about 500 planes behind me, and Colonel Morse J. Lee flew with me because he had to make any decisions if we were to go to an alternate target, but the weather was clear and my bombardier dropped our bombs right on the aiming point. We were fairly low, at 1,500 feet.

We made a right turn to get out over some water, and I was just about to turn south to head back to Saipan when suddenly the plane pitched up violently. I had to cut the power back and we staggered along at a reduced speed. The squadron behind me separated and disappeared. About then the CFC gunner on top of the airplane reported that the right leading edge of the horizontal stabilizer was blown wide open. Colonel Lee went back to look. He came back and said, "Well captain, I think it will stay on," which wasn't very encouraging. About that time the plane shook violently and nosed down. I got everything trimmed back, but the airplane was totally unstable. The right horizontal stabilizer had ripped off. When it pointed down it went down violently, and when it started up it did the same. It reminded me of trying to balance a broom in the palm of my hand. I asked Colonel Lee if he thought we should go into Iwo, and he said, "Well, it's up to you." So I turned on their frequency, and it was terrible on Iwo. There were so many other B-29s trying to get into the traffic pattern there. They had engines shot out; some were low on fuel, or had wounded on board. And as we flew over it we could see this whole string of planes trying to get into the traffic pattern, so I told the Colonel I would try to wrestle the plane all the way back to Saipan. I teeter-tottered the plane all the way back. It was a slow flight, about seven and a half hours.

While we were still over Kobe our left and right gunners both had reported that there was a twin-engine fighter several thousand feet below us. Normally, when the Japanese had fighters pacing us they would be off to one side, directing anti-aircraft fire, but like I said this guy was two or three thousand feet below us. At the time we thought it was rather stupid of him to be directly below us in the line of anti-aircraft fire. We found out later that it was a twin engine "Nick." The pilot was up front, then in the back they had taken the gunner out and put two 20-millimeter cannons, and pointed them straight up. The pilot had some sort of ring sight up over his canopy, and he flew directly under the formation and kept shooting these cannons at us. Unluckily for us, he hit us. Many years after the war I talked to Saburo Saki,* and he said they called them "Gekkos,"— these airplanes with two cannons— and he

**Imperial Japan's leading, surviving fighter "Ace" from the Pacific War.*

*Results of a Japanese fighter — "Gekko"— attack on Ray Brashear's B-29 over Kobe, June 1945. "It was a long trip home."*

said they were quite successful at shooting down American planes that way. It was my guess that it was one of these "Gekkos" that got us that day.

My co-pilot wanted to fly the plane for awhile, but I told him that I had finally got in "sync" with the instability of the plane, so I flew it all the way back. We got into the traffic pattern over Saipan and I wasn't sure what would happen when the landing gear came down, or the flaps, so I flew a big wide pattern and when I came in for the final approach some other B-29 cut in front of me. He landed, and I landed pretty close behind him. Everybody was out to greet us when we landed because Colonel Lee, the group commander, was on board.

Before and after this mission we came back with bullet holes in our plane, but nothing as catastrophic as when we flew that one mission I just described. The Japanese didn't really have any good night fighters to begin with, and we flew many of our raids at night. But later on the Japanese developed a system where when the smoke column was coming up from the city their search lights would play on the up-wind side of that, and when our planes popped out of the smoke they would lock on to them and their fighters would move in on us.

We had a lot of fighter attacks. Some of them were head on, which was pretty scary. Our gunners on my plane didn't shoot many of them down. However, one I remember crossed directly out in front of us. He was ninety degrees from our path, going from right to left. I don't know what he was thinking, but when he got directly in front of us my CFC gunner, the one directly on top, fired at him with both upper turrets. The plane flew straight ahead for a moment, then suddenly

*Brig. Gen. "Rosie" O'Donnell presenting the Distinguished Flying Cross to Maj. Ray Brashear during awards ceremony on Saipan in June 1945.*

pitched over like he had hit a brick wall. We figured our gunner had hit the pilot, and he had slumped forward against the stick and went straight down. I think each of my right and left gunners got a kill, plus I think the left gunner got a probable. It is pretty hard to tell when you are looking at other planes and shooting at one. You can't take ten or fifteen seconds to see what happened to the one you hit.

I usually couldn't see when other B-29s went down because I was usually in front and the rest of the squadron was behind me, but I did see one go down. An anti-aircraft shell blew up right in the cockpit. A good friend of mine, Tom Wilkinson, was in that plane. It blew the whole nose off, right even with the engines. It went into a flat spin and disappeared. Nobody got out. Tom, the co-pilot, and bombardier were blown all to bits.

There was an older pilot, "Pappy" Haines; he was a real character. One time he had to make an emergency landing at Iwo Jima, but the weather was so bad that he had to fly the plane over the island and let everybody bail out. Then he made another pass and bailed out himself. They said he came down through the clouds with a cigar in his mouth. He was very nonchalant about it.

I had the most missions up to that point, so it was decided that my crew could go to Honolulu on rest leave. While we were there they ran out of incendiary bombs in the Marianas, so all the transports that were available were flying incendiary bombs to the Marianas and we couldn't get back. As a result, we spent an entire month in Hawaii. When we got back to Saipan we found that all of the crews who had stayed piled up more missions than we had. Many of them got off with thirty missions and were rotated back to the States. By then they were getting short of crews and we had to stay for thirty-five missions.

While we were in Hawaii one member of my crew claimed he had some malady so they didn't send him back to Saipan with us. He didn't like combat at all, and being shot at. He was petrified. The rest of the men were a good crew — they stood and fought.

By August, LeMay told his chief of staff that we were running out of targets. They kept building up more and more B-29s. We were going to be rotated back to the States after our 35 missions, and a couple of days before that President Truman announced that they had dropped one bomb that had done more damage than we had done during the whole war. Of course everybody laughed at that. We thought that was impossible. On our way to Hawaii it was announced that a second bomb had been dropped. The day after we arrived in Honolulu we heard that Japan had surrendered. You had to be in Honolulu to see the celebration — it was unbelievable.

## B-24 Nose Gunner

### Gerald Shaffer

*Gerald Shaffer was born in 1925 in Mount Pleasant, Pennsylvania. However, he spent most of his life before and after World War II in Coshocton, Ohio. He graduated from high school in 1943, and in September 1943 was drafted into the U.S. military. He was a member of the Eleventh Bombardment Group, which between December 7, 1941, and August 16, 1945, lost 1,063 men killed or missing in action. One hundred fifty-seven were wounded, and nineteen taken prisoner. The percentage of combat crews lost was fourteen.*

On September 27, 1943, I was drafted into the service and reported to Fort Hays in Columbus, Ohio, where the military tested us for about a week. Some time later I was sent to gunnery school at Harlingen Air Force Base in Texas. Gunnery school was just that; we learned all sorts of small bore rifles, the carbine, Thompson submachine gun, .45 caliber side arm, and the .30 caliber machine gun. Our main weapon later would be the .50 caliber machine gun. Some days were spent in the classroom learning about each gun. Other days we spent stripping, field stripping, detailed stripping, and care, cleaning, and oiling of the guns. Other days would be spent out on the range shooting the guns. When we learned stripping of the guns we had an advanced course with gloves on and blindfolded. This was to simulate gun trouble at night and at altitude with gloves on.

They told us a .50 caliber shell cost 25 cents each at that time. I don't remember how many rounds we fired, but I am certainly glad we didn't have to pay for them. At that time, as a private, I only earned $28 a month.

Upon graduation from gunnery school we were promoted to private first class, which was quite an honor at that time. After graduation we were all granted two weeks' delay in going to our next station so we could go home. We were then sent to Lamore Air Force Base in Fresno, California. I reported to Lamore on August 4, 1944. The main reason for going to Lamore was that it was a distribution center. All of the pilots, co-pilots, bombardiers, navigators, gunners, radio men, and engineers reported there after they graduated from their respective schools. The reason for this was to form us into groups of ten which would be our regular bomber crew. Later on we would be sent to advanced air training.

Charles Upstill was our pilot, Jim Daugherty was the co-pilot, Marvin Young was our bombardier. The tail gunner was Tom Yashenko, the radio operator/gunner was Gerald Winger. Bob Conrad was our engineer/gunner. Charles Nelson was our top turret gunner, and Otto Vealse the nose gunner. At that time, I was made the lower ball turret gunner.

Our crew was assigned to Muroc Army Air Force base in Muroc, California. This base is still in existence, but is now known as Edwards Air Force Base. We reported there on January 10, 1944. Muroc at that time had all sorts of airplanes, but their main plane was the B-24 bomber, and the P-38 twin-engine fighter plane. Everyone there was to learn how to fly and work as a unit. I was assigned to the lower ball turret, which was kind of cramped but I liked it. We learned and perfected our skills while at Muroc, and as it turned out we were a pretty good fighting unit.

Upon graduation we received our wings and a graduation certificate, and all of us enlisted men were promoted to corporal. On January 11, 1945, we reported to Hamilton Air Force Base in California. This was an overseas training base and we found here that we would be going to the Pacific area. From there we went to Fort Lawton in Seattle, Washington, on January 27. This was an overseas embarkation base, and on February 4 we boarded the *USS Jerauld* to Honolulu, Hawaii.

On February 12, 1945, we arrived in Hawaii, and from there were transported to the northern island of Kauai at Barking Sands Army Air Force Base. While at Barking Sands a General Harmon got lost at sea and all the planes at that base were assigned to search for him. The search was discontinued around the end of March when they didn't find him.

On our way to Guam we stopped at Kwajalein Atoll to refuel and stayed there over night. We arrived on Guam on April 4, 1945, and landed at Harmon Air Force Base, which was just named for General Harmon who was lost at sea. We were now in the Seventh Air Force, Eleventh Bomb Group, and assigned to the 431 Bomb Squadron. It was our job to learn their ways of doing things to the best of our ability. It was our job to fight from Guam and go as far to Japan as we could. All of the enlisted men were immediately promoted. I was promoted to staff sergeant. I was relieved to learn that 90 percent of the attacks from enemy aircraft against our planes was from the nose position. Originally the B-24 didn't have a nose turret on it. It had a Plexiglas glass front with a couple of .30-caliber machine guns mounted on the side of the forward fuselage. When the enemy discovered that it wasn't protected up there they aimed for the nose. Later the nose turret was added up front to stop those attacks. I was the ball turret gunner, but a few days later I was informed that I would have to take the nose turret position, which was a typical Army way of doing things.

We were thoroughly trained in every aspect of the flying order and in a few weeks we were ready for combat. On April 27, 1945, we were one of twelve new crews to attack Wolaei Atoll in the Caroline group south of Guam. This was a milk run, being that it was our first mission. This was our initiation to combat. We saw our first bursts of flak and found out what that was like, and we dropped two and a half tons of bombs on the island.

The most bombs we ever carried was three tons. We had four bomb bays in our B-24 Liberator, and a lot

*Harlington, Texas, AAFB Gunnery School graduate Gerald Shaffer in March 1944.*

of times three of these bomb bays were taken up by fuel tanks which we needed to get to our targets and back. These tanks were bullet proof rubber tanks that were pulled up into the bomb bay, then hooked up to the gasoline system. One of my jobs was to go into the bomb bay prior to getting to our target, and take the safety wires off the bombs so they would explode when they hit the ground.

Our second mission on May 2, 1945, was over Truk Atoll. Truk was a major Japanese target and there was a lot of activity there. We had planes leave every hour from Guam to harass the Japanese and keep them awake all night. We could only carry a ton and a half of bombs that night. When we reached the island the bombardier couldn't see the island. Then the searchlights came on below. That was an erie feeling. The lights would get close, then far away. Finally one got on us, then they all got on us. Everything lit up in the plane just like we were a big Christmas tree. By the time the bombardier saw the target we were past it, and the pilot was trying to evade the searchlights. So, the pilot decided to go back and try it again. Of course several people tried to talk him out of it, but that wasn't to be. We went back and the Japanese got their searchlights on us again, but we got rid of our bombs, and got out of there.

Sometimes while flying in formation you think they are shooting at the other guys, but when you are in the searchlights by yourself there is no doubt who their target is.

Our third mission was May 7, 1945. Our destination was Marcus Island, northeast of the Marianas, and we carried two tons of bombs. Marcus Island was a 1,910 mile round trip and was one target our bomb

*The Barking Sands AAFB Upstill Crew in Kawaii, Hawaii, February 1945.* Top row, left to right: *Charles Nelson, Tom Barrett, Charles Upstill, Marvin Young, Charles Daugherty.* Kneeling, left to right: *John Lanchak, Otto Veale, Gerald Shaffer, Tom Yashenko, Gerald Winger.*

group had bombed many times. It seemed the more we bombed them the more accurate they got with their anti-aircraft fire. I guess we gave them a lot of good target practice. However, of the eleven bombers on this mission we all returned unscratched.

During the Second World War you didn't hear much about the B-24 Liberator Bomber. The B-17 Flying Fortress was in all the news at that time. Later on it was the B-29. But the B-24 was heard of very little, although there were more B-24s built during World War II than any other plane. The Eleventh Bomb Group was equipped with B-17s at the beginning of the war, but the B-24 had a longer range, could fly faster, and at a higher altitude. So that is the reason it was used extensively in the Pacific later on. The only B-17 I saw during my time on Guam was a rescue plane that had a boat strapped underneath it. In case somebody got shot down they could release the boat. Otherwise rescue was mostly Navy submarines that were always in the area where bombing missions took place.

Our fourth mission was May 10, 1945. We dropped two and a quarter tons of bombs, and again our target was Marcus Island. This time we saw the American submarine that was there in case we got shot down. He was surfaced and I guess watching the excitement on the island. We destroyed a couple of airplanes that were on the ground.

The war in the Pacific was just one big Navy operation. They called the shots; knew what islands they wanted to take, and which ones to bypass. The Japanese thinking was that we would take each island we came to, and they were prepared for that. Instead, we bypassed most islands, and cut them off so they couldn't get any supplies. This made our trip to Japan that much easier. Our effort in the Army Air Corps was to bomb these islands that the Navy picked out for us.

On Guam we lived in tents that had a wooden

*Gerald "Bud" Shaffer at a waist gun on a B-24 somewhere in the Pacific in 1945.*

frame and wooden floors. The tent was stretched over the frame to make a pretty nice unit. The officers lived in one section and the enlisted men in another. We had a Quonset hut for a mess hall. Things were laid out pretty nice, although we had some Japanese around in the hills who never surrendered. Because of that we had to pull guard duty on our planes about once a month. But other than that guard duty we had no other duty than flying our planes and cleaning our guns. We had plenty of free time. Some of this time was spent on going to school. The nose gunner, which was me, learned to be the assistant armorer. What the armorer did was to know all the guns and be able to fix any gun while we were in flight.

I don't want to get into planes being shot down and men dying. You have to realize that we were all kids at that time — eighteen and nineteen — just got out of high school. We had to learn to be men real fast. We did lose planes, and we did lose friends. To this day I can't hear "Taps" played on a bugle. It just makes me sad. More than fifty years later, on Memorial Day, all the veterans remember. I don't know if it is so much remembering; it's just that you can't forget.

Usually in the service you are told every morning what you're going to wear that day, but in our Eleventh Bomb Group there wasn't a dress code. We would cut off our pants and make shorts out of them. We wore no shirts at all. You couldn't tell a general from a private, which was fine with us. Of course on the plane we wore our heavy suits. We had electrically heated pantsuits, shoes, and vest. Over all that we put on our fleece-lined leather clothes. We all had parachutes, but the only one who wore his was the lower ball turret gunner. To get out of the airplane all he had to do was point his guns forward towards the nose and click two levers on his back and that was his escape hatch. The rest of us had our parachutes close by. In my case the only escape hatch was in the nose wheel well. If we did get shot down the Japanese didn't like to take prisoners, so we knew life wasn't going to be very pleasant if we did get shot down.

May 16, 1945, was our fifth mission. Again it was against Marcus Island. We were getting reports that there was quite a build-up going on of Japanese troops on that island.

According to other reports we would be going to Okinawa just as soon as this island was taken, which would put us 350 miles from the Japanese mainland. That meant we could carry more bombs and less gasoline to get to our targets. Although we had not

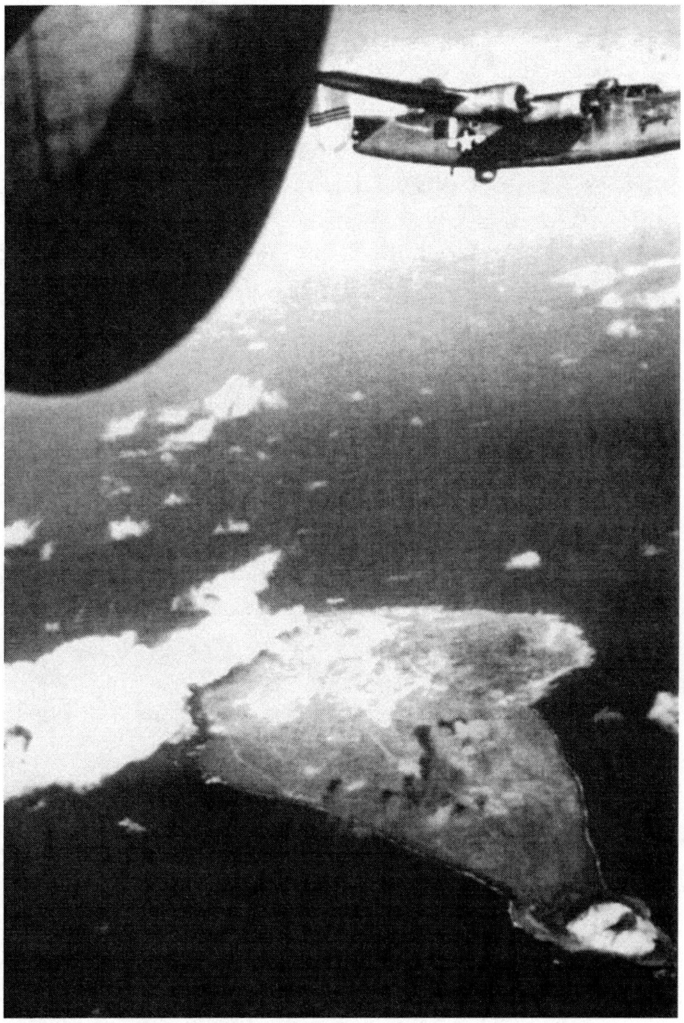

*B-24s from Eleventh Bomb Group over Iwo Jima. The group bombed daily for 78 days. Notice the smoke from bombing. The mountain in the bottom right is Mount Suribachi, where the Marines' picture was taken that later became their National memorial. This photograph was made in May 1945.*

bombed the Japanese mainland yet, it was about to come up.

Our sixth, and last, mission off of Guam was again to Marcus Island. That was June 4, 1945. We carried two tons of bombs. On this mission we took a burst of flak in our plane and it caught fire up in the pilot's compartment. The turret gunner got hit in the leg with a piece of flak — nothing serious— but it got him the Purple Heart. The fire was put out with a fire extinguisher and we made it back to base.

After our last mission off Guam we started to get ready for our move to Okinawa. We were to be located on Yontan Air Force Base. Of course it had to be made to accommodate our bombers. Just as soon as that was completed we were to fly our bombers in, get set up, and be ready to go for Japan. Our ground crews and supplies were loaded onto ships and transported to Okinawa before our planes and crews got there. We arrived at Yontan Air Force Base July 2, 1945. At the time the airstrip was not long enough to accommodate takeoffs, but we could land. The only accommodations set up for us at that time were tents, and we were issued sleeping bags. Our food was C rations.

On July 10, 1945, eight days after we landed on Okinawa, we flew our seventh mission. We carried two and a half tons of bombs to Kitakyushu, Japan. One thing that we weren't used to was when we flew over Japan we got flak from every place. We were used to flying over water and not getting flak until we got to the island we were going to bomb. We would get continuous flak going in and out over Japan. But this was a real pleasure mission for everyone. The Eleventh Bomb Group had fought its way from Hickam Field, Hawaii, during the attack on Pearl Harbor, and we were finally getting to bomb the Japanese homeland and carry the war to them.

We hit the airfields there and started a whole lot of fires. The mission was a complete success and we didn't lose anyone.

One thing nice about flying out of Okinawa was that we didn't have anymore 10 and 11 hour missions. We could hit anything now within eight hours and get home.

On July 17, 1945, we went on our eighth mission. We carried two tons of bombs and went to Changwon, China. On this mission we had fighter escort. Usually we went so far that the fighters couldn't carry enough fuel to protect us.

On July 18, 1945, we went on our ninth mission. It was a weather reconnaissance mission to Formosa. We didn't carry any bombs, just radioed back the weather. One thing we noted was that we did get one Japanese fighter that came at our nose position. I first thought that he had already been shot — it looked like he was on fire. Then I realized that he was shooting at us. So of course we returned fire and discouraged him.

On July 27, 1945, we went on our tenth mission. We carried three tons of bombs to Kagoshima on Kyushu. We really had a nice target this time. It was a marshaling yard, train yards— there were all sorts of train lines coming into this place. When we finished with it I got to see the results as we made a sharp, banking turn. That place was a mess of tangled steel. Everything was on fire.

July 31, 1945, we went on our eleventh mission, carrying three tons of bombs. Our target that day was Nagasaki. This was a strange mission. Our target was the dock area — the gasoline storage dumps. We started quite a few fires and had smoke that went up 5,000 feet. We were intercepted by five enemy aircraft. It was strange; they just came up beside us, but didn't fire. We had experiences lots of times when we would get enemy anti-aircraft fire and there would be enemy aircraft way off out of our firing range. They were there to tell the ground crews what altitude we were so that they could set their ground fire to hit us. But these guys were right there with us.

After we got back from a mission, one of our jobs was to look over the aircraft for holes. We found several flack holes in our wings this time.

On August 6, 1945, we went on our twelfth mission. We carried three tons of bombs to Kagushima on Kyushu. That day we carried incendiary bombs, and the report afterwards was that we wiped out seventy-five percent of their factory district. We had very little opposition that day.

After that mission we heard of the atomic bomb that was dropped on Hiroshima and were hoping that the war was coming to a fast close. On August 9, we flew our thirteenth mission. We had three tons of bombs, and the target was Iwakuni on Honshu. On flying up there, we were over the ocean and noticed a strange, pink haze in the air. We thought for some reason it was the results of the first atom bomb. But as we were flying up the east coast of Japan we noticed a strange cloud formation off to the west. The pilot asked the navigator about where it was coming from. The cloud kept rising and rising. Our navigator estimated that it was Nagasaki. At the time the whole crew estimated that maybe it was another atomic bomb that had been dropped there. The next day we were to find out that that is exactly where it was, and it was an atomic bomb.

*The Eleventh Bomber Group's welcome to Nagasaki, Japan, July 31, 1945. The black puffs are anti-aircraft shells exploding. The formation of B-24s bombed Nagasaki this day and one week later the atom bomb was dropped there.*

As I remember this Iwakuni mission it was at the end of a long bay and we were flying down the middle of the bay. Our orders were to drop our bombs when the lead plane dropped his bombs. It was my job to let the bombardier know when the first bomb came out of the lead plane. I saw the first bomb, told the bombardier, and he dropped his bombs. As a result I think every bomb that the squadron dropped that day went into the bay. Maybe that was a good thing for our side and their side both — we didn't need to kill anymore people.

On August 10, we got the word that the Japanese had asked to surrender, and that was certainly all right with me. As soon as the ships out in the harbor got the word they started shooting their guns up over the island and we had to put our steel helmets on because that shrapnel was coming down on us. Our pilot, First Lt. Upstill, came over and wanted to know if we wanted to celebrate. Two of us had guard duty that night, but we were going to celebrate anyhow. After telling us that, Lt. Upstill got about twenty feet from our position and got hit in the head with one of those pieces of shrapnel. He didn't have his helmet on, so we gathered him up and took him over to the dispensary right away. Fortunately, all it was was a scalp wound, but it scared everyone at the time.

On August 12, we went on our fourteenth mission. This was only a reconnaissance mission off the coast of China. Thankfully, that was our last one. When the surrender was signed on the battleship *Missouri* our planes were fully loaded with bombs and gasoline, and all crews were on the planes ready to take off. We didn't think they would actually sign the thing. But thank God they did sign it and the war was over.

After the Japanese surrender the next order of things was to strip everything out of our planes and send every available plane to Japan to pick up our prisoners of war. These men were living skeletons. They had been through hell. Nobody was going anywhere until those men were completely out of there and on their way home. After the planes were stripped, only a skeleton crew was allowed to go because they needed all the space they could get for the POWs. After the Allied prisoners were picked up they were flown directly to the Philippine Islands. Everybody wanted to go home now, but I think everyone agreed that these guys deserved to go home first. For us, these were the most satisfying missions of the war.

# 10 The Home Front

## When Johnnie Didn't Come Marching Home

Bill Winnekins

*Bill Winnekins was born in Green Bay, Wisconsin, in 1935. After four years in the United States Air Force he became an investigative accountant. He is now retired and lives in Bella Vista, Arkansas.*

December 7, 1941, was a Sunday afternoon. My folks had left for the day to visit my aunts and uncles. My four sisters and I were at home. They had a chance to listen to the radio. That was the only time my father would allow them to. They became very excited—something about a war starting—something about Pearl Harbor. Being only seven years old, it didn't mean very much to me—I didn't understand it. In fact, I don't think my four sisters understood it. I don't think they knew where Pearl Harbor was, or even Hawaii for that matter. But the real excitement started when my parents got home. They were very upset. My father, being a World War I veteran, had been on the battlefields of France. He understood war.

In 1943, my brother John was still in high school and wanted to join the Marine Corps. My parents were really opposed to that. They had to sign for him. There was a lot of stress in the family—a lot of fights and arguments over this. But finally, reluctantly, they signed his papers and he went off to boot camp at Camp Pendleton in California.

One day I got a letter from him. It said he was a Marine now and he was coming home on leave. He had a pass; the most he could stay home was three days because he was traveling by train. It took a long time to get to Wisconsin, and a long time to get back to California by train. He told me not to tell anybody in the family—just to meet him at the train station. He told me when he would be coming in. I told Mr. Falk, the train station master, about my brother coming home but asked him not to say anything to anybody else. He promised not to say anything to anybody, but that he would let me know when my brother would be arriving.

The day came and I took my bike down to the train station. It was a long way from home and there was a lot of traffic, too. Green Bay was about 25,000 or 30,000 people at the time. The train came into the station; I can still remember that steam engine. People got off the train and pretty soon John got off too. He had this green uniform on with a big black leather belt around the middle. I dropped my bike and ran and jumped into his arms. We rode home together on my bike. I snuck him up to my bedroom and hid him there. Pretty soon the rest of the family started showing up from school and work. My mother started preparing supper—the girls were helping her. Pretty soon John came down the stairs. All hell broke loose. I don't even remember eating supper. When you take a look back, three days was not a long time. John had to see some of his friends, and of course my folks were upset if he wasn't around. Then he left.

My father had a large map of the Pacific Ocean. I can still remember that map—it was in the dining

*The grave of John Winnekins on Saipan before being returned to the U.S. mainland for reburial.*

room. He had it on the wall and he would look at it and study it. We didn't hear from my brother for a while. Then we got the news that the Fourth Marine Division took the islands of Roi-Namur in the Marshalls. My brother wrote me a nice long letter when he was on the ship after the battle. He said he had a Japanese dollar, and on it he wrote, "Good luck Bill — John." I still have it.

Every letter that we received from my brother was very important. My older sister Mary would always be the one to read them. Then the letters stopped coming and my dad was looking at that map. I can remember him saying to my mother, "Mary, I think we are in trouble."

The trouble came July 4, 1944. It came in the form of a telegram. I was outside playing with my friends. In Wisconsin in July it is very warm, so all the windows were open. There was no air conditioning. All hell broke loose in the house. My sisters were jumping up and down and crying, and my dad was throwing stuff all around the house. Then I was told that my brother was killed and that more information would be coming shortly.

The news spread fast. The house filled with all kinds of people — aunts, uncles, neighbors, my brother's high school teachers. As a little boy of nine years old I didn't get any attention. It was really hard to understand what was going on except that my brother was killed. I guess death to a nine year old — you don't understand it, you don't believe it. I can remember my mom saying often after that, "Don't worry about John. He can take care of himself."

John was a real sportsman — football player, basketball — he played in the band, boxed. I got all them pictures of him from his high school days. He was always self-reliant. My mother would always say, "John can take care of himself. He'll come home. He'll come home." John was such a good football player that he was the only high school kid in his freshman year to make the varsity team, and first string at that. And he still holds the record in that school for the longest pass thrown. He threw the ball 62 yards.

My older sister Mary was 19 or 20 years old at that time. She had enlisted in the Navy and had gone to Norfolk to become a nurse. Oh, my parents were upset. That was the latter part of 1943. She only came home on leave one time that I can remember. She was not allowed to come home from Norfolk when we received news of John's death. You gotta remember this: the landing on Saipan was June 15, 1944. On June 6, 1944,

*The reburial of John Winnekins in Green Bay, Wisconsin, after World War II. All of the Americans killed in action on Saipan and Tinian were exhumed after the war and returned to the mainland United States or Punchbowl Cemetery in Hawaii.*

Normandy was invaded by Allied forces. So in July 1944, my sister was overworked with the wounded coming back from the Normandy beaches. They could not afford to let her come home.

Well, the war finally did end and my brother did come home in 1948 — in a box.* Down to the train station we went — the whole family. I think half the town was there. There was a Marine Corps guard and an escort. We took the body to a funeral home. That was the second funeral. The first one was back in 1944 —church service only. The Marine detachment in Green Bay had been named after my brother.

When you are 13 years old things register more with you and you are a part of it. I can remember burying John in the family plot. I remember the rifle volleys; I'll never forget "Taps." That bugle still puts pimples on the back of my neck and arms. Every Memorial Day it's like going through it all over again.

*Americans killed on Saipan during World War II were buried there, but disinterred after the war to be reburied in their home states.*

All during the 1940s my mother would travel from one Navy hospital to another, looking for someone who could tell her about her son and what happened to him. She never did get any information. My sister Phyllis was 15 years old at the time. She wrote the Marine Corps demanding to know what happened to her brother. Some chaplain wrote back trying to pacify the family, not knowing that history would catch up to him. I promised my mother, "I'll go to that damned island of Saipan, and I'll bring my big brother home."

Now we know that within a hundred miles of 1160 Thirteenth Avenue, Green Bay, Wisconsin, there were nine guys from "G" Company that came home, but not a one of them came to see my folks. I ain't blaming them; I'm not angry with them. I understand it would have been hard for them to do so, and they wanted to forget the war like everybody else. So I don't hold it against them, but they aren't going to tell me what happened at 1160 Thirteenth Avenue. It was not a nice sight; I did not have a childhood. My mother was consumed with trying to find out any little scrap of information about her son, John. When the body came home she said, "Well, we know it's not John but we will take care of this mother's son as if he were ours, and we hope that whoever receives my boy will take good care of him too."

My mother died at the age of 60 in 1962. My father died ten years later. He was very bitter. He was in World War I and he knew how useless war was, and how devastating it could be. That is why when I came home in a uniform years later he couldn't stand it. He didn't like any kind of a uniform, even a policeman's uniform. Very seldom did my parents talk about my brother's death in front of us kids. My father would have nothing to do with the $10,000 insurance money. As far as he was concerned that was blood money and the United States government could take it and shove it. As far as I know that money is still sitting there and I won't touch it either.

How my mother could have rested in peace if she had talked to Verne Davis and Albert Lee. She could have rested in peace if she had talked to Ray Hickman in Arizona. He was on a burial detail on Saipan and he once assured me, "That is your brother. There is no way we could have screwed that up. He had dog tags—his name was on his blouse."

If my mother had known all this maybe I would have had a different childhood. I was on my own mostly. I ate and slept there at home, but that was all there was to it. My sisters were the same way; they were on their own. We had our school chums and that is how we survived.

The fifties came. I turned 18, 19 years old and I wanted to go into the Marine Corps. Wow, did that cause a stir in the house! My parents were so angry and so upset. Of course I didn't know it at the time but I came under the Sullivan Act. The Sullivan Act was enacted by Congress that the last male child in a family would not go into the service. There were the five Sullivan boys back in 1942 who were all on one ship and killed — all five from one family. It had caused such a stir in the country that Congress passed a law called the Sullivan Act. So when I went down to the Marine Corps recruiter my parents raised hell. My dad went down there and threatened that "son-of-bitch." He was really mad. The Marine Corps recruiter explained the Sullivan Act to me and said there was no way I could go into the Marine Corps.

I ran away from home and enlisted in the Air Force. Finally my folks caught up with me. I remember coming home on leave. My father wouldn't even acknowledge that there was someone else in the house. He was that angry. I had a ten day leave. My father went off to work one morning. I had my bag packed and my uniform on. My mother said, "Where are you going?" I said, "I'm going back to the base; I'm going home." That hurt my mother terribly. It was a very uncomfortable situation. I understand my father's feelings now, and he acted the way he did because of those feelings.

I served my four years and was discharged. But I never forgot what I told my mother — I would go to that damned island of Saipan. I would bring my big brother home. I often wondered, How would I get there? I could see myself going there on a small boat and there would probably be natives there — not one speaking English. They wouldn't even know why I was there. That is how much I knew about Saipan. However, I didn't dwell on it too often, or for too long. I knew it was a long way away and I was getting older — reality sets in. Then in 1993, one of my neighbors talked me into joining the American Legion. I went to the mailbox one day and I had received my first *American Legion Magazine*. I was halfway up the driveway, paging through it, and it jumped out right at me! Saipan Reunion Canceled! Now, if you look at those announcements of reunions in the *American Legion Magazine* they are in fine print. This thing jumped right out at me. I said to myself, "Canceled, my ass!"

In one hour I made five long distance phone calls and finally got through to a guy by the name of Bill Eger. He lived out in Denver, Colorado. He was in charge of this Saipan reunion — Fiftieth Anniversary. I told him who I was and what I was. Then he told me that there was a Fourth Marine Division Association, and he gave me a name and phone number. I decided to write to John Stone, the executive director. I sent in a picture of my brother and I wrote a little article about how I would like to see if I could find some people who knew my brother, John. The only thing I knew at that time was that he was in the Fourth Marine Division. When that news letter hit the mailboxes my phone was busy — damn busy. One of the first calls I got was from Tommy Gleason. He was a big international attorney in New York. He lost his leg on Saipan. Then I got a call from a guy by the name of Walter Shipley from New Jersey. He said he knew my brother, but as far as telling me what had happened to my brother, he did not know. But Walter said, "You know what? I'm coming to Saipan with you." So Walter and I went to Saipan. We became very good friends. He was instantly like a big brother to me because it didn't take us long to fight and argue about things.

The hotel we stayed at was the Pacific Island Club. We started to unpack. From my window I could see the ocean and the beach. So without even unpacking I walked out under the palm trees and there it was, Yellow Beach One and Two with a marker stating that was where the Fourth Marine Division landed. Having never been on Saipan, then walking up to that monument and knowing I was standing on the very spot.... Emotions ran heavy.

The day after we arrived on Saipan I went to pay our bill for breakfast. The manager came out and said, "You Marines?" "Yep," I said. "Marines don't pay," he said. I told the guy, "You crazy? There's 180 of us here." "Marines don't pay," he said. "Bring all Marines. No pay." Wherever we went, it was free.

Walter was wounded on Saipan about the fourth or fifth day, and evacuated. In fact he was wounded bad enough that he was back in Seattle before the island was really secured. Walter and I kept in touch after we flew home. I told him that John Stone had given me a list of men from G Company. "Why don't we try and find some of them," I suggested. Then in the mail I got a copy of some embarkation orders for the Marshall Islands campaign dated January 1944. They had all the names and the next of kin for the men who were in G Company at that time—198 names. So I start looking for these people. I would go down to the library, use their computer, get print-outs, call, and write letters. The process was slow and very expensive, but it was well worth it. Right now I have the names of over 500 men who went through G Company. There were 105 killed in action. I have located about 150 living. Another 150 are deceased and about 100 others are AWOL.

People react to things differently, even these Marines. I contacted one guy and he said, "Hell, I got along without you for the last fifty years; I can make it the rest of the way." Then he hung up on me. Another one said to me, "Look son, they drafted me and put me on Iwo Jima. You can take your United States Marine Corps and shove it up your ass!"

I started receiving thousands of pictures. One guy sent me copies of newsletters that were put out on the USS *Sheridan*. Then word came to me that there were enough guys found from G Company and that they wanted to have a reunion. It was scheduled for

*Fourth Marine Division Cemetery on Saipan in 1945.*

November 1995, in Atlanta, Georgia. I asked my sister Phyllis to go with me.

Just before the reunion strange things started to happen. I got a call from Carl Pilstick in Ohio who is now assisting me in finding other "G" men. He said, "Bill, here's a number. His name is Vernon Davis." Carl said to me, "The minute I mentioned Bill Winnekins to Vernon he got upset. He was your brother's platoon sergeant." I gave Vernon a call. We had a long talk. He knew my brother well and told me the whole story — how they no more than hit the beach and down my brother went. One of the amtracs ran over Anthonio T. Marriro. Verne was pounding on the amtrac, trying to get it off Marriro. There was just chaos on the beach. A sniper was shooting at him. He checked my brother out — said he was lifeless, apparently dead. The sniper kept shooting at Verne, so Verne took off. He told me the whole story, but he wasn't going to come to the reunion. The reunion was only three days away.

Marriro is still alive and lives in the Bronx, New York. We don't hear from him. I guess he prefers to keep all of that in the past, like many of the guys. I talked to him only once and he made it obvious that he would like to be left alone.

Then I got another call from Pilstick that very same day. He said, "Here is another name, your brother's best friend, Albert Lee." I called Albert — the poor man could not talk to me, he cried so hard. And he too could not come to the reunion. Then just before I was to leave for getting on the airplane for the reunion I got a phone call from both men. "We are coming to the reunion. See you there." I know what happened. I told my good buddy Walter Shipley how disappointed my sister and I would be at not seeing these two men at the reunion. By this time Walter Shipley had been nicknamed "The General" because he gives orders and he doesn't give a shit if the Commandant of the Marine Corps likes it or not. He gives orders to the Marine Corps and anybody else, and they damn well better carry them out. He is just one of those old sergeants from way back when. I know Walter got on the phone and told those two guys they better get their butts to Atlanta.

The day came and the first one to arrive after us was Albert Lee. My sister Phyllis was there. She was a cheerleader in high school and was close to my brother because they were close in age. I sat her little butt down in an airport bar, then went out and picked up Albert Lee — put his little butt down next to hers. Then I went off to another gate to pick up Vernon Davis. All this happened in about a half-hour to 45 minutes. I put Verne down on the other side of my sister. Then I said, "Okay, I want you two jokers to tell my sister exactly what happened — the whole truth, nothing but the truth. As bad as it is, don't worry about it. Just tell her exactly what happened." Then I took a long walk down the concourse and let the three of them talk. I had already heard the story. I wanted my sister to hear it from them, face to face, eyeball to eyeball.

That evening they both left. Verne Davis' wife contacted me later and said, "Never contact him again. He couldn't handle it." I can call Albert Lee maybe every six months and he talks to me, but he never initiates the contact. Neither one of them has anything to do with G Company anymore and I think it is because of me. I look like my brother John. In fact there are guys in G Company who think I am my brother and I'm tired of trying to tell them who I really am, so I just let them think what they want. At reunions I'll be in the hospitality room and a guy will come up and put his arm around my shoulder and say, "Hey, do you remember that girl we picked up over in...." "Yeah, I remember it real well." I just go along with them. Or, "Do you remember Sergeant Ruth?" "Yeah," I say. I don't try to explain to them anymore that I'm not John because sometimes I have to explain it three or four times to the same person.

These guys from G Company are no different from the Marines I went to Saipan with. If you weren't there they don't want to tell you anything about what happened. They will tell you the funny stories — the craziness that went on, but the blood and guts — no way. Example: On Saipan I came down to the lobby of the hotel. There were 40 or 50 of these Marines sitting in the lobby early in the morning. I walked into the group and it only took about 30 seconds to discover that I wasn't wanted. Some guys were crying, others were laughing. But when I walked in there it turned to total silence.

I met another Marine there on Saipan. We had gotten together on the flight over. He walked the invasion beaches with me on June 15, 1994. He was an amtrac driver and explained to me what he saw on the beach in 1944. We would walk along, and we got to a certain point on the beach, and he would fall down on the sand — beat the sand and cry. By this time I knew to just walk on, look out at the surf, and let him go. In 15 minutes he was back at my side and we would troop on down the beach. We would sit and talk for a while, then he would start crying again. I learned not to try and console them, not to put my arms around them, not to say, "I understand." Because we don't understand. He told me some stories—not very nice stories either. For example, on June 15, 1944, there was equipment all over the beach, bombed out equipment, and bodies all over. He went up to the beach master and said, "I'm not coming in here any more. I'm not going to be running over all those bodies." Now, the Japanese really had that beach zeroed in with mortars and artillery. He said the minute he stopped that amtrac the Japanese opened up like no tomorrow. He said, "Bill, I ran back to that amtrac because I had about twenty guys in there. They could have gotten killed real easy. I got my ass out of there so fast—bodies or no bodies."

He was taking these guys up to the front and there was a wounded Japanese soldier in front of him. He stopped—he wanted some of the guys to jump out and pull this wounded Japanese off to the side. Nobody would get out because they could hear the bullets pinging on the outside of the amtrac. He said he had no choice but to run over that man.

Dick Freebie from Texas told me a story about how they were crossing this open sugar cane field. All of a sudden a machine gun opened up—Nightingale got hit. He was wounded. The rest of the Marines were hiding behind a berm and the Japanese kept firing at Nightingale, not to hit him, but to irritate his buddies. Dick Freebie threw down his rifle and ran out there. Of course as soon as the Japanese saw that they killed Nightingale—shot him. Freebie wasn't hit, but they sure riddled his back pack. He said it was full of bullet holes, but he wasn't hurt. I found out later that he got the Silver Star for that.

After a while some of the guys started to trust me; they could tell me these things. I never pushed it on them. The only time I ever really pushed something on them was when I asked them to explain to my sister what happened to John.

When we had that reunion in Atlanta—that first one in '95—the master of ceremonies was thanking everybody. He said, "I'm not going to mention names, because we know who you are and you know who you are, and if I forget somebody I'll get in trouble. But I am going to mention one name. His name is Bill Winnekins." Have you ever had 70 Marines give you a standing ovation? I stood up to acknowledge them. Then I went to sit back down. "No, no! Come forward." They had a huge plaque with my brother's name on it, his picture, and my name, making me a Company G Marine. Another 15 minute ovation followed. How proud and relieved my folks would have been. After that, one of the guys came up to me and put his arm around me and said, "Now, you are one of us." And I have been treated that way ever since.

# Already I Miss You as Much as I Thought I Would

## Jane Broome Plante

*Mrs. Plante was born Jane Louise Leininger in 1921. She grew up and went to school in Bronxville, New York. She married Roger Broome of Virginia in 1941 and had two children by him before his death in 1945 as a result of wounds he received during the fighting for Saipan. She now resides on Hilton Head Island, South Carolina.*

In 1941 I met Roger Broome. He was from Charlottesville, Virginia. I was 19 years old and he was 25. He was a newly commissioned second lieutenant in the United States Marine Corps Reserves and was stationed at the Philadelphia Navy Yard. We met through mutual friends in New York in March 1941. A classmate of mine from school knew a Marine from the Philadelphia Navy Yard who brought Roger to New York for the weekend. The four of us had a wonderful time. Roger and I were attracted to each other from the very start and continued to see each other almost every weekend. When we weren't together we wrote to each other daily, a habit we continued whenever we were apart for as long as Roger lived.

In June 1941, I graduated from Lennox School in New York. A few days later, on my twentieth birthday, Roger asked my father for my hand in marriage. In August our engagement became official with a large party at my home, and the next day Roger left for Quantico, Virginia, where he joined the Headquarters Detachment. When we married in November 1941, Roger was still at the Marine barracks. On his nine days of leave we got married, had a four day honeymoon, and then drove to Quantico where we set up housekeeping in a tiny house in Fredericksburg, Virginia.

Roger and I were on leave in Charlottesville in early December 1941. Roger suspected he would be going overseas and wanted to say goodbye to his family.

While we were there on Sunday, December 7th, the Japanese bombed Pearl Harbor and he was ordered to return to Quantico immediately. The next day I watched him fly off very early in the morning to what turned out to be four months in Brazil.

While Roger was in Brazil I returned to my parents' home in Bronxville. During this time I was appalled to discover people hoarding foodstuffs for themselves while our husbands and sons were away fighting the war and giving up so much. I knew people who had shelves of canned goods stashed away in their cellars. It seemed to me to be the wrong thing to do and I made myself unpopular by saying so. I felt that we at home could at least make a small sacrifice to support the war effort.

Thinking back, I am surprised that Roger was able to tell me where he was during his journey south. From Miami he wrote that he would be in San Juan, Puerto Rico, the next night, and Trinidad the night after that. When he wrote from San Juan he said all of his mail would be censored in Trinidad by the British, which would hold it up for some time.

Most of the time that Roger was in Brazil we were trying to arrange for me to join him. This was made difficult by the British censors who made neat, triangular windows in the letters. This added to our frustrations and we were never able to make the arrangements. Anyway, after four months the entire company was sent back to the Marine barracks at New River, North Carolina. Roger returned with malaria and spent the next 15 days in the hospital in New River. His malaria recurred several times during the following year; it seemed I was always dashing to the hospital with him.

When he was discharged from the hospital we lived in a housing project in New River until the first of June 1942, when we drove to Newport, Rhode Island, where he was attached to the Marine barracks, Naval Operations Base. I was feeling quite relaxed and happy with the assignment because I understood that he would not have to go overseas again due to the malaria, but I had not reckoned with my newly commissioned first lieutenant husband. I was unaware of all the strings he was pulling in an attempt to get overseas duty. I guess I was preoccupied with becoming a mother for the first time. Our son, Roger Gravel Brook Broome, IV, the same name as his father, was born in Newport Naval Hospital on April 15, 1943.

As it turned out, the time we spent in Newport was the only time in our married lives that we were able to try and make a home together. Although we were married three years and two months, our total time together was just over two years. And of that time, Roger was hospitalized nearly four months.

We left Newport in June 1943, and Roger was assigned to Camp Lejeune, North Carolina. He was attached to the newly formed Fourth Marine Division. The baby and I stayed with my parents while Roger looked for somewhere for us to live. We found a wonderful house at Atlantic Beach, Moorehead City, which we shared with another Marine couple. This idyllic existence lasted for only one month, and we were off to the West Coast as was most of the Fourth Division. We drove across country with the baby, who was only three months old.

For the next five months Roger was at Camp Pendleton. We lived in a complex called Dana Villa very near San Juan Capistrano, right on the ocean. It would have been perfect except that we knew the next move would separate us for a very long time. Roger would be going overseas. I think that worried me more than it did him.

I'm not surprised that Roger picked the Marine Corps. He was of the stuff that Marines are made of. Traditionally, the Marine Corps was the first choice of many Virginians as well as many of Roger's close friends.

On January 13, 1944, the Fourth Marine Division sailed from San Diego. The next day, aboard ship, Roger wrote, "Already I miss you as much as I thought I would. It took everything I had to leave. When I get back this time it will be for good."

While Roger was steaming towards battle I was driving back east with young Roger, now nine months old, and a friend who didn't drive. And as I discovered even before the end of the journey, I was pregnant. Everything was hard to come by during the war, including accommodations. Motels in 1944 were hardly known. Roger made me promise not to pick up hitchhikers, not even soldiers.

It took us 12 days to cross country from California to New York, and as it was winter we took a southerly route. Roger wrote, "While I am at sea you are driving all the way across the country. I pray for your safe arrival each night. I will feel better when the time it takes you to get home is over. You are doing a very big thing and your pioneer ancestors have nothing on you." He would also write, "I expect today you are bowling along somewhere in Alabama or Mississippi." He was at sea for all of January with nothing to do, he said, except play a little chess. They went directly to the Marshall Islands with no stops in between.

On January 30, 1944, the night before the landings

on Roi-Namur in the Marshall Islands, he wrote, "My life of ease has been shattered. For the last few days I have been very busy indeed. Tomorrow we start fighting. You will read about it in the papers long before you get this, and you will probably hear much more about it than I will be permitted to write." Roger also wrote about the native people and how badly they were treated by the Japanese. He said the Americans would treat them much better, but the people didn't appear to trust anyone anymore.

From Roi-Namur the Fourth Marine Division went to Maui in the Hawaiian Islands to regroup, and do more training. While Roger was on Roi-Namur I saw in the Army-Navy Registry that he made major, but he didn't know about it until he got to Maui some weeks later. He also didn't know that he would soon be a father again. I sent him a set of major's leaves and said, "Isn't it amazing; I'm a major's wife at twenty?"

I was now living in Virginia in the house that Roger found for us before we left for the West Coast. After several months on Maui, Roger told me he wouldn't be able to write quite as often any more, but he said he knew I would understand, and of course I did. I also knew that the time for the next battle was coming closer and we had no idea where it would be. It was scary. I wrote, "I will be worried to death, and all the time I will be praying twice as hard as usual." On June 14 he wrote his last letter to me in his own hand. The next day I wrote Roger that I had heard on the radio and saw in the papers that Saipan in the Marianas had been invaded. "I've been saying my prayers more than ever these days. Please don't take any unnecessary risks."

We knew of the Saipan landings, but the papers only said American forces had landed. They didn't mention the Marines, but since the reports came through the Navy Department we felt sure the Marines were involved. I was worried sick and wrote, "I can't wait until I hear from you." I was also concerned about how I would let him know when the baby arrived. I guessed it would be through the Red Cross. Fortunately, I was very busy at that time and didn't have much time for worry. I had one ten-month-old baby to take care of and another on the way. I had a house to fix up and Roger's mother and younger sister to care for.

By late June 1944, the papers were full of stories about the landings and battle for Saipan. I was complaining in my letters that they didn't mention which outfits were there. Later, I wrote Roger that I had read that they had gained 800 yards on Saipan in one day and that it sounded as if it were a perfect hell there. In the same letter I wrote that his mother suggested that we name our first little girl Kathleen Bruce, and admonished him that he never did tell me who he wanted as the godfather.

By the end of June, *Time* magazine had a complete account of the fighting on Saipan. We at home were scouring all the media, looking with great care, hoping to get as much information as possible, and always hoping against hope to actually see someone we knew. *Time* said that there were two Marine divisions on Saipan, but didn't say which two. It was so frustrating. Finally, on July 4th, I heard on the radio that the Second and Fourth Marine Divisions were on Saipan. That was the first mention of what units were doing the fighting. The report said that the heaviest fighting was yet to come. This was harrowing news, and I wrote to Roger, "I worry so much and will not breathe easy again until I hear you are safe and well."

Another time I complained that the Charlottesville paper had not mentioned Saipan in three days, and if it wasn't for the Richmond paper we wouldn't have any news. I hadn't heard from Roger since his last letter written June 14, the night before the invasion. On July 6, I received a short "V" mail note saying, "I am alive and well and very happy to be so. You can tell our boy that his dad is too mean to get hurt. Your picture is always with me. Your loving husband." That note had been written on June 21, and when I replied I wrote, "That is the best letter I ever got." I also told him that another Marine had written his wife that he had seen Roger on "June 23, and that you were okay." I also told him that I was saving all the clippings from the newspapers and putting them in a scrapbook for him.

On July 8, the day Roger was wounded, I wrote, "I guess the worst of the fighting is over, but I won't feel relieved until I hear from you." But most of the letter was filled with jolly news about his sister visiting, swimming parties, buying watermelons, and other trivial things. In hindsight it seems terrible that we were so lighthearted while he was suffering so much.

The next letter I received was from Roger's close friend, Lt. Col. Charlie Hagin, written the day after Roger was wounded. In it Charlie wrote for Roger that he was getting along all right. "I was hit in the thigh yesterday afternoon and sustained a pretty bad fracture of the femur." He expected to be in a hospital the next day and would most likely be in the States in a month. He still had his sense of humor. He finished his letter by saying, "Hagin is writing this for me, so you probably won't be able to read it. I will write myself in the next few days. Don't be alarmed because I didn't write this one. I'm not yet accustomed to the cast on my leg, and writing is a little difficult." In fact, he was never able to write another letter himself. The next thing I heard was in the form of an official Navy Speed Letter, written on July 16, eight days after he was wounded. It came from the chief pharmacist, U.S. Naval Hospital #10, Hawaii. It read, "Your husband, Roger G. B. Broome, USMCR, admitted this hospital July 15, diagnosis fracture left femur, is seriously ill. Will advise of all important changes." I can't remember now which message I received first, but I believe it was the one from Roger. He made it seem not too bad, so I was devastated when the other letter came saying my husband's condition was critical.

I was mighty grateful and full of admiration for the Red Cross case workers who were filled with compassion, and wrote often to me about Roger's progress to comfort me. They answered questions that the cold official speed letters did not. They told me of the total and constant nursing care he was getting. They said he had a beautiful room which they kept supplied with native flowers— blue water lilies, hibiscus, and bird of paradise. I was also grateful to the Grey Ladies who wrote the letters for him when he couldn't write for himself.

In August, as a life-saving measure, it became necessary to amputate Roger's left leg. His doctors realized that it was close to the time of my confinement and took the trouble to convey the shocking news to my doctor in Virginia for him to judge whether I should be told of the amputation at that time or not. I appreciated their extremely sensitive concern. I was also glad my doctor decided to tell me. Roger and I had always been up front with each other, and I was grateful that my doctor realized we wanted to continue that way. Naturally, it was a terrible blow but we were still optimistic about our future together. Roger was a lawyer, and I couldn't see why he couldn't carry on his practice of law just as effectively. A Grey Lady wrote me soon after that and said, "Your reception of the news, and your attitude towards the future have been major elements in your husband's improvement."

Soon another speed letter came that said, "Please to advise you, condition of your husband, Roger G.B. Broome, much improved but still considered serious." At the beginning of September I got the last speed letter. It said Roger's condition was no longer considered serious. On September 10, 1944, he was flown back to the United States, to the Bethesda Naval Hospital in Maryland. He was still a stretcher case and had to be accompanied by a corpsman. He arrived just the day before our daughter, Kathy, was born. I was so relieved that he was home at last but frustrated that I couldn't be with him. The doctors wouldn't let me travel for a month, and I felt so cheated that everyone got to see him before I did. His mother, who was a very emotional person, was the first person to visit him and I was worried that her visit would distress him, because she lost complete control over the news of his amputation. However, I think he was too ill to notice and was comforted by having some family with him again.

For a period of 11 days both Roger and I were in the hospital. However, it was arranged that we could talk to each other by phone from hospital to hospital. I will never forget the joy of our first conversation. During this time his father visited him and I was glad he was there when Roger was presented with the Purple Heart. Roger's father was so proud of his son; all of this while I languished in my hospital bed. Even though we could talk to each other every day it seemed so hard to be apart. I continued to write every day as well, but I remarked that it was harder to write now since we could talk every day by phone. I did write a detailed description of our little girl. "She has a round face, dark eyes, and dark hair. She has terribly long, narrow feet and lovely long hands." In another letter I was concerned about bringing the children up right and told Roger he would not be allowed to cuss any more, as young Roger was beginning to repeat everything he heard.

The days were dragging and I was so anxious to get to Bethesda. At last I was able to go and I moved Roger's mother and the two babies up to Arlington, Virginia. I swapped houses with Roger's sister who lived in Arlington. She moved to my house in Charlottesville. Since she had two babies about the same age as mine we didn't have to move any equipment. It was an ideal situation. Arlington was only a 45 minute drive from Bethesda and I was able to go to the hospital every day while Roger's mother took care of the children. I have to admit that the details of those last three months have been blacked out over the years. I often wish I could get the memories back, as painful as much of it was.

I remember how bad the weather was that winter and the daily drive to the hospital was very difficult because of the icy roads. It's sad I can't remember how Roger and I passed these days— what we talked about or plans we made. I do remember we did listen to the radio a lot. I took young Roger and Kathy to see their father once and I can't remember anything about it. I hated the days I was not with Roger and was ashamed of my ungenerous feelings towards his mother on the days she went.

Christmas came and went and I don't remember it at all. The next thing I remember, and I remember it vividly, was on January 18, 1945. It was 6:30 and I was giving Kathy her early morning bottle when the phone rang. A voice said, "I'm calling to tell you your husband just died." This call I have never forgotten — the message, and the unfeeling way in which it was delivered kept ringing in my ears for many weeks. In fact, after 54 years I can hear it just as clearly as I did that January day. It remains the most shocking message I ever got, and the lack of compassion has been unequaled in my life. That call put me in a state of frenzy. It resulted in unbelievable action and organization. Before waking Roger's mother to tell her the heartbreaking news I ran next door to get my neighbor to stay with Roger's mother and the children while I rushed to the hospital. I don't know what I expected to find or to do, but I remember a policeman stopped me for speeding just as I entered Maryland. However, he saw the state I was in and when I explained the reason he escorted me the rest of the way. I don't remember anything else except running into Roger's room and finding it empty. I'm told I signed some papers and made some arrangements. They told me Roger could be buried at Arlington National Cemetery, but I thought he would rather be buried in the small country church yard by St. John's Chapel in Poindexter, Virginia, with the rest of his family. I had another decision to make at that time. The doctors asked permission to do an autopsy. I knew that his mother would never permit it, but I thought it should be done and gave my permission. I was told that I had made the right decision because they had the authority to do it anyway. I never told Roger's mother. According to Roger's death certificate the principal cause of death was, "Amputation, traumatic." The contributory cause was "pyelonephritis."

I called my mother and father in Bronxville. They somehow got on a plane immediately for Washington. I don't know how they did it because in wartime plane reservations were almost impossible to get. I drove to Washington to pick them up at the airport, but I have no recollection of how we got back to Charlottesville, nor do I remember making arrangements for the funeral.

Roger's close friend, Marine Col. Carleton Penns, escorted Roger's body to Charlottesville, and the service was held in St. Paul's Episcopal Church. My only memory of that day is the playing of "Onward Christian Soldiers."

I was at least thankful that Roger knew he had been awarded the Navy Cross. The presentation was delayed because of Roger's death. But on the 24th of February, 1945, the Navy Cross was presented posthumously to me and our 22-month-old son by Rear Admiral Monroe Kelly at Navy Headquarters in New York. The citation was signed by Gen. Holland M. Smith.

The children have no memories of their father for they were much too young. It was difficult for my parents to have me at home with two small babies, so after a month or so I moved into a house of my own. Eventually, I married again and moved to England. Kathy, particularly, often during her teen years, expressed her feelings about being cheated by having lost her father. Both Roger and Kathy have grown into splendid and talented adults in spite of their loss. I often think they might have been quite different people had their father lived. They likely would have had more discipline, which might have led them on much different paths, not necessarily better ones.

I was very fortunate for many years to be in letter contact with one of the two men who rescued Roger after he was wounded. He was Gunnery Sergeant William O. Coonts, fondly known as "Willy-O." We wrote letters and sent family pictures at Christmas time. His letters were always full of praise for Roger. During the years I was in New York I lost track of the men of the Twenty-fourth Regiment. Fortunately, two years ago, through the Internet, I was put in touch with them again. I discovered that the survivors of Roger's weapons company, and the men of the Twenty-fourth Regiment, were having reunions each year, and always remembered him with a moment of silence at their meetings.

In 1997, I went to their reunion in Cowsbell, Montana. I was hoping to meet "Willy-O" at that time, but learned that he had died two years before. The reunion was a step back in time and an extremely emotional one for me and some of the men of Roger's company. They always fondly referred to Roger as "The Major" as they told me about their being his driver, radioman, or scout. They poured out their personal memories of him. This sparked off a desire to learn all I could about that period of Roger's life. I remembered that I had hundreds of letters packed safely away somewhere. Rereading them later brought back the past so vividly and led to a search for the other man who helped save Roger when he was wounded on Saipan. He was Pvt. First Class William A. Crane of Texas. After the war he lost track of the outfit and never heard another thing for almost 50 years. He didn't even know that Roger had died until one day two years ago when out of the blue I called him. He could hardly believe he was talking to

Major Broome's wife. It was terribly emotional for both of us, but especially for him as he was taken by surprise. He broke down over the phone after just a few minutes. We had to cut our conversation short, but we have been writing and phoning since.

Last year the reunion was held in Houston, Texas, and I skipped out one morning with three other Marines to drive to San Antonio to meet Crane. He was not well enough to attend the reunion. It was a grand moment for all of us.

That baby, my daughter, who was born the day her father returned wounded to the U.S., is now a professor of history, her specialty being military history. Recently, she has been able to interview Crane and has written his story of the rescue of her father. Gunnery Sergeant Coonts received the Navy Cross, in part for his role in the operation. But Crane's contribution has not been recognized. We are hoping that Kathy's account of it will change that situation. Crane certainly deserves to be recognized.

During the last two years I have spent much time reviewing the past. Roger was only 29 when he died. I have read that those who die young are forever young. Reliving those early days has had a strange effect on me. Sometimes, just temporarily, I feel more a part of those years than of the present. Reading those hundreds of letters after almost 60 years has filled me with many emotions. There is sadness for all the hoped for and unfulfilled plans Roger and I had for the future together. We wrote eagerly about our home and how we would furnish it. We wrote about how marvelous it would be to live in Virginia in the spring. There was also pride in the superior job he did as commander of his weapons company, and there is comfort in knowing that he finally got the job he wanted. He was, as he wrote, "elated to have it, and it's the best job for a major in the Marine Corps."

# Index